THE HOSTAGE CHILD

THE HOSTAGE CHILD

SEX ABUSE ALLEGATIONS IN CUSTODY DISPUTES

LEORA N. ROSEN / MICHELLE ETLIN

INDIANA UNIVERSITY PRESS ■ **BLOOMINGTON & INDIANAPOLIS**

The paper used in this publication meets the minimum requirements of
American National Standard for Information Sciences—Permanence of
Paper for Printed Library Materials, ANSI Z39.48-1984.

Manufactured in the United States of America

Library of Congress Cataloging-in-Publication Data
Rosen, Leora N.
    The hostage child : sex abuse allegations in custody disputes /
Leora N. Rosen and Michelle Etlin.
        p.   cm.
    Includes bibliographical references and index.
    ISBN 0-253-33045-9 (cloth : alk paper)
        1. Incest—United States—Case studies.   2. Custody of children—
United States—Case studies.   I. Title.
HV6570.7.R67   1996
346.7301'7—dc20
[347.30617]   95-47113

    1   2   3   4   5   01   00   99   98   97   96

We dedicate this book to our children,

Joshua Z. Rosenthal

and

Daniel Ariel V. Etlin

CONTENTS

ACKNOWLEDGMENTS

We have gone through the usual authors' process of encouragement, discouragement, and growth during the gestation of this book, and naturally, some of the individuals we acknowledge helped in the traditional ways—providing support, assistance, knowledge, and invaluable guidance. For these contributions we thank Abbie Kohn, whose rigorous intellectual research set foundations for much of the theoretical work; Dwight Noble, whose clinical knowledge and common sense remained like astronomical points of reference for our journey; and Tonya Pinkins, whose lifelong dedication to morality as a basis for action was a constant inspiration. We would also like to offer our special thanks to two anonymous reviewers of an earlier draft of the manuscript for their invaluable suggestions and insights.

There are, however, two special categories of people without whose work we could never have written this book. First, activists and professionals whose sense of justice constitutes the only hope that sustained us in our work: among them, Alice Monroe, Glenni Rohelier, E. Sue Bloom, Joan Pennington, Sherry Quirk, Barbara Norris, Alan Rosenfeld, Garnette Harrison, Nannette Sachs, Fran Moore, Judy Weigel, Jack Straton, Louise Armstrong, Jania Somers, Daisy Morrison-Gilstrap, Jean Brothers, Lloyd deMause, and Chris Gardner. Second, we cannot adequately thank the protective parents of the hostage children whose plight gave rise to this effort. For every mother named in this book, a thousand other protective parents sacrificed their own welfare and braved unimaginable terrors to protect their own children, and many of them somehow managed to help others as well. We thank these protective parents.

But a special and specific acknowledgment is due to Norman Rosenthal, who is responsible for the very idea to write this book. Husband of author Leora Rosen and prominent psychiatrist, Dr. Rosenthal conducted many of the initial interviews that ultimately gave shape to the book. Throughout the process of researching, writing, and promoting The Hostage Child, his work has been not only invaluable but irreplaceable.

In advance, we thank every adult who, as a former hostage child, will read this book and consider his or her place in the unique history of the movement it represents.

INTRODUCTION

Child sexual abuse—once a taboo subject—is now a familiar topic of daytime TV talk shows, docudramas, made-for-TV movies, and thousands of newspaper and magazine articles. Celebrities make public service announcements on television and radio; and in commercial breaks during Saturday morning cartoons, animated characters tell children that if someone touched them where their bathing suit covered with a "bad touch" instead of a "good touch," they should tell, because they will be helped and protected. Officer Friendly has appeared in classrooms educating a generation of children about the kindly understanding treatment they can expect if they disclose sexual abuse. The same message was conveyed by Oprah Winfrey in an HBO program that aired in September 1992. Adult survivors of incest told their stories. It seemed that appropriate action was always taken when reports were made to the proper authorities. Victims were protected; perpetrators received punishment and/or therapy.

The campaign to encourage disclosure (including increased sensitizing of parents to possible warning signs of sexual abuse) bore fruit. Reports of sexual abuse skyrocketed, so much so that authorities are still wondering whether this reflects improved reporting methods or an actual rise in the number of abuse cases, or some combination of the two. But the results of this effort were not all positive. The accused were not predominantly dirty old men in trench coats lurking around school yards; they were family members, child-care providers, teachers, priests; they were the pillars of society. Not only was the fledgling system of child protection overwhelmed with cases to investigate, but it was now being confronted with indignant, self-righteous, often powerful adults who claimed that they had been falsely accused of heinous crimes against children. Some highly publicized criminal cases against day-care providers involving both successful and unsuccessful prosecutions led to cries of "witch hunt" among certain segments of the public. Questions were raised about children's suggestibility and the techniques used to elicit information from young witnesses. Though improved education and training for professionals in this area became increasingly available and a considerable body of clinical literature began to develop, methods of detection remained an inexact science, and experts with widely differing approaches were taking the witness stand—often against each other—in both civil and criminal cases.

While many experts insisted that children seldom lie about sexual abuse, others claimed that young children often failed to distinguish between fact and fiction and might be susceptible to suggestion and pressure on the part of investigators.

As more of these allegations arose in custody and divorce cases in which one parent was being accused, the issue of deliberate malice and vindictiveness on the part of the accusing parent became a matter for consideration. Were these parents intentionally coaching their children to lie in order to punish a hated ex-spouse or to gain advantage in a divorce settlement? There were many professionals—lawyers, judges, clinicians, psychiatrists—who became convinced that this was the case. Articles in respectable publications like *Time* and *Newsweek* cited statistics indicating that fictitious allegations made by divorcing parents were on the rise, and lawyers were quoted describing sex abuse allegations as the "atom bomb of custody disputes."

There were also parents—predominantly mothers—who found evidence suggesting a good possibility that their children had been sexually molested by ex-spouses. Sometimes a child's disclosures or physical or psychological symptoms led a mother to seek medical or psychological advice. Often the suggestion that abuse had occurred came not from the mother but from a doctor or a psychologist. Initial shock and disbelief on the part of these mothers was followed with the hope and expectation that the proper authorities, to whom suspicion of abuse was reported, would conduct appropriate investigations and take the steps necessary to protect their children. Rapidly they found that the system's response was very different from what they had expected. As protective mothers in cases against fathers, these women were automatically labeled vindictive, malicious, and paranoid, regardless of evidence to the contrary. Suddenly they found themselves in a Kafkaesque labyrinth of courts and state-run systems, among lawyers, judges, social workers, and experts, where the end result was almost always the same—returning or delivering the child to the alleged molester. Could this really be happening in America?

Coverage of high-profile cases in the respected print media tends to reflect the attitudes of a handful of very vocal, self-styled "experts." They have fueled the widespread public perception that false allegations of child sexual abuse are appearing with increased frequency in custody cases. Despite scientific evidence to the contrary, this belief has been adopted by many in the legal profession and by a sizeable segment of the mental health community.

The purpose of this book is to challenge these misconceptions. Sex abuse allegations that occur during custody disputes are frequently presumed to be false because they have arisen during or just before a custody case, regardless of the evidence. Because of this presumption on the part of private professionals and public officials, when children who suffer incest become the subjects of custody disputes, often their outcries are not believed and they are not protected. Custody of such children is likely to be given to the very adults accused of molesting them.

In recent years grass-roots support and advocacy groups have been providing help to protective mothers facing custodial challenges. In Part One of this book we describe five cases of this kind that have come to our attention, and in Part Two we look at "The System."

Chapter 6 examines the scientific literature on true and false allegations of sexual abuse, in divorce as well as in other contexts. That literature suggests, despite popular belief to the contrary, that sex abuse allegations made by children, even in divorce cases, have a high probability of being true. We then explore explanations for the persistent belief that these allegations are usually false. Chapter 7 traces the historical pattern of the discovery of incest, followed by the denial of its existence and prevalence, and the minimization of its consequences. The modern mental health establishment vacillates between "discovering" incest (and documenting and treating its ravages) and "delegitimizing" disclosures of incest (and denying that it is a social or psychological problem). Thus, the denial of sex abuse allegations in custody disputes is part of a trend to deny the incest problem following its "rediscovery" in the 1970s and early 1980s.

In Chapter 8 we view the problem as part of a growing anti-mother bias in custody decisions. This bias is fostered by aggressive fathers' rights advocates and facilitated by the feminist movement's lack of support for women who opt for the role of mother. Chapter 9 is a detailed analysis of the fundamental flaws in our current system of child protection, which is geared more toward preserving family unity and the rights of patriarchal heads of households than to individual children within the family. "Solutionizing" (creating a false impression of a real solution) and various rhetorical responses to child abuse, however, create the public perception that something substantive is being done to protect children. Impediments to child protection in our current legal system are also discussed, and we evaluate various solutions proposed by other advocates.

In the final chapter, we describe a unique solution we have developed, legislation known as CARCO—Child at Risk Classification Office. The essence of CARCO is that it takes child abuse out of the legal arena and places it within the public health domain, where protection is based on medical risk assessment rather than on legal proof of abuse. In our case histories, proof of abuse did not bring protection for incest victims who were the subjects of custody disputes. On the other hand, the criminal justice system cannot be permitted to punish family members for sex crimes against children without the most compelling evidence—a form of protection that is inherent in our Constitution and that must not be disturbed. CARCO does not punish offenders for crimes; it simply protects children from risk. Since most Americans find it unacceptable that many incest victims are ordered by the courts to live with their molesters, we believe that the public will see CARCO as a means of protecting children as well as preventing unfair punishment of the falsely accused.

A WORD ABOUT NAMES

As activists, we believe in naming names whenever possible in order to make public the identities of those who have helped children at risk as well as those who have helped their accused molesters gain control over such children. As authors, however, we have chosen to change the names not only of the accused (who often start frivolous lawsuits to intimidate persons who oppose their aggressive tactics) but also of the innocent victims, protective parents, and professionals involved. We feel it is more important to preserve the privacy of the children. We are not trying to tell individual stories or assign responsibility for particular injustices; we are trying to inform the public about problems we have seen within the system and to initiate ways of solving them.

We have used the real names of persons who are already identifiable from prior publicity or publication. The following names are fictitious:

Mary H and Dan H	Karen Carter
Judge Martin Brown	Ellen Trevor
Judge Barry Camden	Jesse
Dr. Fred Sutton	Donald Harper
Judge Clinton White	Larson & Harper
Dr. Dick Gruber	Dr. Kristen Overlook
Betty Neufield	Dr. Stanley Emerson
Linda Jamison	Judge Jill Somerville
Marianne Jamison	Joe G
The "Lord of the Sky" religion	Ted
Sky Village, Georgia	Judge Susan Lindhoff
Darlene Painter	Dan Green
Judge Rita Connolly	Sarah Galloway
Dr. Ronald Sand	Janet Ferguson
Dr. Maureen Manchester	Barbara Clott
Dr. Arlene Nardi	Judge Victor Scranton

Holy Name Hospital

Gary Brentano

James Cunningham

Mark Wade

Anne Weaver Backman

Albert Backman

Tina Backman

Al Backman

Calvin Nederman

Charleen Bender

Judge Boston

Judge Wooten

Dr. Marina Monkberry

Judge Cynthia Williamson

Raymond Silver

Judge Daryl Coombs

Judge Arnold R. Singleton III

Sandy Moore

Antonio Valdez

Fanny Jenkins

Derekville, Texas

Judge Gordon Mitchell

Eleanor MacIntyre

Judge John Kastengood

Annette Garner

Jane R.

PART ONE CASE HISTORIES

In August 1987, the evening news in Fairfax, Virginia, showed Dr. Elizabeth Morgan being dragged off to jail in handcuffs and leg irons. Her crime: hiding her daughter, Hilary, from her ex-husband, whom the child had apparently accused of raping her. Alice Monroe of Fairfax saw that newsreel, felt an enormous sense of outrage, and began to look into the facts of the case. She learned that Morgan had adduced evidence to show that her daughter's disclosures were valid, but the judge refused to protect the child from unsupervised contact with the alleged perpetrator. When Morgan resisted, the judge ordered her jailed until she delivered her child to the father. Monroe then began the work that led to the formation of the organization called Friends of Elizabeth Morgan, which was devoted to securing Morgan's release from jail and bringing public attention to her plight.

As the organization grew and its newsletter reached more and more people (eventually 15,000 nationwide), letters of support poured in from all over the United States and even from abroad. The authors of this book joined the Morgan campaign in various roles. Another phenomenon quickly became apparent to the campaign workers: Morgan was not alone in her plight. Thousands of mothers throughout the country were facing the same problems but had not been able to get publicity. They wrote to Morgan in jail and to Monroe, often sending documentation from their own cases. A network was born. The cases poured in at a rate that quickly overwhelmed the volunteers. Many protective mothers participated in the campaign. Dr. Anne Backman (the mother described in Chapter 4), Mary H (Chapter 1), and Karen Carter (Chapter 3) were among those who either spoke at campaign rallies, sent their information to the Friends of Elizabeth Morgan, or were identified by others as mothers who shared the problems facing Morgan. Alice Monroe provided many mothers with names of people who might be able to help and support them, and upon receiving documentation of the Sandy Moore case (Chapter 5), she forwarded that documentation to Michelle Etlin, asking if she could help. Gradually, as the Morgan case heated up and repeatedly appeared in broadcast and print media, similar cases received publicity in other parts of the country, and grassroots organizations were formed elsewhere, joining the network of individuals with a network of organizations. Through this network, Etlin became known to several New York organizations and was invited to speak to a panel composed of New York State legislators on the subject of the well-publicized Neustein case, which had taken place in Brooklyn. Another speaker on that platform was protective mother Linda Jamison (whose case is described in Chapter 2). Meanwhile, protective mother Amy Neustein was contacted by over 300 other mothers in her situation.

Since that time, several organizations have started collecting cases to show that the problem has reached a certain critical mass where it must be dealt with. Using the adage "one case does not a problem make," attorney Sherry Quirk, of the American Coalition for Abuse Awareness, collected 80 cases to present in a memorandum to Attorney General Janet Reno in November 1993. Attorney Joan Pennington of the National Center for Protective Parents has been contacted by 5,000 protective parents and guardians since 1991. The Alliance for the Rights of Children has identified 2,000 cases since it was formed in 1992. Child-Help was reported to have received calls about thousands of cases in 1994 alone. The Mothers' Alliance for the Rights of Children actually documented approximately 200 cases by late 1991. Mothers Against Sexual Assault in California identified over 1,000 cases, about which they reported at a national conference in 1993. Criminology professor Hal Pepinsky of Indiana University included information from more than thirty of these cases in course work for undergraduates. Local and national organizations are counting, compiling, and photocopying, as it becomes more and more obvious that there is no lack of cases: this is a widespread and persistent problem. Each time the word goes out that somebody is collecting cases, mothers and other protective parents run to the photocopy centers to package up and send out their data, hoping that the effort will result in help at a local, state, federal, or divine level. Still, there is a lack of belief at the government level that the sheer number of cases has implications for this society, and still, there is a lack of an organized and appropriate response by the society at large.

By early 1994, the present authors had information on 206 such cases to review for possible inclusion in this book. In those 206 cases, 204 of the protective adults were mothers or maternal relatives (such as grandparents) and two were fathers. Of the 206 cases, only fourteen children had escaped being delivered into the custody of their named alleged perpetrators after custody battles at which the allegations were said to be "false" or at which the evidence was described as "not enough."

We have selected five representative cases to relate in detail. They illustrate the five most common ways a sexual abuse/custody case can go wrong. (The names of the individuals have been changed to protect the parties involved.)

The Mary H case is the clearest and easiest to understand in terms of proven guilt of the perpetrator and a judge who can destroy a case regardless of the evidence. It exemplifies the proposition that the rights of even a convicted child molester are held superior to those of a child who may be at risk in his custody.

In the Linda Jamison case, a supposedly competent validator (who had previously been the prosecution's expert in a well-publicized day-care sex abuse case) made it impossible for a child to be protected. It shows that a child's disclosure of sexual abuse is vulnerable to "invalidation."

The Karen Carter case was chosen to show that even undeniable, unrecantable physical evidence of rape is not sufficient to guarantee justice, and that an unsympathetic lawyer can manipulate the system so that it imperils the child. Karen Carter has been particularly vocal; of all the mothers, she has devoted the most time, energy, and money to getting the word out on cases like her own, and we wish to recognize her efforts.

The Anne Backman story disproves the persistent but erroneous belief that a child molester is more likely to abuse a stepchild than his own biological child. It also demonstrates that a mother's credibility is not respected with regard to her children's situation, despite her obvious competence in her profession and in the larger world. It also shows how an aggressive team backing the alleged perpetrator can "grind down" the protective parent with a variety of legal maneuvers.

The Sandy Moore case shows how far our society will go to punish a protective mother of a molested child. Women who kill because they have been beaten often obtain pardons; women who kill to protect their children often do not. In the Moore case the CPS agency that prevented the development of evidence is symptomatic of a legal and social services system that presents a clear danger to protective mothers and dooms their efforts to failure.

1

H versus H

PRE-HISTORY OF THE MARRIAGE

Mary H was born and raised in Kentucky horse country and was a trained show judge in the art of dressage. By profession she was a social worker. Her first marriage was rocky and unhappy, but she had two daughters, Christie and Debbie, four years apart. Mary's first husband did not seek custody of the children upon divorce; he never wanted responsibility for them. Mary described him as an alcoholic whose intentions were not evil but whose effect was. Nothing in her first marriage or first divorce, unfortunately, prepared Mary to recognize or protect herself or her two daughters from abuse. Her second marriage was to Dan H.

Dan H's first wife—who was also named Mary—had died of cancer in 1979, leaving Dan with four children from her prior marriage. Mary-the-First practically left her four children to Dan in her will. The local priest described a touching scene of Dan sitting lovingly beside his dying wife as she bequeathed her children to him. He comforted her and promised to take good care of them. (Questions were not asked, at any point in this proceeding, about the identity or whereabouts of their father, whom Dan H seemed to have totally replaced in their affections and loyalty.) So Dan became the loving custodial stepfather.

Dan met Mary-the-Second, then a single mother with two young daughters, at a performance of *As You Like It* in Lexington, Kentucky's "Shakespeare in the Park." Mary was impressed with his deep appreciation for culture and literature, but she reported being "repulsed by him" at first, because of his inconsiderate behavior. He had brought two big dogs with him and allowed them to run loose and annoy everybody during the event, even causing concern to the park staff. Mary also mentioned that Dan was with a woman who cried as he spoke with her intensely. At that meeting, Mary-the-Second was not at all attracted to him.

The friend who accompanied Mary to the play had played tennis with Dan H for seven years, and described him as an expert tennis player and a renaissance man. He also told Mary that Dan's wife had died two years before, that he was "raising all these kids by himself," and that he was still broken up over the loss of his beloved Mary-the-First.

> And so the maternal stuff in me goes, "hmm, well, that's a plus," you know, it's kind of adding up pluses and minuses, and you know, to me that was plus, and he had . . . four stepchildren and one biological son, that were apparently living at home [with him], although the two oldest stepchildren were not in the house, they were gone, as adults, by that time.

Mary, who was impressed with Dan as a loving, paternal, overwhelmed, sad guy, agreed to go back to his house with the company after the theater. There, her sympathy was tugged on even more urgently.

> Anyway, so when we went back to his house, I mean it was a wreck, it was just a mess. So of course, my antenna goes up and says, "oh, you know, hmm, we need a woman around here," you know it was this same old enabling type of stuff. And I had dealt with that in my first marriage but still didn't recognize it at that point.

In that "mess" of a house, Dan had an antique Steinway piano in the dining room. Mary loved classical music, especially Chopin. Dan played "wonderfully well." And that was "a plus." Dan kept adding pluses, and in a few weeks he asked Mary out on a date, something she had not done since the break-up of her marriage. She went, impressed with Dan's culture, respectability, and apparent parental responsibility.

> And we talked. He's a very good conversationalist, and he's actually a good companion. And I found out later why he's such a good companion was because what he does is, study people, finds out what they need, and then gives it to them, if he wants something from them.

What did he want from her? His children from Mary-the-First were grown or nearly grown. Mary-the-Second had two pre-teen daughters:

> I think he probably wanted my children. I don't know that he particularly wanted me . . . he may have. Um, . . . but you know, I had two daughters, which he knew, and he had heard a lot about me, also, he thought I had money, family money, which I don't.

Dan may have assumed that Mary had family money because she was in the horse world, the so-called mink and manure set of old Kentucky. She had ridden horses most of her life, had owned some, and was an American

Horse Show Association Judge and Technical Delegate. Whereas most judge/delegates may come from wealthy families, Mary did not, and never pretended to, but Dan may have formed his own conclusions. Mary thought that was the case, for she remarked that once they were married, when Dan was in some financial stress "after the honeymoon was over," he revealed this motivation to her in a heated argument:

> He very angrily told me one day that I really fooled him. He said, "You really got me, you really fooled me." I said, "What do you mean?" and he said, "Well, I thought you had money. You really fooled me." He was angry about it.

In a six-month courtship Dan managed to make Mary's apprehensions fade. He swept her off her feet with his patient attentiveness, his skill at social conversation, his beautiful piano playing, his appearance as a model father, and his romantic qualities as a lover. Whatever Mary needed, he was there to provide it. She was actually unaware that he was "servicing her needs" as the relationship developed. Later, looking back, she saw things much differently.

> What he did was, I realized after the fact now, he did a lot of questioning. And I thought it was just, oh, you know, there's somebody that's actually interested in me, . . . *in me*! He questioned and questioned and asked about, oh my girls, and pretty much, found out what my needs were. And then he set about meeting them.

Mary's needs were fairly urgent and fairly obvious after her failed marriage and two years of attempted recovery while bearing the responsibility for her children alone. She needed companionship. She felt her girls "could use a father, a male figure, in their lives." Dan arranged outings with Mary and the girls. "And in front of me, anyway, he would try to prove very caring towards them. And that sort of thing." But the girls did not like him. Christie in particular disliked him, but she did not say so strongly (it would have been impolite, and Mary had taught her children to be polite) until much later. Debbie didn't take to Dan either, but she was only seven and did not express herself much on that subject. Altogether, Dan made himself appear "an interested parental type."

Added to that, Mary had never had a satisfying physical relationship before. Her ex-husband "would go five, six months, without ever looking at me or touching me or anything, and that was in the good part of the marriage" before his alcoholism completely destroyed the family. Dan waited from summer until late fall to approach Mary sexually, and then he did it very skillfully. "He was very good in bed," commented Mary tactfully, "and I had never had that. It was like, gosh, you know, this *is* okay."

HISTORY OF THE MARRIAGE

Mary's recapitulation of the courtship and marriage was, finally: "So you know he just put his pieces in place in the puzzle and roped me in, and we married." A new blended family was quickly arranged: marriage, house, household.

Whereas the courtship seemed to be centered lovingly and sensitively around Mary and her childlren, her needs and her children's needs, the new arrangement operated like a solar system around Dan H. Dan had just accepted a job at a federal installation. Mary, her family, and Dan and his children prepared to move to Maryland almost immediately after the wedding. Mary says they "ended up with a big house, a 17-room one" within months. Mary could not tell if they could afford the house or not, because Dan was so secretive about his money. "He would lie to me, and I didn't realize that in the beginning." Dan had actually been on food stamps and Aid to Dependent Children after his first wife had died; and Mary said, "He had saved a bunch of money off the—the FDC or whatever it was." He had also sold the house that once belonged to his first wife in Kentucky, using that for the down payment on the semi-mansion in rural Maryland.

Dan drank every night, but he was never a "fall-down drunk" like Mary's first husband, so she did not think he was an alcoholic. Then she noticed that he drank more and more, that he recorded how much he drank but underestimated it regularly, and that on weekends, he would carry a shaker of margueritas around with him starting before noon and ending when he fell asleep. Mary said that Dan never went to bed, never fell asleep, without drinking. Only later did she realize that his prodigious tolerance for alcohol did not mean he was not an alcoholic. At age 49, ten years after her calamitous marriage to Dan H, Mary described herself as "kind of naive, I guess, about some things."

Besides drinking heavily and being disrespectful toward the feelings of others, Dan had other faults, which showed up quickly after he and Mary were married. He liked to make fun of people and mocked them cruelly. He subjected the children to ridicule and mean forms of "teasing." When he began to drink on weekends, he would at first "get real happy" but then "get real cruel." Mary said that the kids would "just scatter" on the weekends to stay out of his way. He saved a special kind of relentless cruelty for his one biological son, who had a "lazy eye" that had not been treated. Dan hounded him and degraded him at the dinner table every night, calling him "wall-eye." Mary called it "sick stuff." As he drank, and as it got later in the day, Dan got "meaner and meaner." By nightfall, his time alone with Mary, he was a menace, and she was frankly terrorized by his sustained state of verbal cruelty and near-violence.

Strangely, Dan was able to keep Mary from drawing her own conclusions about his behavior by telling her the opposite of what he was showing her.

She admittedly helped him out in that regard because, she said, "I presumed I was in love with him." When Mary would complain about his mistreating her, his response was that he cared about her deeply, that he really thought women were wonderful, and that she was probably just mistaken about his behavior because of the "scars" from her first marriage. She accepted that, still suffering a loss of self-esteem from years of self-doubt and oppression, and she concluded, "At least he was noticing me."

According to Mary and her daughters, the H house was not the family home; it was Dan H's castle, which his wife and children were to maintain to his specifications. They saw him as distant and autocratic. He and his older stepsons spent a lot of time in the barn, which was littered with beer cans and smelled strongly of marijuana. He beat the children, with the exception of his oldest stepson, a physically large boy, who was more a companion to Dan than a son. Mary was Dan's servant. The other children were his occasional victims and his slaves. Dan beat his own biological son especially frequently and severely. The beatings were not even administered for serious infractions. According to Mary, they were

> For anything. He, um—it was a very—he is a very ritualized kind of person. He does everything almost in a ritual, in a set pattern. And I mean, even in bed that—he was that way. And I did not recognize it for a long time because I did not have the experience to recognize it. But we would sit at the dinner table and here I would fix all these wonderful meals and everything, and sit down, and before the meal even started, he would start bringing up everybody's transgressions. And meting out the punishments. He would say, "Christie, meet me in the living room after dinner. You get two whacks for—"oh, whatever the infraction was. The infraction might be, one thing that he did that Christie still remembers, that she testified to in court, was she was supposed to vacuum the living room. And OK that was no big deal she would vacuum the living room. But he would take—he would clip his, like his toe-nails and take them in and sprinkle them under, for instance, underneath the table. [And he would punish her for missing them. But] Christie would say, later she would say, you know, I remember that I did vacuum under that table. Well what he would do—it happened too many times, for him not to be [planting] those things in the living room, or he'd put a penny under a cushion, you know to trap people. And, then he would get to punish them. And he did this, and he would say, well you didn't obey me, or you never swept in the living room or you didn't sweep well enough, so you get two whacks for that. And then, he had his fraternity paddle.

Dan had a definite sadistic tendency to his sex life after marriage, according to Mary, whereas his sexual conduct while he was courting her was tender and attentive. But as is sometimes the case with a predatory pedophile, Dan was sadistic and controlling. His history was full of situations in which he became the administrator of punishments to weaker "family" members. Dan had a favorite souvenir from his college days, a fraternity paddle, which he used when he was the "disciplinarian" at his fraternity. Evidently, he routinely administered punishment, in the form of spankings on bare bottoms, to any offending frat underclassmen. Dan had pleasant tales to tell about the eager and contrite freshmen who dropped their pants with all due respect and humility to him as he wielded the wooden paddle.

He still enjoyed using the punitive relic. For instance, Dan might sentence Debbie, after a dinner-time interrogation, to four strokes with his paddle. He would then order her to wait in the living room for him to arrive, caressing his paddle and reminding her of her crime, 20 minutes to half an hour later. He would draw out his victim's agony by making her wait for her punishment in silence. He would then show up, lecture her on the need for this punishment, and administer it with mock chagrin alternating with real relish, stopping and starting as he chose, to produce a more pronounced effect.

Mary also reported being battered and even sexually tormented by Dan. Desire was, to him, as much a matter of physical and mental torture as a matter of sex. His main desire was for control—of every conversation, every relationship, every opinion, every penny spent, every activity of every member of the family he had acquired. Punishment was the activity he could most control, and the one that could produce—by the squirms, apologies, and cries of his "subjects"—the highest degree of satisfaction.

Mary admitted in sober tones to being unable to protect her children from Dan's alcoholic rages. She was exhausted and shocked by the change in her new husband concurrent with her move to Maryland. Many things contributed to Mary's paralysis: seventeen rooms, four children, two adults, Dan making no contribution to household finances, Mary's work substitute teaching and traveling to judge horse shows, and the nagging uncertainty she felt about the nature and severity of what was happening to her family. Before marriage, she and Dan had discussed his "helping" with discipline for the children, but Mary did not suspect he would assume the right to beat them, since she herself never did. She spent an initial period in confused denial, which was frozen by continuous tension and naked fear.

> From the time he started doing this with any regularity, he had already started abusing me, and it was like, the girls and I don't remember some stuff, it's—you know, we kind of have blocked it out, but now, it's like if anybody ever touched one of my kids again I think I would just absolutely—fall all over them, immediately. But at that time, . . . I just couldn't. I couldn't. It was almost like there would be a little voice in the back of my head, "Oh, don't let him hit me, don't let him get me, don't let him hurt *me.*" And I would see that he was going to paddle one of the children, "Don't don't," you know, just "Don't," and I would just kind of withdraw within myself.

When Mary was finally able to deal with the issue of his beating the children, Dan showed the skill he would later use in avoiding the consequences of his behavior, by admitting his offense and pretending to reform. Mary learned the reform was pretence:

> When I did confront him on it, there at the end, I thought he had quit. [But he hadn't; he just continued in secret.] He would wait till I was out of the house and he would [beat them then]. . . . he would wait till I was out of the way somewhere, or not in the house, and then he would do it.

Mary's daughters were protective of her and didn't tell.

> The girls were afraid. OK, they knew that he was unkind to me. So they were afraid if they said anything, that, that he would get me worse. And I was afraid that if I said anything, that he would get them worse. So I submitted to what he wanted and they submitted to what he wanted. And we didn't find out until later. And he's a great divide-and-conqueror type of guy, because he would tell them that I didn't like them, like Debbie, you know, "You're special," and all that stuff, same old stuff you read in the books. "You're special, your mommy doesn't love you but I love you and I'll—you know your mommy doesn't protect you but I will. She's not a good mother but I'm a good father and I will do this and do that," and she still—cause this is my middle child—she still to this day has problems expressing anger toward him. She's able, very easily to express anger toward me, but she can't handle to express it toward him.

In June 1992, a Maryland psychiatrist recorded Mary H's description of the intense psychological prison that had been established in the household:

> M.H.:   Yeah, well he was busy paralyzing me in the bedroom, and—more and more of that's coming out now in therapy. It's pretty awful. . . . Very difficult.
>
> Dr.:   Difficult stuff, huh?
>
> M.H.:   Very very difficult. And I'm remembering more and more, and—it's really very very hard. I mean I can see why I ended up with being unable to defend my children.
>
> Dr.:   He was actually abusing you too?
>
> M.H.:   Yeah.
>
> Dr.:   Physically hurting you?
>
> M.H.:   [almost inaudible] Yeah.
>
> Dr.:   Hmm. And when you say it's coming back, you had actually blocked that out?
>
> M.H.:   Yes. A lot of it.
>
> Dr.:   You disassociated that out?
>
> M.H.:   Yes, repressed it and disassociated. And, so—
>
> Dr.:   So, were you afraid for your own self?

M.H.: Yes. And when he would do the inquisition, as we would call it, at the supper table, every night, in this big formal dining room in this beautiful old house, you know, big table, and all that, he sat at the head, he had the only chair that had arms on it, you know, and he would sit at the head of the table and he sort of held court every night at supper . . . and . . . meted out the punishments. Or he would verbally attack you know, one of the children, at the table. I didn't talk a lot at the table, and the girls and I didn't talk a lot at the table. The men [Dan H and sons] usually did all the conversation. And he would . . . mete out the punishments, and it was sort of like, you know, . . . don't let it be me. . . . Which sounds really awful, but I felt just like one of the kids, but—I knew I would get mine later.

Dr.: Really.

M.H.: You know, he didn't mete out punishments to me at the table, it was only the children.

Dr.: But you got yours later in the evening.

M.H.: Yeah.

. . .

Dr.: He became physically hurtful to you?

M.H.: Yes he did.

Dr.: Let me ask you Mary, are you—are you disassociating right now?

M.H.: I'm paying attention to my food.

Dr.: I see, OK, that's very healthy, to focus on your food. [laughter]

M.H.: OK. [laughter] focus on my food. OK, let me think. It's really funny because, you know, it's sort of like, when you talk to—you know I had a lot of children, you know as a therapist, and—when you talk to an adult that had an abusive childhood, they will have major gaps in their memory. I have trouble remembering a lot of the marriage. And, for whatever reasons, you know, I just—I don't remember. I remember some parts but as far as like . . . [silence].

In spite of the obvious problems in the marriage, Mary became pregnant by Dan in 1985, but she had a difficult early pregnancy and miscarried. Her doctor advised her to avoid another pregnancy, at least for a year. Dan refused to allow that. According to the physician, Mary was too old to use oral contraceptives, and Dan forbade the use of any other method. Mary became pregnant again within the year, much to Dan H's approval, although she suffered hypertension and gestational diabetes.

In July 1986, after having beaten the girls many times and having gone to therapy with Mary a couple of times, Dan H sexually abused Debbie. Mary had sent her to the barn to tell Dan that it was dinnertime. He ordered her to take off her clothes, in a "soft but commanding" voice. Dan is over six feet tall and weighs more than 200 pounds. Debbie obeyed him and undressed. Dan "began to lick her all over her body" with his tongue and then "fondled" her and told her she was "special." He penetrated her vagina with his tongue and a finger. Then he let her go. Debbie was so frightened and confused she did not react. According to Debbie, he repeated these actions at least twice more, once adding a violent beating while warning her never to "tell." Her physical welts and bruises were extensive.

In late 1986, Mary was six months pregnant and in need of money for the continued royal upkeep of the House of H in a rural county in Maryland. She had contracted to judge a horse show in Kentucky, but before she left, Debbie, then eleven, was clingy and tearful and begged her mother not to leave. This was unusual behavior, since the girls were accustomed to Mary's traveling and usually accepted her absences without much ado. This time Debbie tore off a piece of an envelope and scribbled something on it, shoving it into Mary's purse. "Don't read it 'till you get there," she begged in a hoarse whisper. Not until Mary was in the airport in Kentucky did she uncrumple the scrap of paper and read in her child's shaky handwriting, "HE MOLESTED ME."

Dan's oldest stepson had molested Christie when she was eleven, Debbie's age, but Mary and her then newly wedded husband had let the incident pass without much ado, considering it teen-age misbehavior that was best corrected and forgotten. The inherited son had blamed the misdemeanor on Christie, who was six years younger than he and who had no prior sexual knowledge or experience. Christie's embarrassed response was to try to get away delicately and then to tell her mother, who told Dan, who laughed off the incident as a manifestation of his theory that "boys will be boys." He did promise that the behavior would not be repeated.

But when Mary's eyes fell on her younger child's anguished words, she was much more apprehensive than she would have been if she considered this a repeat of the stepbrother's misbehavior. "HE" seemed to mean Dan H this time. She went to the nearest pay phone and dialed home. "Who was HE?" she asked. Debbie had indeed meant Dan.

> Inside I went, Oh, God! . . . I . . . asked her what he'd done, and—uh— she told me, and uh—I said, well, I said, you know, I can't get back right now. What I need you to do, you and Christie, is stay away from him, and do not go near him, stay away from him. And of course my mind was immediately racing, OK, now, how can I get those kids out of that house? Um, without causing some big furor. . . . And then I said well let me talk to Dan, and she got real upset and said, "No, no, don't say anything to him don't say anything to him he'll get mad." And I said, no, don't worry about it, I said he will not hurt you and he will not touch you again. He got back on the phone. . . .

Mary used careful words to tell Dan she knew "what had happened." Dan knew exactly what she was talking about. He did not seem overly alarmed or upset. He was not apologetic. He maintained control. He didn't cry. Mary continued, exerting effort to keep her voice moderated:

> I said, "When I get home, I want the status to be *quo*!" I said I do not want you to get near the girls. *You stay away from them!* And I said we'll deal with this when I get back. And um, . . . he never denied it. He never said anything except, "well, why didn't you—if you knew about this why didn't you say something to me before you left?" And I said because I didn't know before I left. I had Debbie's note in my purse. So he didn't say anything. And so that was sort of the end of the conversation and I warned him again. I said, you stay away from the girls.

As Mary stood in the airport, with the receiver still in her hand, realization—and self-recriminations—crashed in on her. Why had she not known? Why had she held her tongue and allowed Dan to send Debbie into the dining room night after night for prescribed "punishments"? Why had she endured sadism in the master bedroom while the children of Mary-the-First and her own children cried themselves to sleep in separate bedrooms in the expensive new house she kept for the brutal, tyrannical government toxicologist? Why hadn't she left him after the first shocking beating? Why had she taught her daughters submissiveness in the face of abuse, rather than self-defense? Mary was filled with fear and guilt.

She tried to get a flight home the same night, but nothing was available. She needed to find someone to pick up the girls and take them away from the house until she returned. She stayed up all night calling people; nobody she knew and trusted was home. Finally, at 8 the next morning, she located friends who agreed to pick up the girls around 11 A.M. Mary called home again and told Christie that friends were picking up her and Debbie to go riding, so they should pack their saddles, hard hats, and a change of clothes, in case they got dirty. Friends picked up the girls before noon, pleasantly pretending to be taking them on a recreational outing. "And that was the last time they were ever in the house with him," said Mary.

MARRIAGE TO DIVORCE:
THE BOUNDARIES OF ABUSE ARE NOT FIRM

Family, kinship, fraternity, brotherhood—the brotherhood—the fraternity paddle, all meant essentially the same thing for Dan H: control and victimization. As Mary was to learn, the same principle existed in the brotherhood of the family court system. Marriage as "obedience to the owner of the fraternity paddle" under pain of terrible punishment for you or those you love was replaced by divorce law as "obedience to the owner of the gavel" under exactly the same circumstances. But when Mary first faced the situation—a molested daughter, a dangerous husband, her initial natural faith in the legal system—she had other expectations.

When Mary got back to town, she refused to move back into the house with the girls until Dan moved out. He moved in with neighbors across the street. Mary thought at first that Dan would have the "good sense to stay away until we could sort everything out," and she hoped to keep the problems within the context of divorce and therapy. But Dan was not practicing the same brand of "good sense" Mary expected. He repeatedly came to the house, let himself in, and conducted himself like a privileged owner. He agreed to go to Johns Hopkins University to see a nationally recognized expert in the treatment of sex offenders, but he did not deign to conduct himself like a sex offender. He still wanted contact with Debbie and Christie. Another "incident" occurred. Dan came into the house while Mary and Christie were home. Christie absented herself quickly and Mary took Dan upstairs to talk.

> I went upstairs and I sat down to talk with him, and he started to cry. Well he cries easily, um, when it suits his needs. And put his arms around me and said oh you know, we can work this out and you know, shouldn't live separately, and you know, I can just move back in here and we can take care of this. And I said no, this can't be worked out with you in the same household with the children. I said we'll work on it with you living out of the house. And he turned off his tears and jumped away from me, and you know, it was like, huh! And you know, zipped back across the street. And uh, then we moved back in, when we were sure he was gone, and uh—he didn't stay gone very much. He would break in on us.

They had tried therapy before, and it was doomed to failure because Dan was adept at pretending to deal with his behavior while carrying it on in secret and manipulating the therapists—almost like a Machiavellian game that actually increased his power. All the while he had been physically abusing Mary. In the late summer, right before she found out about Dan molesting Debbie, she learned how skillfully he could protect and even increase his abusive activities right under the nose of the therapists.

> I um, had—you know he was beating on us, beating on Debbie in particular, and he used his fraternity paddle and a raw oak thin plank, and he left—she was just a mess from her knees to her waist the last two times he did it. . . . [Again,] under the guise of punishment, you know, so many whacks, for whatever infraction it was. . . . I warned him not to touch the girls again. . . . I said it's child abuse and I will have you arrested. I just said, stop it. So he said he had stopped it but the girls tell me that he didn't. He would do it secretly when I wasn't around. . . . [They didn't tell because] we were all pr—thought we were all protecting each other. I would let him get away with a lot of the things with me, when he—because if I didn't let him do what he wanted with me, . . . he did [take it out on the girls]. . . . [So] I just didn't refuse him anything, if I tried, well he got angry, he would be really vicious. And the girls thought that they were protecting me, because they knew he was abusive to me, so it was pretty—pretty interesting, we didn't find out a lot of that until after the fact. . . .

Mary had tried the therapy route, hoping against hope.

I wanted him to go to marriage counseling with me. And you know . . . I got the therapist aside [beforehand] . . . and said look, he is beating my childlren, and I want to see if we can do something here because I don't understand exactly what is going on, and, don't like what's going on. So the therapist knew, [what was] going on, that he was abusing the girls. [The therapist] spoke with I guess somebody in the county because of the child abuse issue. They did not act on it, [because they said they] felt that I was doing what needed to be done by trying to get him into therapy. We went twice it was with a psychologist, we went once individually and once together.

So Mary believed they were making progress. Dan did not admit that he was continuing to beat the girls, in secret. But then Mary learned from the girls that he had been doing so. "And then I found out about the—about Debbie and ended up calling the therapist back and saying we won't be back for a return trip, because we have to deal with this in a different way."

Things would not be worked out. Dan "was harassing us so much." He turned off the utilities when Mary was sick, pregnant, and couldn't work. She said, "You never knew when you came out of the house whether he was going to jump out of the bushes at you." Mary endured these conditions for the remainder of her difficult pregnancy. In late 1986, she gave birth to a healthy baby girl, over whom the "parental rights" of Dan H hung like a pall.

THE RESPONSE OF THE CRIMINAL JUSTICE SYSTEM

Since Debbie was not the biological daughter of Dan H, but his step-daughter, the law enforcement officials involved in the case took it seriously. A grand jury indicted Dan with four counts of child abuse—three for sexual abuse (in ascending order: child abuse, second-degree child sexual abuse, and third-degree child sexual abuse) and one count of assault and battery. Dan H was arraigned on February 17, 1987. On March 3, he posted $20,000 bond and was given strict conditions: no contact with Debbie, the child witness; not to go near the house where Mary and the children lived; not to bother, harass, or threaten the family; and to support the family.

Two days later, through his Maryland lawyer, Dan filed a motion for visitation before Judge Martin Brown. And on the same day, immediately after his fellow judge had ordered Dan to have no contact with Debbie and while the restraining order keeping him from the house was still hot off the courthouse press, Judge Brown granted Dan visitation with his victim's newborn baby sister in an "oral order." Mary was precluded from giving testimony in that proceeding. The decision was made in chambers, not in open court. Details of the logistics of permissible visitation are absent from the file, and may never have been put in writing. They had a serious effect.

On April 11, 1987, when Mary was gone on a brief trip to the gro-cery store, Dan entered the house and "came into contact with the alleged victim [Debbie]." Christie "sought emergency assistance through 911." A detailed police report of the incident filed that day notes that the defendant, Dan H, "left the premises" after the police arrived. The report noted that Dan was "very threatening to 12-year-old Debbie" and that his actions were "having a detrimental effect on her well-being." Dan was not taken to jail but allowed to return home to start more legal proceedings, which he promptly did.

By the time the prosecutor brought a motion to revoke Dan's bond for dis-obeying its clear conditions, a letter appeared in the criminal file from Dan's attorney opposing bond revocation. The letter requested that the criminal matter be reassigned, from the judge who had set the conditions on his bond to Judge Brown, "inasmuch as he has prior knowledge of prior orders of the court [not the criminal court, but the divorce court] which directly relate to the matter requested by the [prosecutor]." In the alternative, Dan's lawyer asked that the case be rescheduled at a time when Judge Brown could *appear and testify as a witness for the defense.* A copy of the letter was sent to the prosecutor.

The petition Dan H filed in court shortly thereafter to oppose the revoca-tion of his bond "vehemently denied" the charges that he had molested Debbie, and blamed them all on Mary. Dan characterized the charges—which had been brought by the grand jury—as false allegations made by Mary to gain leverage in her divorce case. This had no bearing on the case because the child witness was not involved in the divorce between Mary and Dan, since her legal and biological father was Mary's first husband. But the groundwork was being laid for Dan to change the criminal child molestation case into a "bitter custody battle" and to avail himself of the easy rhetoric of the molester defense bar, complete with "crazy mother" and "vindictive ex-wife" paradigms. One short month before Dan admitted under oath that he had performed oral and digital sex on a child, he said:

> The instant [criminal] case is an outgrowth of a domestic case . . . and the Defendant vehemently denies each and every allegation of the indict-ment. . . . the instant charges were precipitated by the [mother] as an attempt to force a more favorable settlement in said domestic matter. . . . [T]he State's Attorney's Office . . . is aware of . . . the right of the Defen-dant to have visitation with *his* child.

That would be the baby, Shari. Dan was fighting a no-holds-barred battle to get out of the charges for molesting Debbie, to beat Mary into legal submis-sion, and to gain access to Shari. What is also clear from the petition is that Dan never honestly took responsibility for what he did to Debbie or to anyone in the family; he was prepared to swear to whatever was expedient, to cry when tears were necessary, to storm when threats were useful, and to harm others in order to protect his own interests or obtain his own satisfaction, legally or illegally, in or out of court.

Less than three weeks later, another order appeared in the file, signed by Judge Barry Camden, who was obviously not part of the cover-up. That order maintains the $20,000 bond and adds an extra condition: "Obey ALL Court Orders. Absolutely Stay Away From [the victim's home]. Stay away from [Debbie]" [Emphasis in the original].

The custody case over Shari had already begun, almost immediately after the criminal case for molesting Debbie was initiated. In many such cases, the criminal case is then subordinated to and actually incorporated into the custody battle, and the criminal charges are dropped; but since Debbie (the complaining witness in the criminal case) was not a subject of the custody battle, the prosecutor would not drop these charges. Plea bargaining began. Three counts were dropped and Dan was allowed to take a special plea provided for by Maryland law—a "Statement of Facts." That essentially admits the facts while denying the charge, allowing the court to sentence the defendant; it is the legal equivalent of conviction. This was the solution of choice for Dan because, according to the judge, there would be "job repercussions" if Dan's employer, the federal government, learned that he had pleaded guilty to a sex offense.

Dan H was allowed to take this gentle route out of his criminal charges because he "admitted" the facts—that he had orally and digitally raped Debbie, *once*, in the barn. His sentence was either five years of probation if, within two years, he completed sex offender treatment, refrained from contacting Debbie, supported the family, paid for therapy (for Debbie and all family members) needed because of his conduct, and had only supervised visitation with the infant Shari; or fifteen years in prison if he did not comply with all these conditions. Dan's admission of the facts and the sentence were memorialized in the written record on May 11, 1987.

By August Dan had missed four of the weekly therapy sessions he was ordered to attend. The record also reveals that he did not support the family and reneged on his obligation to pay for therapy for Debbie. In defense, he demanded to know why Debbie was still in therapy after he considered that she should have been long over her trauma. After all, Dan was over it. Within a year he sought to have the criminal finding stricken so he could gain unsupervised visitation with Shari. As to his speed in therapy, he had apparently recovered from pedophilia faster than Debbie had recovered from child sexual abuse. Dr. Fred Sutton, head of the County Mental Health Sex Offender Program, testified under oath that he considered Dan H to have already been "rehabilitated" because he cried in therapy; but Dan had cried before therapy. After a lot of aggressive-defensive litigation from Dan's lawyer and a few half-hearted attempts to revoke bond, probation, and other advantages, the State of Maryland apparently gave up on trying to make Dan H pay his debt to society.

THE BEST DEFENSE TURNS INTO A VERY GOOD OFFENSE

Judge Clinton White presided over the custody case of Shari H. He did not consider the conviction of Dan H for molesting Debbie relevant to the custody issue between Dan and Mary because Dan had already undergone therapy. Therefore, he considered Mary's fear about Dan's pedophilia (actually diagnosed as "paraphilia" by a sex offender specialist) a sign of mental illness on the mother's part. He ordered unsupervised visitation between the baby and the convicted child molester while Dan H was still on probation for sex crimes against her older sister.

The case soon turned into a battle between Mary (seen as a disobedient, trouble-making, and recalcitrant "crazy mother") and the judge, with Dan playing the role of an innocent whose rights were being denied. On March 15, 1991 Judge White said:

> I made previous findings that there was not a basis to deny visitation, other than the fact that Mr. H was not acquainted with his daughter since he had never met her. . . . We have now had 16 supervised visits . . . [and since no problems were reported] . . . there is no reason to subject Mr. H to this [continued supervision].

On June 13, Judge White said, "I recognize Mrs. H's fear, and I quite frankly am convinced that a substantial part of the problem is fear. . . . Mr. Roosevelt said there is nothing to fear but fear itself. Sometimes fear is totally overpowering." Judge White became incensed that Mary H had checked her daughter unobtrusively after visitation with Dan, to see if her genitals were visibly harmed. The judge did not want the child's genitals observed by her mother even during a diaper change: "[T]he only evidence of touching, Mrs. H, and what I feel is inappropriate, is by *you*. . . . Your checking this child out to see if she was abused is totally inappropriate. I think it creates additional problems for the child." Judge White summed up his theory about child sexual abuse and child protection in the following colloquy:

> So, if the only thing important in life, if there was only one objective, and [that was to] go through life without being sexually abused, then life would be fairly easy. Put the child in a locked cage and have several people to open the door and feed them and what have you, and then they wouldn't be sexually abused, and that would be it. But when that becomes the overriding criteria [*sic*], I saw the child a couple of times yesterday. . . . She's not afraid of me. I stuck my head in the jury room door and I said "Hi," and she said "Hi" back. When I started into the courtroom she came to say good-bye. So, she's not afraid of men. . . . So, I think that we have got a pretty healthy child here at the moment, and I think that [if] we evaluate this child, we may destroy her with that.

As to what actually endangered Shari, if anything, he declared: "If she lives out the rest of her life and only sees her father in a supervised setting, she will be *screwed up*."

Finally, Judge White accepted Dan H as a good parent and "not a sex fiend" because he had already admitted molesting Debbie. The judge seemed to regard pedophilia not as a crime or a perversion, but as a sexual preference. As long as Dan H was out of the closet about the abuse, Judge White did not appear to think he should be penalized. He apparently could not appreciate Mary's critical and frightened behavior about the past sexual abuse.

> In terms of who [is present during Dan H's visits], [Dan's] son is accept-able. . . . There may be some conspiracy of [Dan H] and his son to go out and trail little children [as alleged by the mother] but I have no evidence of that. Just as likely that Mrs. H is the secret abuser, *the closet abuser*.

Now Mary, who has never been suspected, accused, or convicted of child sexual abuse, is equal to Dan, who has been all of the above—and absolved. The more Mary fought off unsupervised visitation between convicted moles-ter and defenseless baby, the more she was seen as a crazy mother harboring unexplainable fears and unacceptable grudges. Judge White sent her to a hand-picked court-appointed psychologist, Dick Gruber of Annapolis, for as-sessment of *her* psychological condition because of her continued fear of Dan H's unsupervised access to Shari. Dr. Gruber rendered a shockingly un-professional report in which he opined that the only reason Dan required supervision would be to protect *him* from unfounded charges made by Mary, whom he pronounced to be psychiatrically impaired to the highest degree. On February 18, 1992, Judge White said, "The only reason I had not trans-ferred custody to [Dan H] long ago was because of his having had the conviction of child abuse."

Mary saw the inevitable future. Her youngest daughter would be handed over to Dan, and she would be cut out of her child's life for being "crazy." While motions were pending to force Judge White to recuse himself from the case, and Mary was forced to allow unsupervised visits, she took Shari to Mercy Hospital in Baltimore, where a genital examination revealed that she had already sustained sexual injuries during visits. The court advised the medical expert not to show up in court, telling him that he would not be asked to testify. Mary was facing contempt charges. Her daughter was facing sexual abuse and the loss of her mother. Dan was doing very well in the liti-gation and in having the criminal charges neutralized.

Mary went "on the run" before Shari's fifth birthday, and before custody of Shari was handed over to Dan. Shari had seen her father twenty times, on supervised and unsupervised visits, each of which was the result of lengthy and energetic litigation. After the unsupervised visits, Shari had suffered marked signs of sexual abuse. Later, in therapy, after more than a year of safety, Shari told Dr. Otto Kaak, a child psychiatrist at the University of Kentucky Medical School, what her father had done to her—approximately the same as he had done to her sister while she herself was still in utero.

DANGER ON THE RUN

While Mary was in the "underground," she was kept in many different places, endured many different problems, and at one point stayed in a "safe house" that she described as extremely unhygienic. During that stay, a cat that had no inoculations leaped out at her and clawed her breast after a shower, drawing blood. A cyst grew there and developed into a malignant growth. For more than a year, Mary suspected that she had breast cancer, but she was unable to get appropriate medical treatment or the benefits of early detection because she had no access to medical care.

Mary lived by the kindness of strangers and by her wits. To avoid detection, she sent letters to her lawyer by mailing them to other people to remail with different postmarks. She called various child advocates from unknown locations using public phones. She received small donations of money wired through Western Union using a code. Mary and her endangered child lived in substandard conditions. She had been forced to send Debbie, as troubled as she was by Dan's abuse, back to her own father, whose alcoholism had not abated and whose care of the disturbed teen-ager was, at best, benignly inadequate. The entire family descended into abject poverty and lived in terror while Dan H received relief in court and sympathy from people who excoriated the "kidnapper" mother, Mary H, who had disobeyed a court order.

Meanwhile, attorney Mercedes Samborsky continued to fight Mary's case without payment, carrying it through the Court of Special Appeals of Maryland, trying to fend off the legal disabilities being heaped on Mary as the mother struggled to maintain her hiding place and heal her wounded pre-schooler. This pro bono attorney ultimately succeeded on appeal, making important new law in Maryland. The decision in H v. H is one of the most significant appellate decisions in the nation dealing with these cases. But had Mary not run away with Shari and endangered her own health, the appeal would not have saved Shari from sexual abuse, at least not during the year and a half that the Maryland Court of Special Appeals pondered the situation while Judge White's orders were in effect. The orders would have been enforced by police officers, who would have physically delivered Shari to Dan over Mary's objections and on command from Judge White or Judge Brown. Nor would the appeal have saved Mary H from jail for contempt during the same period while her daughter was in the "care, custody and control" of Dan H.

THE HISTORY OF THE CAMPAIGN

The present authors were among the advocates who heard from Mary during her exile. Just after the Mother's Day March on Washington in 1992, Rosen informed the Alliance for the Rights of Children that Mary H's case was again coming up for hearings in Maryland, and that Dan H expected to get not only sole custody but also a "pick-up order"—like a title to a car— that would entitle him to physically take Shari from anywhere he might find her, without the need for court or law enforcement intervention. About a dozen members of the Alliance prepared picket signs and descended on the county on May 21. They learned, first, that Judge White had recused himself and had been replaced. In his place was Judge Martin Brown, the proposed witness for Dan H in his criminal case, who was as much a part of the problem as Judge White himself. In this way the court could "look fair" but could deny all rights of fundamental fairness to mother and child, by judicial pre-arrangement.

The advocates wrote an *amicus curiae* brief and attached signature pages for the names of citizens of the county. Alliance members gathered in front of the courthouse at 7 A.M. and gave leaflets to passers-by, explaining the situation and collecting signatures on the brief to submit to the judge later in the day. More than 60 individuals signed, but fully four times as many declined to sign because they were afraid of Judge White and Judge Brown, whom they characterized as capricious, arbitrary, and vindictive. Only three persons actually took issue with the demonstrators or disbelieved their description of the case. It had been covered in the local newspapers in this small, traditional, religious neighborhood. Many citizens offered their prayers for mother and child and blessed the activists in their work.

In the bright summer weather the protest took on a 1960s civil rights ambiance. Banners and signs proclaimed, "STOP CHILD ABUSE BY THE COURTS," "PUNISH PEDOPHILES, NOT PROTECTIVE PARENTS," and other strongly worded messages. On the courthouse lawn Leora Rosen performed songs she had written for Shari, Mary, and other endangered mothers and children.

Inside the courthouse, Michelle Etlin tried to present the *amicus* brief to Judge Brown. It urged the court not to turn over the child to the convicted molester until and unless he had been evaluated by the doctor at Johns Hopkins (the first expert who had seen Dan in connection with his criminal charges) and pronounced "safe" as a caretaker for a young child. This was a stop-gap measure; the doctor had already informed Etlin that *no* person who had molested a child could *ever* be considered safe as a caretaker. But he had not been asked to testify in the custody proceedings, in spite of his expertise.

Judge Brown refused to read the *amicus* brief. He pronounced Mary psychologically impaired and gave Dan full custody, including the right to "regain" Shari anywhere and anytime he might find her. The timid guardian *ad litem* begged the court to alter its orders just slightly, so that the child, when found, would be placed—temporarily—in foster care rather than being turned over to her father. She argued that Shari "might be frightened" of her father because of her mother's (admittedly wrongful, by her own estimation) actions in telling her bad things about the custodial parent. She pointed out that a five-year-old child could be traumatized by being placed in the custody of someone she feared, and that if Shari were picked up on a Friday it might take until Monday for the lawyers to ask the court for assistance for a very frightened child.

Judge Brown refused to grant that relief, commenting that from Friday to Monday was not a very long time. A shocked murmur ran through the courtroom, and the word "Shame!" echoed. Dan visibly snickered.

Etlin ran out onto the front steps of the courthouse, took the microphone from Rosen, and told the collected demonstrators and the crowd that had gathered about the judge's words. The second-floor window of Judge Brown's courtroom was open, and it was apparent that those inside were listening. Enraged, Etlin's voice, enhanced by the microphone, carried up to the window, across the street, and down the block: "So a weekend is not much time? Well I want you in *my* garage over the weekend, Judge Martin Brown, so I can teach you something about the value of time!" Fists and shouts went up as spectators invited Judge Brown to spend weekends in their garages, learning about the quality of time.

The press was there. The *Baltimore Sun* and the *Lexington Herald Leader* carried stories and editorials about the case within days. Public opinion was definitely anti-molester and pro-mother. News reports called Mary a heroine, yet both activists and journalists realized that, while the battle for public opinion was being won, the battle for Shari's safety had already been lost.

Meanwhile Etlin followed leads developed by Mary's hometown friends in the State House and the Cabinet for Human Resources of the Commonwealth of Kentucky, where Mary was presumed to be hiding. She finally managed to reach Masten Childers III, the Counsel for the Cabinet for Human Resources. In a lengthy and productive conversation he informed her that the Cabinet could do a lot to rescue an endangered Kentucky child, but he did not know of a mechanism to protect her against a judge in another state who claimed to be exercising jurisdiction properly. Judges respect each others' turfs. In the end, Childers found a way to accomplish the goal of, as he put it, "the Commonwealth stretching out its arms to take in this child from the cold." Kentucky law, he said, allowed a person to turn a child over to the Cabinet for safe-keeping if that person could not adequately protect the child from harm.

Childers, an attorney representing one of the largest and most powerful state agencies in the country, flew to Baltimore and argued before Judge Brown Kentucky's plea to be allowed to intervene and help. "He was like Perry Mason," commented a court observer. Judge Brown backed down. He ordered a 30-day stay on his previous order (characterized by the activists as the "snatch-and-molest order") so that Kentucky could attempt to resolve the matter. When Childers, eloquent and expansive, proclaimed that the Commonwealth wanted to help the child and the mother, the defense counsel for the molester protested that it was inappropriate to try to help the mother. Again the cries of "Shame!" rose in the courtroom, and again Dan snickered.

Rushing out of the courtroom, Childers handed his card to several of the advocates. He asked them, if they had any "network connections," to make Mary aware that the Commonwealth of Kentucky wanted her to consider turning Shari over to the law in his state. Etlin said, "I'll try. I hope she trusts me enough to call in." He said, "I hope so, because we have gone a long way to try to bring her in, to help her. Tell her we are doing this for the child."

Conversations took place from public phones, to other public phones, at specified times. Sometimes connections were made and "passes were completed"; sometimes vigils by lonely pay phones netted nothing. Finally, Etlin made contact with Mary, and told her about the signatures of the citizens in Maryland, the efforts of her friends back in Kentucky, and the extraordinary efforts of Masten Childers. She added that prayers were being offered for Mary's and Shari's safety in at least ten states of the Union, as the story had appeared in newspapers in various cities. Mary knew that. With both fear and hope, with her sleeping child in the car packed with all her belongings, trusting one last time in the promise of help instead of betrayal, Mary made a dangerous decision—to risk it—and a dangerous automobile trip to bring Shari in to the Kentucky authorities. The Commonwealth of Kentucky took Shari into its jurisdiction and into its protective custody the next day.

A genuine in-depth evaluation of Dan H, including prior difficulties he had encountered with law enforcement authorities in Kentucky and elsewhere, revealed that he would not be safe as a custodial or visiting parent for Shari. Although Shari was not allowed to live with her mother at first, but was placed in foster care until she and Mary were fully evaluated, she was at least not molested, not turned over to her father, not deprived of visitation and contact with her mother, and not frightened. When the social workers from the Cabinet determined that Shari was becoming seriously depressed by the separation from her mother, they arranged for her to live with her mother again, under the protective auspices of the Cabinet.

Meanwhile, Mary was afraid to reveal her health problems, thinking that a diagnosis of a life-threatening illness would deprive her of custody of her now seriously depressed child. She hid the cancer that was growing in her breast and she traveled, when she could afford it, over state lines for intermittent and inadequate medical care elsewhere. Finally, when she revealed to social worker Betty Neufield that she was ailing, Neufield rallied to her assistance as strenuously as she had to the child of whom she had become so fond. Before the end of 1992, Shari and her mother were reunited. Debbie and Christie also returned to live with their mother in Kentucky. Social services and therapy were made available to them through the Commonwealth, and Mary was found to be "not crazy." She obtained employment as a counselor, underwent chemotherapy and radiation therapy, and began to mend her badly tattered family. She also tried to help other sexually abused children and their protective parents.

Meanwhile, Dan applied for visitation with Shari in Kentucky. His petition was considered and denied.

THE HISTORY OF AN APPEAL:
THE MARYLAND COURTS SAVE FACE

Mercedes Samborsky had done excellent work in the appeal of the custody case in Maryland, whose court still claimed to be correct in its bizarre and dangerous custody ruling. Without payment or fanfare, with no honorable mention in any of the newspaper articles, Samborsky achieved a decision in the Court of Special Appeals of Maryland dated November 10, 1992, No. 77. Justices Bishop, Bell, and Fischer said, in a *per curiam* (for the entire court) opinion, that they reversed the circuit court order of August 1991, which had caused fifteen months of fear and chaos in the lives of innocent parties. The Court said:

> Mr. H has admitted sexually abusing his 11-year-old stepchild in 1986. This particular instance of sexual abuse was one event, but there is overwhelming evidence that other instances of excessive punishment with sexual overtones had occurred prior to this incident. . . . Criminal charges of sexual molestation were brought against Mr. H for the incident involving his stepchild. As part of the plea bargain entered into by Mr. H . . . he agreed to, among other things, supervised visitation with the parties' child. . . . The trial judge granted Mr. H unsupervised four-hour weekly visitation periods [nevertheless]. . . . After one of these visits, the . . . child reported . . . [sexual abuse involving genital touching]. . . . DSS had the child examined at Mercy Hospital . . . [resulting in] . . . abnormal Genital Exam consistent with but not conclusive for fondling of external genitalia. Possible healed sexual injury. . . . Prior abuse cannot be excluded. . . . Dr. Raifman characterized Mr. H as having a "paraphiliac coercive disorder," a child physical abuse pattern characterized by thoughts and behavior of a coercive nature, called frotteurism pedophilia. . . . therefore, his child is at risk. . . . We hold that, given the circumstances presented in this case, the decision of the trial judge was clearly wrong. . . . Where the evidence is such that a parent is justified in believing that the other parent is sexually abusing the child, it is inconceivable that that parent will surrender the child to the abusing parent without stringent safeguards. . . . [The Judge] abused his discretion in failing to . . . protect the child. . . . We will reverse [the decision] but see no reason for a further review, and suggest that any further actions in this case be confined to the courts of Kentucky

which apparently have assumed jurisdiction and where the child has resided since . . . 1991.

Costs were charged against Dan H for the appeal.

THE LEGACY OF H v H

In August 1993, Carol Bowers received a Society of Journalism award for her coverage of *H* v. *H* as it unfolded in Maryland and Kentucky. Three days earlier Bowers had written an obituary of Mary H. Mary had been so weakened by chemotherapy and radiation treatments that she could no longer tolerate that medical route, physically or psychologically. She decided to try an alternative therapy, for which she had to travel to California at intervals. On her first trip, she took Shari with her. The homeopathic treatments seemed to give her back the vigor she had enjoyed before her marriage to Dan H. A picture of her and Shari taken at that time shows rosy color in both faces. On her second trip, Mary left Shari in the care of her two older sisters, Debbie (now eighteen and "emancipated") and Christie (22 years old, with a job as a horse attendant, doing the work she and her mother both loved). Mary died in Mexico, where she had gone for cancer treatment.

The newspapers again carried the story of the heroic mother and her endangered daughters. Prayers were again said in cities all over the United States. Debbie once again suffered the loss of her mother, this time permanently. Christie once again suffered too-early responsibilities brought about by the extraordinary need to protect her little sister in her mother's name. The day after her mother's death, Christie went to court, and with the help of social worker Betty Neufield, she was awarded custody of Shari.

There are many heroes in the *H* v. *H* story; their efforts, time, money, and very souls had to be tried to the breaking point because of the support the system gave a known criminal who preyed on children. Masten Childers III, now Secretary for Human Resources for the Commonwealth of Kentucky, blazed a trail that had never been taken before in the service of children at risk. He promoted his innovative legal attack on a complex problem with an advocacy born of passion. Betty Neufield, with a quiet voice and a solid knowledge of child psychology and social work, patiently helped mother and child heal from a nearly incurable assault on their health and welfare. Journalists Carol Bowers and Valerie Honeycutt used the mighty pens of their profession. In the office, the study, and the library, in the courtroom and the imposing appellate halls, attorney Mercedes Samborsky prevailed by the excellence of her presentation and her devotion to the merits of her client's case and a child's life. Personal friends and supporters of Mary H played both silent and vocal roles throughout the events, giving with no thought of return, helping with no thought of consequences, using "whatever means necessary" in their attempts to protect and defend the innocent. Sixty ordinary citizens of the county signed a petition early one morning in spite of the fact that the judges were feared and the mother and child were unknown to them. A dozen members of the Alliance for the Rights of Children stood on the grass in front of the courthouse and made it clear to Judge Martin Brown that they were outraged at his judicial behavior.

We will never know what combination of events produced which results, and although Mary died because of the rigors of her effort, the victims in this case were finally protected.

2
In the Interest
of Marissa, a Child

THE FAMILY, THE IMPERATIVE, AND
"WHAT IS A SECRET?"

Linda Jamison called a family meeting two months after separating from her husband, Ronald. She hoped to work out certain domestic problems amicably. Accustomed to an extended family life-style, she invited her estranged husband; her own mother, Marianne Jamison; her mother-in-law, Mildred; her husband's friend Arthur and his wife, Aline. Linda recorded the meeting and later listened to the tape over and over, as if trying to convince herself of the reality of her situation. An African American woman with a Christian heritage, Linda did not want her daughter brought up in the new Lord of the Sky cult that her husband had joined. Ronald had been indoctrinated into the cult by Arthur, and was expecting to be ordained as a minister, as his friend had been. Linda held herself apart from these activities, but during the last stages of her marriage, Ronald had persuaded her to undergo an "exorcism" under their auspices. Because of her despondency after the death of her own father, her husband and his new religious friends insisted that she needed a cult-performed ceremony to purge her grief, but the proceeding had terrified and humiliated her. Without giving details, Linda said that she had refused to continue with the ritual, but that her husband and his friends had forcibly completed it to their own satisfaction. "What they did," she almost whispered, "was actually illegal; they did not have my consent." All three of the cult members then tried to prevail upon Linda to stay with Ronald and to adopt the religion; they wanted, above all, to make sure that she would not bring charges against them. But she wanted to separate herself and her child from the cult and its practices. She sought her mother-in-law's intervention and her husband's agreement, hoping to handle the problem through divorce rather than the police.

Linda struggled to convince her mother-in-law that she had to divorce Ronald unless he could keep his religious conversion to himself. She didn't want their baby, Marissa, then two years old, to be indoctrinated into the new religion or treated the way children were treated by the fanatical cult members. She objected to some Lord of the Sky practices that she believed were sexualized and inappropriate. She did not want to relocate to the ultrareligious commune in Sky Village, Georgia, where Ronald had been invited to be ordained as a priest.

Mildred was not happy to hear her daughter-in-law speaking about her own interests rather than her husband's reputation. Ronald, who was his mother's favorite child, was a successful Certified Public Accountant. Mildred had grown fairly close to Linda during the marriage, and the two had confided in each other. Although Mildred was not delighted with the cult herself, she now scolded Linda, insisting that family problems must never be made public by divorce.

Mildred had lived through precedents in her own life, both with keeping secrets and with revealing them. Her own mother had prosecuted the superintendent of her apartment building for molesting Mildred at a time when such prosecutions were almost unheard of. The family had said that Mildred and another relative had been "lowered into the basement" to provide oral sex for the pedophile and forced to endure other indignities and sexual assaults. Mildred said she had had to stay out of school for a long time, having contracted a venereal disease. She said things had happened to her that she "would take to [her] grave."

Ronald's father had been a religious fanatic, insisting that his wife and children attend church six days a week. He sent them to at least eight different denominations, from church to church, on a harrowing schedule. He also beat Mildred viciously during the marriage, so much so that Ronald, whose reputation she now ferociously defended, had once physically confronted his father to protect her. His father called the police and had Ronald kicked out of the house, as his mother watched helplessly. Ronald's father had often held "family night," when he sat the children down, at ages as young as five, and preached at them for hours in a bellowing voice, while they were paralyzed with fear, forbidden to speak or move. Yet Mildred never divorced him; even now they live separately a few blocks apart and they have never "aired their dirty laundry in public."

Mildred's voice eventually became raucous on the tape, which lasted 90 minutes. She did not want her daughter-in-law to divorce Ronald. She cried that she would never see her little granddaughter again. She would say or do anything to protect Ronald, to preserve his reputation, and to keep Marissa—anything. Linda spreads out notebook after notebook of orderly tabbed, indexed exhibits and documents. "Anything," she explains, in a sweet, wavering voice,

> can include lying, committing perjury, making false allegations against others to protect herself from the truth, intimidating my baby girl not to tell what has been done to her, taking Marissa away and handing her over to a cult of child abusers and pedophiles, allowing my beautiful child to be

molested and even raped just as horribly as she herself was so many years ago. "Anything" can include all that.

And Linda has evidence of "all that" in her notebooks and in her five-year history in the child protection system.

THE SYSTEM: "WHAT IS AN ISSUE?"

Linda and Ronald had separated in April 1990; the family meeting was held in June. Convinced that the animosity could not be resolved, Linda decided inalterably that she had to divorce Ronald to protect Marissa from Lord of the Sky activities. Ronald was taking Marissa on visitation every other week, from Friday until Sunday evening, and on Mondays and Wednesdays of the alternate weeks. Linda had some misgivings but she did not interfere. Since she had no evidence of actual sexual abuse, she maintained a watchful eye and continued to encourage liberal contact between father and daughter.

In December 1990, however, Marissa returned from visits with a persistent vaginal discharge. The pediatrician referred Linda to the Albert Jacobi Hospital emergency room for children. Just beginning to become verbal, Marissa described a game her father played with her, putting her pacifier into her genitals to illustrate his behavior. The doctors diagnosed a urinary tract infection but could not confirm sexual abuse. They said Marissa was too young to interview with anatomically detailed dolls, and although Linda had notified Child Welfare Authority (CWA) of a possible problem, they failed to provide an age-appropriate validation study for her, simply observing that Marissa "looked healthy."

The next day, after her bath, Marissa told her maternal grandmother that her daddy put Vaseline on her when he "hurt her." Marissa showed Marianne Jamison in body language that her father had hurt her anal area, her vaginal area, and her undeveloped breasts, after spreading Vaseline on those parts. Linda did not question her daughter, but reported the incident to CWA.

The caseworker sent to the house told Linda to give Marissa her doll and some Vaseline and say, "The baby doll is hurt, what do you do?" Marissa at first described the baby doll's injuries as being a result of "Uncle Arthur" hurting her, and then showed how her own daddy had hurt her, the real baby, by pulling up her dress and pointing to her anogenital area, correctly saying, "in my vagina" and "in my buttocks." Linda had always taught Marissa the correct words for her body parts. The caseworker advised Linda to get an order of protection and not to allow any more contact with the father, or she could be charged with child endangerment. As Christmas approached, that caseworker went on vacation and the case fell into limbo. On New Year's Eve, he called, saying he had interviewed Ronald and found out that there was a divorce proceeding pending. He immediately decided to close the case and advised Linda to "take up the matter in divorce court." When Marianne

Jamison called him to argue that it was not a divorce matter but a child abuse matter, he accused her of negligence and refused to help. As far as CWA was concerned, he said, the investigation was ended because sexual abuse was merely "an issue on divorce."

Linda points out that CWA and the court hearing the divorce case ignored the fact that she was providing liberal visitation for Ronald before the disclosure of sexual abuse and the urinary tract infection that signaled sexual abuse. "They all say this is about me not wanting him to visit his child," she protests, "but he was visiting his child until he molested her. This is about me not wanting my child to be molested."

Linda immediately felt the hostility in the family court, but at first, she thought the law guardian, Darlene Painter, would help. As soon as Painter was appointed, she expressed concern about Arthur and Ronald having molested her child client. In February 1991 she invited Linda, Marianne, and Marissa to her own home in Mahopec, New York. Painter took Marissa into her bedroom and interviewed her for about an hour while Linda and Marianne waited, entertained by Painter's mother. When Painter came out of that interview, with Vaseline all over her hands and arms and Marissa practically covered with it from demonstrating what her father had done, Painter was prepared to tell the court that Ronald had molested Marissa and that she was "obsessive" about Vaseline and sexual abuse. On March 13, 1991, Painter informed the family court that she wanted all visitation between Ronald and the child supervised by a licensed agency, to prevent further problems. She documented the fact that, on February 27, 1991, Marissa had disclosed sexual abuse by both Arthur and her father. A court date was set for April 8, 1991 to review the visitation situation.

On March 28, 1991, Marissa's teacher sent Linda a letter saying she was concerned about certain behaviors that Marissa was displaying in school. Linda took that to court with her as well. On April 8, when Linda showed up for court, she was led to a witness room for a conference with her attorney, and suddenly the entire nature of the proceeding changed. Her lawyer admonished her in urgent tones to "stop talking about the sex abuse issue right now." The lawyer said Painter had "changed her position" about the sexual abuse; therefore Linda had to do the same. Linda objected, unable to understand how a "change in position" could have occurred, since Painter had not conducted a new interview of Marissa. Linda described her attorney as "shaking with fear, really frantic to get me to drop it," badgering Linda to "forget about all this and get on with your life." The lawyer even insisted Linda had to convince Judge Rita Connolly that she no longer believed her daughter had been molested. Linda would not agree, pointing out that if she did so, Ronald would again have unsupervised visitation and Marissa would again be abused. The lawyer pulled out of the case immediately.

Judge Connolly was annoyed with Ronald and his lawyer for being late. Without a hearing, she granted Painter's request to have a validator interview Marissa. Thus, Painter did not have a chance to describe her "turn-around" to the court, and Linda was not asked to "convince" the judge that she had abandoned her belief. Linda would have time to find a new lawyer, and, she assumed, that Marissa would be taken to a psychological validator and thus protected.

At that time, Linda belonged to a mothers' group called 21st Century, because their children would be eighteen by that time. The group had speakers, seminars, and activities. A local pediatrician, Dr. Ronald Sand, had made a presentation to the group about children's health, and Linda was impressed with his expertise and gentle manner. When she took Marissa for an examination on June 6, 1991, Dr. Sand said his findings were consistent with a history of sexual abuse. He immediately called in a mandated report to the child abuse hot line, saying he was concerned because the "child did not have a hymen." This would indicate that Marissa's descriptions of digital (and/or other) penetration into her vagina were accurate and were now corroborated by medical evidence.

But the decision seemed to have been made, somewhere, by someone, that the case would be considered "unfounded." CWA's response to Sand's mandated report was an immediate attempt to discredit the pediatrician and supersede his report with someone else's opinion. CWA ordered Linda to take Marissa to Dr. Maureen Manchester at a metropolitan hospital; if she did not do so, she would immediately lose custody for disobedience. The threat of loss of custody was already being used by the authorities to discipline Linda. Although a second examination for physical evidence of child sexual abuse is not advisable, according to American Medical Association guidelines, it was clear that this "second opinion" was part of a plan upon which Painter and CWA had already embarked. Linda took Marissa to the hospital as ordered. She and Marianne went into the examination room with Marissa and finally got her to agree to let Dr. Manchester examine her genitals and take pictures with a special camera, called a colposcope. Linda saw Dr. Manchester take at least four pictures with the colposcope.

After the examination, Dr. Manchester would not meet with Linda, but a hospital staff member tried to convince her that Marissa might not have been molested; instead, he suggested, she might have become "sexualized" by watching porno films. He could not, however, explain other evidence that she had been mistreated—a friction burn on the child's buttocks and the many scratches across her back. No CWA caseworker was on hand, although that had been promised. Linda was finally dismissed with instructions that the photographs, to be developed later, would reveal the conclusion of the examination.

The hospital refused to turn over the records to Linda or her counsel, and she received no information until seven months later, when Dr. Manchester appeared in court. Hired and paid by Ronald as his witness, the doctor testified that in her opinion Marissa had not been molested, based on her own determination about the absence of physical evidence of penetration. She did not have her file with her, and at first she testified that she had not taken any pictures. Confronted by Linda's attorney on cross-examination, she said that she had taken pictures, but the equipment was broken that day.

Nearly two years later, Linda was waiting in a courthouse in another jurisdiction, where she had accompanied another mother to provide support and comfort during a sex abuse trial. Dr. Manchester was scheduled to testify in that case. Again, CWA had hired her to do a second-opinion examination after definitive evidence of penetration had been discovered and documented. Linda and three others in the waiting room burst into tears when the mother emerged from the court room saying, "Guess what—Manchester did it again—no evidence, her equipment was broken again!" No explanation was ever demanded or given as to why this physician, relied upon so heavily by the New York child abuse authorities, did not reschedule exams after such "broken equipment" days.

Painter had been ordered to find a validator to interview Marissa. After two months, she finally did. Linda took Marissa to Dr. Arlene Nardi, who determined in one session that there was probable cause to suspect that the child had been sexually abused. Nardi immediately Faxed a letter to the judge, saying that she suspected sexual abuse and that there was enough risk for her to strongly urge that Marissa not be exposed to her father unsupervised until the investigation was completed. Judge Connolly did not react—on the record. The letter was in fact suppressed until Linda's third attorney discovered it in the file nearly three months later. All that time, visitation proceeded in spite of the risk and in spite of Dr. Nardi's express concerns.

Since CWA had told Linda to deal with the sexual abuse in the divorce case, her new lawyer started a custody and visitation proceeding in divorce court based on the allegations. Painter showed up at that proceeding, in tow with Ronald's lawyer. Although she had no legal role to play in divorce court, being a family court law guardian appointed in a child abuse investigation, she voluntarily intervened, assumed a role, and addressed the court. She told the judge that Linda had "dragged the child to six doctors," although, in truth, Linda had only voluntarily taken her daughter to one doctor, Dr. Sand; CWA had ordered her to go to Dr. Manchester. Painter insisted that the proceeding be referred back to the family court. Clearly, she had an interest to protect at this point. Whose?

Marissa's visitation with her father continued unsupervised, and her behavior continued to attract attention from the concerned adults in her life. On September 13, 1991, her teacher made a mandated report to the child abuse hot line and filled out an affidavit for the Bronx District Attorney. She was very concerned about the "sexualized behavior" Marissa exhibited after weekends she spent with her father, and reported disclosures Marissa had made about him. The CWA caseworker refused to investigate the teacher's mandated report. The next day, Painter suddenly called in a mandated report of suspected sex abuse of Marissa against Marianne Jamison, Linda's mother. Painter alleged that she had just gotten information that Marissa was sexually abused by her maternal grandmother inserting a thermometer into her vagina. Painter's source of information was Ronald, who had been told it by his mother. Less than two weeks later, without a validation report or an evidentiary hearing, the family court cut off all contact between Marianne and her granddaughter, based upon that allegation. Still the mandated report from the teacher remained uninvestigated, although Painter admitted that a child's teacher would be "a good source of information" about her behavior.

Judge Connolly did not allow Marissa to return to Dr. Nardi, the psychologist who had already reported her suspicions of sexual abuse by the father, and Nardi never completed the validation process. Linda again made a motion, through her new attorney, for validation. Time passed.

The court appearances became nightmarish by sheer quantity alone. Linda recalls 102 separate court dates. The Assistant District Attorney testified that there was sufficient evidence against Ronald to prosecute for child sexual abuse, but he could not get CWA to cooperate. Painter ripped him apart on the stand. Marissa's teacher testified about her concerns, with her detailed notes in front of her. On March 25, 1991, Marissa woke up from a nap, screaming. Questioned, the child said, "Daddy scares me and he scares me in the bathroom." The teacher's log showed the dates in 1991 when there were incidents suspicious for child sexual abuse: February 22; March 1 and 22; May 20, 22, 24, and 31; June 7 and 21; July 19; August 9; September 13 and 20. Then, chronologically, came the hearing at which all contact between Marissa and her maternal grandmother had been severed because of the "thermometer allegation." Still, suspicious incidents continued unabated: October 18 and December 5, 1991; January 24, March 27, May 15, July 10, and July 17, 1992. Thirteen incidents occurred before the thermometer allegation, seven afterward. Unsupervised visits with Ronald, his family, friends, and religious cohorts continued during this period.

On July 13, 1992, Marissa's therapist called in yet another mandated report to the hot line of the State Central Registry, saying Marissa had disclosed sexual abuse to him, including telling him that "her father recently licked her privates." Later that day, the therapist informed Linda's attorney of the disclosure the child had made to him, and said he had already phoned in a report to CWA. Two weeks later, a CWA caseworker was assigned to investigate. Finally, the therapist called the CWA supervisor, dissatisfied with the way the investigation was proceeding—because it was not proceeding. According to the supervisor, the caseworker was on vacation and had not filed an abuse report. The therapist objected to delay, noting that the child was still seeing the father unsupervised. The supervisor agreed that the caseworker should have "stopped the contact from the father" under those circumstances; but still, nothing was done.

Painter rushed into the family court and repeated her concerns about the thermometer abuse, although all contact with Marianne Jamison had ended nine months earlier. Visitation with Ronald was continued but was ordered to be supervised by Ronald's mother, over Linda's vociferous objections.

Judge Connolly then ordered a videotaped interview of Marissa, although CWA objected. When Linda's lawyer moved to have Painter kept away from Marissa until after the interview, the Judge responded that the law guardian need not see the child "unless there was some emergency."

THE CREATION OF AN "EMERGENCY"

On August 8, 1992, a day when Linda was ordered to turn Marissa over to Ronald for a visit at 10 A.M., Painter called the therapist's office at 7:10 A.M., asking him to call her immediately because there was an emergency. Marissa was with her mother, who had not reported any emergency. The therapist reached his office at noon and began to call Painter from that time until 10 at night, but he got no answer and no answering machine. He called again all day Sunday and got no response.

At 10 A.M. Saturday morning, Linda turned Marissa over to Ronald for court-ordered visitation, finding out only later that Marissa was taken to Mahopec, to Painter's home, for a new interrogation in her father's presence. On Monday, Painter made a new mandated report against Marianne Jamison, again alleging thermometer abuse. She also told Marissa's therapist she was trying to put the child into foster care.

On August 31, 1992, Linda took Marissa to CWA for the court-ordered videotaped interview. A week later, Linda's attorney watched the video, on which Marissa apparently disclosed oral sexual abuse by Ronald three times and said that she was warned by "Grandma Milly"—Ronald's mother, Mildred—"not to tell." After speaking with the Bronx D.A., the therapist, and the teacher, Linda's attorney filed an order to show cause in the family court to have Ronald's visitation supervised by a qualified agency. No decision was ever made on that motion. Painter made a cross-motion saying that Marissa had revealed on the videotape that her grandmother Marianne Jamison had inserted a thermometer into her vagina. According to Linda's attorney, that is not on the tape. The tape was never aired in court.

THE "VALIDATION" EVALUATION—"WHAT IS A LIE?"

In October and November 1992, at last, Marissa was taken for a validation interview by CWA's choice of validators, Ellen Trevor. Trevor had become somewhat famous—or notorious—for her role in prosecution of the Wee Care day-care sex abuse case in New Jersey, leading to the conviction of

Kelly Michaels, who was later exonerated on appeal by the New Jersey Supreme Court. In this very high-profile case, Richard Gardner was a witness for the defense, and the press were intimately involved (see Manshel, 1990).

After Trevor testified about the conclusions of her interviews with twenty children between the ages of three and five, a jury convicted Michaels, a young, female day-care worker, for 115 counts of child sexual abuse. They believed, beyond a reasonable doubt, what Trevor said she believed: that Michaels had horribly molested and even ritually abused those children in the day-care center, while escaping notice by her fellow instructors, none of whom were accused of complicity in the crimes. In the Wee Care case, Trevor validated allegations that Michaels licked peanut butter off the children's genitals, made the children drink her urine and eat her feces, and raped and assaulted them with knives, forks, spoons, and Lego blocks. Trevor believed that Michaels had performed these atrocities on the children during nursery school hours over a period of seven months, during which time no parents had reported disclosures from their children or suspicions aroused by marks, injuries, behaviors, fears, or odors of urine or feces. Trevor's interviewing techniques had been attacked by the defense counsel as leading and coercive. A rash of articles criticizing her methods appeared. Similar articles are often used to support the theory that disclosures of incest are invalid because validation methods are so inappropriate and misleading.

The same validator refused to believe Marissa's disclosures in spite of corroborating evidence from her mother, grandmother, therapist, and teacher. Trevor, who believed the Wee Care children's disclosures uncritically, invalidated Marissa's statements, calling some of them "not realistic." For example:

> In the second session . . . [Marissa] spontaneously said . . . "One day I told my Mommy I was mad cause my Daddy told a lie on me." When the content of the lie was probed, Marissa said "I told my Mommy to tell the Judge but she is going to tell him." With further probing about the lie, Marissa stated "I told [the therapist] that. That Daddy did something, I did not like it." Her speech pattern changed at this point to a slower, more faltering pace. When asked what she told [the therapist], [Marissa] took a deep breath and said "He hurt me" with downcast eyes. She then moved back to her play. In an effort to test her suggestibility, I asked if the father had punched her in the nose, which she denied saying "no. He did something that was not very nice." When asked again what he had done, she said that he hurt her "so much he did not know he was watching the step." When asked what that meant, Marissa stated "he had to watch cause he was telling a lie on me and that's why I get mad at him." She then said that "he touched me in my private part." There was no change in her affect in making this statement. [Marissa] said that he touched her vagina with a stick, that he had taken from the ground.

The use of sticks and various "magic wands" in sexual abuse is fairly common in cult rituals. Many adult survivors of such organized sadistic abuse report that, as children, they were mistreated with a variety of sticks, wands, canes, bats, walking sticks, vibrators, "scepters," and even crucifixes, apparently to convince them that the objects were powerful magical tools that could be used to punish them if they revealed abuse. Such a "stick" or "wand" might be left around the house "innocently" or even hung on a wall or placed in a toy chest, as a constant reminder to the children of their obligation to remain silent about the rituals they endured.

Also, in this part of the report, we detect a conflict in the child with respect to her father's accusations against her for "lying"—showing that on unsupervised visitation, it is quite possible that the child was being threatened and manipulated so she would not reveal the abuse. Nevertheless, her disclosures did continue:

> [I] directly asked "what did he do to your vagina?" and Marissa answered "he looked in my vagina" and she added that he said "yhew."
>
> [I] gave Marissa a Teddy Ruxpin bear and asked her to demonstrate on the doll what had happened to her. She said "Pulled down my shirt. Pulled up my skirt, then he pulled down my panties and I did not like it" . . . "then he pulled them all the way down" . . . then "he stepped on me" . . . "on my head. He stepped on me." When asked what he did then, Marissa stated "I think that's it. I don't know the rest. I think I forgot. Then he licked me in my vagina. Then he put some Vaseline." When asked what happened then, she said "I don't know the rest. I forgot. I want to color." There was no noticeable change in her affect or play when she made these statements.
>
> . . . Marissa was asked where Daddy had licked her vagina and she said "in the living room, he was trying to hide so Grandma Milly did not see him." She said she was laying [sic] down on a cover when this happened and that "he was sneaking so he could lick me and that's why he licked me and that's all, my Mommy, that's all I told my Mommy." She was asked what the story was with the Vaseline and she said she did not know. Marissa expressed that she was tired and wanted some apple juice. No further inquiries were pursued in this session.

Apparently, Trevor did not follow up on Marissa's statement that "that's all I told my Mommy." Most of the children in the Wee Care case had not disclosed abuse to their parents. In light of Marissa's concern about her father and grandmother not wanting her to reveal secrets, it would have been appropriate for the interviewer to discuss with the child her fear about "telling." It came up in the following exchange:

> In the third session . . . [I] informed Marissa that [I] had met with her father. Marissa appeared very concerned about this and said "what did he tell you? Did you tell him that he hurt me?" [I] told Marissa that [I] had not

told the father what Marissa had said, to which Marissa replied "Don't tell him cause he might get mad, okay?" . . . [I] asked Marissa how [I] could help [her] with her Daddy and Marissa said that he was "not doing that to me no more." When asked what he had done, Marissa said "before he was hurting me and that stuff." When asked what he hurt, Marissa said she did not want to talk about that, but rather that she wanted to play.

The child continued to be responsive and credible. Trevor wrote:

She was asked if she would like to show [me] what had happened to her using a doll. Marissa said she would . . . and was asked to select any doll in the playroom. She selected the anatomical dolls and said "want me to show you?" as she pulled down the pants of an adult, male, Black doll, and said "Yuck. I don't have a penis. I want a girl and a boy doll." She pulled down the underwear of the girl doll and said "he hurt me back here (vaginal area) and back here (buttocks). He said, pshh, oh penis. My Daddy pulled down his pants and he pull off his shirt." Once again, there was not a noticeable change in her affect as she made these statements.

Although some evaluators believe that the anatomically explicit dolls are themselves suggestive, in this case there were other disclosures which did not depend on the use of such dolls. Marissa had already described abuse to a CWA worker, law guardian Painter, her grandmother, her teacher, and her therapist. It seemed as if she had been placed on a treadmill and would have to keep disclosing over and over until she either gave up and recanted or gave some indication of "inconsistencies" that could be used to invalidate the whole process. Meanwhile, she was visiting her father, and the issue of "lying" came up:

When asked if she thought that some adults sometimes tell lies, Marissa said "sometimes my daddy tells lies." When asked "what about" she said "I don't know. Sometimes he lies and lies and sometimes he tells the truth. Sometimes he does not listen to me." When asked for an example of when he did not listen, she said "because one time he told me—you told a lie and [sic] me and that was the lie.

This paragraph points up how expert an expert has to be in understanding "Childrenese." In our opinion, Marissa meant, in the last sentence, "because one time he told me, 'you [meaning Marissa] told a lie on me,'" and that [the accusation against Marissa for allegedly telling a lie "on" her father] was the lie. In other words, we believe that Trevor did not comprehend the childlike description of the father's "lie." It seems likely that the following scenario had taken place: Marissa had disclosed sexual abuse by her father; then she was exposed to him under the "supervision" of his own mother, Grandma Milly, who had previously warned her not to "tell." We believe her explanation means that her father said to her, "You [Marissa] told a lie on me [Ronald]!" Confronted about her disclosure, without a supervisor's protection, facing censure from her father and grandmother, Marissa would have been unable to defend the truth of her prior disclosure. That is why, we believe, she later declared that his accusation of her was "the lie," and that is why, we believe, she was "so mad now."

Our interpretation is, we believe, perfectly compatible with all the other facts known. Linda kept audio tapes of Marissa raging about "how mad" she was after her father badgered her during a visit, after her therapist testified as to her disclosure. In the midst of being called a liar and interviewed over and over, Marissa expressed herself to Treacy:

> "He told cause I did not tell the lie on him and that's why I am so mad now." Marissa denied that children sometimes tell lies and she denied that she had ever told a lie in her life. When presented with eight inquiries designed to objectively assess a child's ability to differentiate truth from lies, she correctly responded to all eight. . . . On . . . inquiries regarding the difference between "real" and "make-believe," Marissa correctly responded to five of six.

The child knew not only the difference between truth and falsehood but also the difference between reality and fantasy. She was also credible in that she did not have a neatly packaged list of complaints to make about her father, she displayed conflict when asked to tell Trevor about him hurting her, although she did ultimately make herself perfectly clear. The following notes appear at various places throughout the report:

> She was asked what happened next and she said that her father does not like her, but she could not explain this perception any further.

> When asked again about the location, she said that it happened at her father's house in the living room while Grandma "Milly" . . . [was] present. She was asked to describe what he did and she said "He hurt me with a stick and I did not like it and he laughed when he did it and I did not think it was funny. I never hurt my Daddy." When asked what he did with the stick, Marissa said "He hurt me too much and I say stop it, stop it and he did not stop." When [I] asked what the father did in the living room, Marissa said that the father punched her on her foot and that it "hurted."

> She also told [me] that she still loves her father. Marissa talked about the visits to her father's home and said that she liked these visits. [I] asked Marissa how [I] could help [her] with her Daddy and Marissa said that he was "not doing that to me no more." When asked what he had done, Marissa said "before he was hurting me and that stuff."

Marissa was aware that there was conflict between her father and mother, but she attributed it to the fact that her father had hurt her, rather than seeing it as a separate troubling issue:

> [I] asked if her father likes her mother, Marissa replied that her mother tries to talk to her father, but that the father will not listen to the mother and that was "how my Mommy gets mad." When she was asked if the mother likes the father, she said "no, not actually when he hurts me."
>
> When she was asked what her mother thinks about all of this, Marissa said "she says did Daddy hurt you still and I said no." Marissa also said that she forgot the first person she told about all of this.

It should have been apparent that Marissa was not being coached by her mother or being turned against her father for vindictive purposes. When first invited by Ellen Trevor to "tell on" her father—by being asked about good and bad touches, but before she was engaged and fully comfortable with the interviewer,

> She reported that her Daddy gave her a lot of good touches and when asked about bad touches, she said "I don't know. Nobody gave me a bad touch." She did appear somewhat anxious at this point and turned her back to the evaluator and this was the first time that she had done so in the session.

Marissa had already told her own therapist, her teacher, and her relatives about the "bad touches." The result had been a lot of sound and fury but no change in her unsupervised visitation with her father and grandmother. It is undeniable that a child who had previously disclosed sexual abuse and then had to face the alleged perpetrator unprotected, to be confronted about it, would thereafter be reluctant to repeat the process. This does not invalidate the prior disclosures or her subsequent ones.

After all this, Trevor, who had believed the Wee Care children about elaborate sexual and ritual abuse by Kelly Michaels during nap time in the day-care center, concluded:

> After reviewing the various reports and records in the present case, as well as the present assessment process, this case cannot be found to be consistent with child sexual abuse. . . . The child's statements to various professionals have not been consistent in central action details through time or setting.

Yet Marissa had told her therapist the same things she now told Trevor; she had told her teacher the same thing she had told her grandmother; she did not necessarily tell each person every single abusive incident or detail each time, but she was going on visits for seven months while being repeatedly interviewed. Trevor wrote: "In the present interview, the child was unable to provide a consistent recollection of the alleged events."

Here, it may be that Trevor is harder to understand than the child she interviewed. Marissa's recollection seemed consistent for a child her age: her father had hurt her by touching her private parts with a stick and otherwise; he had undressed her and touched her private parts; he had licked her private parts; he may have physically abused her during or between these incidents. But then Trevor deals the final blow to the disclosure, a completely subjective decision; *she* does not believe it: "Some of the activities that are described are not realistic." Was there anything less realistic than the acts allegedly performed by Michaels against the twenty children Trevor had believed?

"Her affect in making the statements was not consonant with her remarks." Marissa's affect was at first refractory, as she refused to admit or discuss sexual abuse. She sometimes said she forgot, and wanted to color; sometimes she was tired and wanted apple juice. Later, her affect varied, including slower and faltering speech, downcast eyes, being very concerned (at the suggestion that Trevor might have told her father she had "told" again), and several times answering that she didn't want to talk about her father hurting her; she wanted to play. These are perfectly consistent with the disclosures and with what is known about children who have been molested.

We submit that Marissa's affect was not the real issue. Toward the end of the report, the following language shows what Trevor's concern may have been: "These difficulties in the case are further compounded by the context of the case. The mother and father are embroiled in a bitter dispute over the custody of the child." Trevor was influenced by the context of the case. She was not faced with twenty children accusing an unrelated adult female of hideous abuse; she was faced with incest. She turned away from the obvious finding, in an official move strangely reminiscent of the child's original reaction of turning her back on the evaluator. To cover her retreat, Trevor churned out the stock commentary about the harm that can come to children from divorce and litigation:

> The child is caught between two parents that she loves. Family therapy with both parents and the child should be strongly considered. Marissa is a child with a tremendous amount of potential. There is no question that her overall development will be compromised unless she is allowed to grow without the lingering litigation and its accompanying acrimony.

There is a certain phenomenon attending the judicial reception given to reports and conclusions of validators: if they say that they believe a child has been molested (as Dr. Nardi had done earlier in this case), there is usually no immediate action, and the opinions of other professionals are sought to see if they agree with the validator. If, however, the validators say that they disbelieve a child who has disclosed sexual abuse (as Trevor now did), their disbelief is acted upon immediately and the opinions of other professionals who may believe the child are disregarded. Thus, if a validator wants to be thought of as credible, the easiest course is to disbelieve children who say they have been molested by parents. To avoid hostile and threatening cross-examination, possible lawsuits, and exposure to all manner of enmity and opposition, the safest route for a validator to follow is the route taken—for whatever reason—by Ellen Trevor, not in the sensational Wee Care sex-abuse case, but in the case of Marissa.

THE DIVORCE: "WHAT IS CUSTODY?"

Linda was promptly made the focus of blame for her daughter's problems. She was ordered into a Parenting Skills Course provided by CWA, and when she successfully completed it, the judge was notified of her "graduation." Now Ronald was on the offensive. Although the Crime Victims Assistance Unit of the Bronx D.A.'s office already regarded Linda and Marissa as victims of sexual assault, the D.A.'s position and even the testimony of the Assistant D.A. who had interviewed the child were disregarded by the judge.

Marissa's therapist soon noticed and reported negative effects upon his patient: "Lately, stories she tells involve adults breaching faith and betraying trust." Meanwhile, Linda sought a psychological evaluation of herself to defend against the "crazy mother" charges. A board-certified psychologist evaluated her and reported that there was

> no evidence in this testing to support the supposition [that] . . . [Linda] is delusional. Her affect, in this testing situation, was not "flat" and she was very appropriate. She was highly animated and talked spontaneously with this Examiner. She appeared to be very much "at ease."

The psychologist noted that Linda suffered from a generalized anxiety disorder, obviously brought on by the sexual abuse of her daughter. He concluded that "the child in question should remain in [Linda's] custody unless there is evidence to the contrary."

This is not what happened.

At hearings convened by New York State Senator David Paterson on May 14, 1993, Linda reported, in a calm but sorrowful voice, that Judge Rita Connolly had taken custody away from her with a handwritten one-paragraph order. She would be allowed only six hours of visitation per month, supervised by the father, to take place where and when the father allowed it. No finding of fact was included about the possible sexual abuse of Marissa; no mention was made of the lengthy sexual abuse investigation. Linda, having lost her job during the eighteen month trial, was ordered to pay child support to Ronald out of her unemployment compensation.

When Linda filed her notice of appeal, she made an application to have the trial transcripts—which would cost over $40,000—prepared free, since she was a pauper within the meaning of New York law. The New York City Corporation Counsel opposed her getting free transcripts because her appeal was "without merit." Not having seen those transcripts, it is unclear how the Corporation Counsel came to that conclusion, for Linda had filed with them a book full of exhibits showing that the allegations of child sexual abuse were well documented and fully corroborated.

Marissa lives with her father and lives the life he sees fit for her. She sees her mother only under her father's stern gaze on alternate Saturdays in public places of his choice. Linda says that Marissa, a musical and creative child, makes up songs to cover her sorrow. "Someday we'll be together," she sings, "and we'll be so happy, together, for-e-ver, the two of us, you and me, Mommy, you and me-eee-eee Mommy, so-ome-day."

3

We Believe Jesse

Karen Carter led the Mothers Day March for the Children in Washington, D.C., in 1992. Hundreds of protective parents, adult survivors of incest, and child advocates gathered on the south lawn of the Capitol to hear the speakers, before marching sixteen blocks to the White House, loudly chanting "We believe Jesse!" and "Two, four, six, eight, no more baby rape!" On Mothers Day, 1993, Karen again stood in Lafayette Square, updating the crowd on the status of her daughter's case and the cases of other molested children around the country. In 1994, the March for the Children was held in Grant Park, Chicago, and again, Karen was the lead activist.

Karen came from an Iowa farm family of six children, all devout Roman Catholics. Her sister fashioned a handmade christening gown for Karen's baby, completely covered with an elaborate design of seed pearls, white lace, and embroidery. A large photograph of Jesse wearing the gown hangs in the living room of Karen's modest house-trailer in Iowa City, next to framed pictures of Jesse as a toddler in an ornate, frilly ballerina costume; Jesse with members of the extended family; Jesse at play; Jesse hugging her mother.

Custody of Jesse was taken from Karen before her third birthday, by the Johnson County, Iowa, Juvenile Court. Karen was then denied visitation for nearly three years because she continued to believe and to verbalize her belief that her daughter had been molested. During the legal battle over the next five years, even the authorities admitted that Jesse had been molested.

THE MARRIAGE, THE DIVORCE

Karen described her husband, Bob Fulton, as verbally abusive to her as soon as they married, in May 1981. She tolerated it, but said that the abuse intensified during her pregnancy, when Bob threatened to take her baby away. She sought pastoral counseling. Bob sought legal advice, apparently planning divorce. After six years of marriage, when Jesse was only six months old, Bob sued Karen for divorce and custody, and a bitter struggle ensued.

In the first stage of the divorce proceedings, unbeknownst to Karen, a guardian *ad litem* was assigned to the infant Jesse: Donald Harper, a well-known Iowa City lawyer with the firm of Larson & Harper. Of course, Jesse, at ten months, was not yet verbal and was not able to express her wishes to her new lawyer. Harper did not consider that a drawback, since he never tried to meet his client, even when she learned to talk. By the time he testified under oath in 1994, nearly seven years later, he had still not tried to meet or interview his client.

Karen's lawyer told her that Harper was hostile to her almost from the start. Also, forensic evaluator James Cunningham was very positively impressed by Bob Fulton. Nine months after Harper's appointment, Karen reached an agreement with Bob for joint legal and physical custody with neither parent seeking child support or alimony. She said she was under pressure to avoid trial because the guardian *ad litem* was so firmly set against her. Fifty-fifty custody was the preferred arrangement in Iowa, anyway; the law so strongly favors mandated joint custody that it is recommended unless there is some overriding reason to avoid it. The politically influential Fathers' Rights organizations in that region had introduced and backed joint custody legislation for years. The judge hearing Karen's divorce commended the parents and blessed their stipulation, saying joint custody was in Jesse's best interests. So starting on June 2, 1988, Jesse was a commuter baby. Every Friday, she was picked up at 5:30 P.M. from one home and transported to her other parent's home.

"I began to see changes in Jesse in the late summer," said Karen in a solemn voice. She mentioned night terrors during which Jesse screamed, "No no no!" She said the baby was terrified by the doorbell and cried when she was told Daddy was coming to pick her up. Karen described frequent regressions and age-inappropriate sexualized behaviors. Eventually she sought the advice of a psychologist, who said such problems sometimes indicated child sexual abuse, and who directed her to call the Department of Human Resources for guidance. DHS confirmed that these behaviors could indicate child sexual abuse, and gave Karen instructions for the next week. She was to take Jesse directly from her father's home to the local hospital for an examination by Dr. Kristen Overlook, head of the Children's Protection Center.

THE SLIDES

On September 2, 1988, Karen and a friend (going along to help and as a witness), picked up Jesse from her father's house and drove her immediately, without a diaper change, as instructed by DHS, to the CPC. While Karen held Jesse prone, Dr. Overlook examined her internal genitals and took slides with a colposcope, a photographic device made especially for that purpose. The slides were to be returned Thursday of the next week, one day before Jesse's next scheduled transfer to her father's house. At that time, the doctor told Karen there was a bump by the hymen, that the opening was enlarged, and that there was "Desitin in the vestibule." Overlook asked if Bob would "push it," if Karen refused to return the baby the following week. Karen said he definitely would "push it." Instead of reporting her admitted suspicion of abuse to the authorities who had referred Karen to her, Overlook told Karen to return the baby to Bob as scheduled and to "document the behaviors [which presumably would continue if there was abuse] and then this will be a sexual abuse case."

Overlook later admitted under oath that she was suspicious of sexual abuse at that first examination, but she was "on the fence" as to whether the damage to Jesse's hymen was a definite "positive," indicating penetration of the genitals. Overlook's reaction was noncommittal and equivocal.

Iowa law requires any doctor or child-care worker who suspects—not confirms—sexual abuse to report that suspicion—not certainty—to the authorities. But Overlook failed to make such a mandated report, even though she was director of the Child Protection Center and fully familiar with the procedure and the law. Therefore, it can be presumed that if sexual abuse were found after her examination, she might be liable to civil or criminal penalities for her failure to make a mandated report of her suspicions when the slides from the genital examination were returned. Karen guessed that part of Overlook's motivation in later minimizing her findings was to avoid negative consequences or liability to herself. If DHS or a court had found that Jesse was molested before Overlook's examination, but proper steps were not taken to protect the child from repeated abuse after it, the doctor's reputation, at least, could suffer. Years later, when Overlook was challenged in court, her lawyer filed a motion on her behalf to quash a subpoena issued by Karen. That lawyer worked for the same firm as the guardian *ad litem* who had reportedly disliked Karen from the early days of the divorce case.

Subsequent analysis of these slides by top experts in the country (including the professor of pediatric medicine who had trained Overlook in colposcopy) differed radically from Overlook's own interpretation. On September 15, 1989, Dr. Edward N. Bailey, Chairman of the Department of Pediatrics of Baystate Medical Center in Springfield, Massachusetts, wrote, after viewing the slides:

> Th[is] opinion . . . is based upon my personal experience with large numbers of children seen over the past decade for evaluation of sexual abuse in our program here at Baystate Medical Center. It is also based upon . . . [my examination of] slides taken in Iowa. . . . On September 2, 1988, at a time when she was of normal height and weight, Jesse was examined by a professional using a colposcope. . . . [N]ine of those pictures have been for-

warded to me for my review. . . . The hymen is quite asymmetric with an opening of approximately 5mm. in the horizontal direction. Between 12:00 and 3:00 o'clock and between 6:00 and 9:00 o'clock, there is thickening of the hymen with significant narrowing present as well. Between 4:00 and 6:00 there is a significant bump which appears to run intra-vaginally and which is consistent with but not diagnostic of a synechiae. . . . These are dramatic photographs, consistent with [penetrating injury]. . . . indicative of blunt or penetrating type injury.

Dr. L. Chadwick of the Children's Hospital and Health Center, San Diego, California, gave his interpretation of the slides in a letter written on his hospital's stationery, dated September 3, 1991:

I reviewed colposcopic photos of [Jesse's] genital area, and offered an opinion that she had been a victim of prior *"non-accidental genital injury"* which means that she had previously experienced a penetrating genital injury of the type which is seen in sexual abuse, and which is extremely unlikely to be due to accidental injury or disease. . . . The physical findings stand alone as indicators of sexual abuse. If we saw a child with such findings and the child and all involved adults entirely denied abuse I would still hold the opinion that she had been abused. Not all children who have been sexually abused, have such definite findings, in fact, most do not. . . . The existence of such definite physical findings indicates penetration or vigorous attempted penetration of this child's vagina at some point in time prior to the time when the photos were taken. . . .

Dr. Lori D. Frazier, a University of Iowa pediatrician specializing in child abuse diagnosis, also reviewed the slides. Her signed affidavit of October 4, 1991 reads:

The following hymenal abnormalities are present: there is a hymenal defect from a bump at 5 o'clock, extending to nearly 9 o'clock. This results in an extremely thin rim and nearly complete absence in hymenal tissue in this area. The result is a key hole appearance to the hymen. This appears to extend to the vaginal wall. This represents healed evidence of vaginal penetrating trauma.

Not only did these individual doctors state without equivocation the significance of this genital examination, but also Dr. Chadwick asked his expert colleagues to do the same:

In addition to my own review . . . , I showed the slides of the colposcopic photos to five other physicians who are on the staff of this Center for Child Protection at this Children's Hospital. All of the physicians present are very experienced in the examination of children who may have been sexually abused. It is my opinion, and that of all of the other physicians here who saw these photos, that there is a high probability that Jesse has received non-accidental genital injury. I base this opinion solely on the appearance of her genitalia which show distinct signs of injury. . . . I believe there is a "reasonable medical certainty" that Jesse has been sexually abused.

Each of these reports on the slides declares that penetrating injury to the internal vaginal area caused the injury to the hymen. But Dr. Overlook, after having failed to report suspected abuse, spent the next several weeks having conversations with persons she described under oath as "Ïsome contacts," including some outside the Child Protection Center. She reportedly found herself feeling more concerned about Karen's behavior than about the possible diagnosis of child sexual abuse. She described Karen as being overly concerned about Jesse and too focused on the possibility that her daughter was molested. Dr. Overlook would not identify her "contacts" by name.

THE COVER-UP

Part I. Dr. Overlook

Karen was immediately concerned about Dr. Overlook's failure to report suspected abuse, not because she knew, at that time, how conclusive and shocking the slides were, but because the doctor herself had expressed concern and because Jesse's behavior and disclosures were worrisome. While waiting for official resolution of the problem, Karen was delivering Jesse to Bob every other Friday. On October 28, 1988, she wrote to Dr. Overlook describing Jesse's behavior since the examination:

> The big changes . . . that . . . began first week of August—the no no no no no no in her sleep—screaming nightmares on Sunday nite. She continued no no's in her sleep—the next weekend. . . . We were setting at table (Jesse in her highchair) eating supper when the doorbell rang. Jesse started screaming—mouth wide open—arms up in the air, shaking, while, scrambled to get out of the highchair to me. Jesse had a terrible week at the sitter—wanted her sheepskin, pacifier, popple and her bottle back (which she hadn't had at Kelly's since May), cried most of each day, would lay with eyes closed while awake, wouldn't play.

> Jesse's crying out in her sleep has gone from "no no no no" (usually says it 5 times) to "out out out" to "hurt hurt hurt" and now "help help," over the last three month period. She no longer cries loudly in her sleep, she whimpers instead.

> Jesse usually has 3 to 4 dirty diapers the day after I get her back—her tummy is very tight and distended . . . —she is usually very white and very tired. She usually does not want a bath on Friday nite.

She gets very upset and agitated when I tell her that [her father] is coming and runs around the house in circles—doesn't want her clothes on after her bath on Friday nites, gets very sad after she stops crying before he comes—says "Dad coming."

I could go on and on. Jesse exhibits more and different behavior each week. I need some information please—to what do you attribute hymenal edge thickening? To what do you attribute hymenal orifice dilation? Please explain: "There was some Desitin ointment noted to be in the vestibule." How would it get there? Do you think there is abuse going on here? Thank you, [Karen Carter].

Karen got no response from Dr. Overlook. She sought advice from others, including clinical psychologist Stanley Emerson and DHS. She was referred by DHS itself to Sarah Galloway, a psychiatric nurse-practitioner with clinical expertise treating sexually abused children. Karen first took Jesse to her on October 18, 1988. After four visits, Jesse was willing to play with her in a room alone, with Mommy waiting outside. On December 12, 1988, Galloway wrote:

I was successful in separating Jesse from her mother. I took her to my office where I had an adult male and a child female anatomically correct doll. Jesse immediately named the man "Daddy" and the little girl "Jesse." She immediately took the clothes off both dolls. Again we named the body parts and she called the penis a "pee." When I said to Jesse, "what does the penis do?" Jesse spread her legs and pointed to her genitalia. I clarified by saying, "Does Daddy's penis touch you?" Jesse responded by shaking her head affirmatively and again pointing between her legs. I asked Jesse to show me with the dolls how Daddy's penis touched her. She refused to position the dolls or play with them in any way. However, when I repeated that question she squatted over the leg of the doll and moved up and down. After Jesse revealed this information, I attempted to have her repeat it for her mother. She would not do so. Once again she became quite whiny and clinging and laid her head on her mother's shoulder. . . . I felt that the above information was enough to suspect sexual abuse.

Galloway then did what Dr. Overlook had failed to do; she immediately reported the case of suspected abuse to the Iowa Department of Human Services.

Part II. The DHS Investigation

Since a mandated reporter of suspected child abuse had reported the case to DHS, the DHS intake worker in turn contacted the abuse investigator in Johnson County. His first responsibility was to obtain an injunction against the alleged perpetrator having any contact with the child while the abuse investigation was pending. The investigator was contacted on December 12,

1988 (the same day as the examination), and Jesse was scheduled to return to her father on December 16, 1988 at 5:30 P.M. Waiting until the eleventh hour, on Friday, December 16, to file the necessary petition, the investigator quickly obtained the injunction from a judge in neighboring Linn County. No reason is given for the abuse investigator seeking relief in another county. Since juvenile court judges rotate, it is possible that the investigator had had prior contact with that judge. Instead of Jesse being delivered to her father that Friday, the injunction and notice of the abuse investigation were served on him instead.

When Bob Fulton heard that his daughter had disclosed sexual abuse, he called—not Karen, not the abuse investigator, not the psychologist he had previously seen, not a priest, not a family member, but—Donald Harper, the guardian *ad litem* in the custody case. According to his billing details, Harper consulted with Bob on Friday evening and immediately called the Linn County judge. Without speaking to the mother about the case, Harper appeared in court on Monday, December 19, 1988, for the removal hearing.

Judge Jill Somerville was presented with a father who vehemently denied abuse and appeared amazed that he had been accused; a father's lawyer who was indignant that her client's custodial "perfection" had been doubted; a very worried and upset mother who had demanded action from the system until she got it; a mother's lawyer (newly hired) who seemed overwhelmed; a guardian *ad litem* who had called the judge three days previously, disliked the mother, and was very favorably disposed toward the father; and a male career DHS social worker (Mark Wade). Absent was two-year-old Jesse, now verbal, who, according to the DHS emergency call, had disclosed frank rape in her own childish way to a psychiatric nurse she had seen for weeks before "telling." Jesse had refused to discuss the matter with anyone except the therapist. The judge knew that it would be difficult to get her to repeat her allegations to anyone else.

Judge Somerville ordered that Jesse stay with her mother while the investigation proceeded. DHS would be responsible for setting up and supervising visitation with Bob. During this time, however, nobody was permitted to discuss sexual abuse with Jesse. Her therapist, who had finally built trust with the child, was forbidden to treat her for sexual abuse or even to discuss sexual abuse with her, even if the child disclosed again. Karen was forbidden to discuss sexual abuse with her even in a passive role, so that if Jesse were to reveal more of her fears and turn to her mother for comfort and validation, Karen was ordered by the court to remain silent, which would give Jesse the idea that she could not discuss these matters with her mommy.

Part III. The DHS/Juvenile Court Connection

The first case plan from DHS instructed Karen in how to behave as the mother of a sexually abused child. The subsequent case plans showed that

DHS itself was behaving as if Jesse were not in fact a sexually abused child. Moving backwards through the paperwork trail, Karen discovered that this anomaly could be explained by a memorandum buried in the DHS file.

The day after the emergency removal hearing and prior to any investigation, abuse investigator Mark Wade sent a handwritten memo to the DHS caseworker who would be responsible for Jesse's case. That memo, later designated the "Smoking Gun Memo" by Karen over the indignant objections of Harper and the entire CPS staff, read:

STATE OF IOWA
Department of Social Services
Johnson County
911 North Governor Street
Iowa City, Iowa 52240

MEMO TO Joe G [caseworker]
From Mark 12/20/88
Subject: Fulton Visitation

I don't want to tell you how to do casework, but, in a conversation today with Judge [Somerville] she happened to incidentally voice concerns to the effects that we may have an innocent father and "we" have restricted his time with the child. Thus, it might behoove DHS to give him as liberal visitation as possible under the present court orders. Thanks for your ear! Mark.

The implications of this memorandum are most significant. First, the subject line did not say "Jesse Fulton" or "Fulton Child" or "Carter/Fulton Case," but "Fulton Visitation." Right from the start, the emphasis was solely on the father's rights. The concerns voiced by the judge, again *ex parte* in an "incidental" conversation, do not relate to whether the child has been raped but to the innocence of the father and the negative consequences of restricting "his time" with "the child." DHS was to give the father as liberal visitation as possible and cooperate with the judge to make sure that this presumption of an innocent father does not turn out to be mistaken. In other words, the abuse investigator and the caseworker from DHS were on notice by the judge that the father was best considered innocent.

Wade's abuse investigation file did not include the slides or any copies or analyses of them or their implications. It did include interviews with neighbors and friends of Bob who characterized Karen as "crazy." Bob was not asked to take a polygraph test or a plethysmography, which measures sexual arousal when the subject is exposed to various kinds of sexual stimuli in the form of pictures and narration. In six weeks, on February 1, 1989, DHS concluded that the question of whether Jesse had been molested was "undetermined."

DHS has three possible administrative responses to its investigations of reports of suspected child sexual abuse: "Founded" means the Agency believes the abuse occurred; "Unfounded" means the Agency believes no abuse has occurred; and "Undetermined" means the Agency neither believes nor disbelieves that abuse had occured. That finding is, semantically, the same as Overlook's expression after her examination of Jesse. She said there were cases where she definitely thought there was abuse; there were cases where she did not think there was any abuse; and there were cases, like Jesse's, where she was "on the fence." Now DHS got on that fence with the doctor.

Part IV. Juvenile Court

Judge Susan Lindhoff took over from Judge Jill Somerville when the case was sent back from Linn County to Johnson County. Lindhoff ordered that before each interview with DHS, Jesse have a three-hour supervised visit with her father, to be "fair," and then be interviewed by strangers, to whom DHS would transport her. DHS chose experts from Dr. Overlook's Child Protection Center. No anatomically explicit dolls were used. No attempt was made to find out what had happened to Jesse. Not a single question was asked about her prior disclosures, or about abuse. Jesse was asked if anybody had hurt her—but she had just come from a supervised visit when no "hurt" could have occurred, and she was otherwise living with her mother, where no "hurt" had ever occurred. Predictably, no fresh disclosures were obtained, and without a fresh disclosure, the abuse could be invalidated as long as the torn hymen was ignored. So it was.

In court, Overlook testified that, although she was concerned about possible sexual abuse of Jesse, her concern had quickly turned to the mother's behavior. Subjectively, she admitted, she felt that the mother was "too tuned in" to her baby during the genital examination. Admitting that Jesse's genitals were "irritated," she found herself more worried that the mother was too close to her child. She did admit that there were abnormalities in the slides, which she called "minor changes," but she remained more concerned that Karen was too focused on the sex abuse issue. Overlook said Karen might psychologically abuse Jesse by paying too much attention to the possibility of molestation. She felt Karen might blow the situation out of proportion; it might get out of hand—out of control. In other words, Karen's reaction to her daughter's alleged rape might not be the cool, official, non-responsive approved attitude.

Neither Karen's lawyer nor guardian *ad litem* Donald Harper, nor DHS attorney Dan Green ever brought the slides themselves into the Juvenile Court proceeding. It seems as if they deliberately avoided entering into evidence the one thing that was actual—physical, objective, medical—evidence. The court case concentrated on all kinds of guess-work and equivocal issues, mere opinions or possibilities. When Donald Harper asked Dr. Overlook if the damage to Jesse's hymen, which she had termed "minor changes," could have been caused by Desitin, the diaper cream, this licensed, registered pediatrician answered in the affirmative! When Dr. Marilyn Kaufhold was questioned, years later, as to whether "minor changes" was an accurate description of the keyhole configuration she had seen in the slides, her direct and simple answer was "no." (Michelle Etlin asked the medical research director at Pfizer Chemical Corporation if it was possible for Desitin to cause damage to Jesse's hymen. His answer was that it was absolutely impossible.)

Judge Lindhoff gave the clear message, early in the hearings, that she would "not believe" the sexual abuse allegations. Subtly, without notice to Karen, the proceeding turned from an abuse proceeding with Bob as the subject, to a "blame someone for making problems" proceeding with Karen as the subject. DHS witnesses uniformly concentrated on her supposed faults—that she believed and actually said that Jesse had been molested by Bob. Judge Lindhoff ruled that Karen had "misrepresented the strength of her case from one professional to another." But Karen went only to experts to whom she was referred; and since each professional perused evidence from the prior contacts and added his or her own assessments, the evidence became cumulative. The suspicion of child abuse increased, and Karen's presentations became increasingly stronger. Therefore, to regard Karen's presentation of the "strength of 'her' case" as misrepresentation merely because it increased from one professional to another is itself a specious analysis. Even if she were "guilty" of such conduct, the passion of her presentations to the various professionals would have no bearing on the following pertinent facts:

> There was independent confirmation of the nightmares Karen reported. Both Bob and a DHS visitation supervisor confirmed that Jesse had screaming nightmares during visits to Bob's house.

> Independent witnesses confirmed other behaviors exhibited by Jesse that DHS identified as possible indicators of child sexual abuse, as well as the fact that they grew worse as time passed.

> Karen reported some problematic behaviors to Dr. Emerson, but reported more to the professionals involved later, because during the time (from late summer to Christmas, 1988) between seeing Dr. Emerson and the others, Jesse was still seeing Bob unsupervised. Therefore, if abuse was continuing, it would make the behaviors caused by such abuse grow more pronounced.

> Karen reported behaviors to Dr. Overlook after, not before, the physical examination showed findings and photographs consistent with a diagnosis of vaginal penetration.

> When Karen took Jesse to Sarah Galloway, the case was stronger than when she sought advice from Dr. Emerson, since the physical evidence had since been discovered by Overlook, who had expressed concern, and DHS had also speculated that Jesse might have been molested.

All professionals consulted after Sarah Galloway's examination were made aware of the initial behavioral suspicions, the physical evidence, and the disclosures made to Galloway. Thus, naturally, those professionals did hear a "stronger case."

No proof was presented that Karen had made any "misrepresentation," as Judge Lindhoff proclaimed. But in the world of "validation" of sexual abuse, unless a judge agrees that there was sexual abuse, the allegations are likely to be called "false."

In July 1989, ten months after Dr. Overlook discovered damage inside her vagina, Jesse was removed from her mother's custody and placed, temporarily, in the custody of her father's parents, who had never made a petition for custody and whose fitness had never been examined by the court.

Two months later, the Juvenile Court of Johnson County, Iowa, placed Jesse with her father. Judge Lindhoff ordered that visitation by Karen be very strictly supervised; because she persisted in her belief that Jesse had been molested, she might affect the child adversely. The judge also declared that Karen was not to be trusted and might "kidnap" her daughter, as Elizabeth Morgan had done. "In other words," said Karen, "I was accused, convicted and sentenced for kidnapping without anybody even making the charge against me—on suspicion alone!"

Judge Lindhoff admitted that the conditions imposed on Karen would interfere with the mother-child bond, but she was willing to sacrifice that for the greater good of ensuring that Jesse never again adopted the mistaken "belief" that she had been molested by her father. Karen appealed the Juvenile Court order and lost; the Court of Appeals said Judge Lindhoff was within her discretion to decide that Jesse had not been molested.

Part V. DHS Seals Jesse's Fate

Anyone reading the entire Jesse case would conclude that Jesse was molested, including vaginal penetration, before the age of two; and that Karen lost her daughter and was unable to protect her because of a combination of outrageous legal maneuvers and the misfunctioning of DHS. Eventually, in 1993, guardian *ad litem* Donald Harper admitted under oath that Jesse had been molested, that he had not followed up on the problem because it would be impossible to determine *who* had molested her. But DHS, whose responsibility it was to find out who the molester was, had refused to do so and even refused to allow Karen to do so for them.

Karen had made a timely and legally proper application for an evidentiary hearing in DHS right after it made the "Undetermined" finding. She intended to present the slides and the medical evidence in a contested hearing pursuant to the Iowa Administrative Code. DHS, represented by the Attorney

General of Iowa, notified Karen that it was postponing that hearing until the Juvenile Court proceeding was concluded, which is perfectly legal. When Karen reactivated her request, however, she was informed that the hearing would not be granted because the Juvenile Court had already decided the issue, which was then barred from further consideration by the legal principle called *res judicata,* or "issue preclusion." That means that a matter decided in one court cannot be relitigated in another. However, this has no bearing on the fact that administrative agencies and courts are different forums and operate differently. Administrative decisions are frequently relitigated in courts. But DHS would have it that their job was over once Judge Lindhoff turned "Undetermined" into "No Abuse."

Karen appealed from that administrative decision in the District Court, basing her claim to an absolute right to an evidentiary hearing on a very important point: the standard of proof in the agency is "preponderance of the evidence," meaning that 51 percent proof that Jesse was molested should have changed the "Undetermined" to "Founded." She felt sure that the medical interpretations of the slides would undoubtedly cross the 51 percent boundary. The Juvenile Court, however, uses a standard of "clear and convincing evidence," which is closer to 67 percent proof. The fact that the Juvenile Court did not confirm that there was "clear and convincing evidence" of child sexual abuse would not mean that there was not a "preponderance" of evidence of it. Karen had an iron-clad, quantitative justification for demanding her hearing. Furthermore, she had a meritorious case.

On September 11, 1991, a prominent Iowa child abuse expert with experience in both the public governmental and private nonprofit child protection systems signed the following affidavit:

> 1. My name is John Holtkamp and I am the Executive Director of the Iowa Chapter of the National Committee for the Prevention of Child Abuse (NCPCA).
>
> 2. I was previously employed from November 24, 1987 to July 5, 1991 as the Program Manager for Child Protective Services for the Iowa Department of Human Services.
>
> 3. In the course of my previous employment, I became familiar with a child abuse case involving Jesse Fulton.
>
> 4. Based upon the medical opinion offered by Dr. David Chadwick and his team, and Dr. Lori Frazier (based upon their review of slides taken during a colposcopic examination of [Jesse], it is my opinion that there exists a preponderance of evidence that Jesse has been sexually abused.

DHS denied Karen's right to a hearing. The District Court ruled against her, and she appealed, again, to the Court of Appeals. Its decision was arrived at without addressing the different standards of proof in the court and agency, without commenting on the uncontroverted physical evidence of sexual abuse, and without taking Holtkamp's affidavit into consideration. The court said that only "persons" were entitled to evidentiary hearings in DHS; Karen was not a "person" under its definition because she had not been accused of molesting Jesse. The only "person" entitled to an evidentiary hearing would be the one who did not want an evidentiary hearing—the accused, Bob Fulton. A learned dissent by a female appellate judge did not help Karen get that decision reviewed in either the Iowa Supreme Court or the U.S. Supreme Court. Jesse has gone down in Iowa case law as nonabused, and Karen has gone down in Iowa case law as a nonperson.

DHS witnesses admitted under oath that Karen's visitation was supervised and videotaped because they had to control everything, even Karen's facial gestures. She was faulted for wearing a T-shirt that said "We Believe Jesse"; it was described as "provocative clothing." She was not permitted to explain to her daughter why she was not allowed even to walk her to the car after visits, or to stand on the steps to blow kisses. If Jesse cried when she was separated from her mother, Karen was blamed for making the separation difficult. Once Jesse was even threatened by a supervisor: if she did not stop crying when leaving her mother, her visits would be shortened. Supervisors seemed to be chosen for their degree of hostility toward Karen. Visitation supervisors who did not express criticism and open negativity toward Karen were soon replaced.

A videotape of the last visit Karen was permitted in the DHS office building shows that three officials stood behind a one-way mirror, filming Karen for more than ten minutes and conferring solemnly, writing notes on a clipboard, before Jesse even entered the room. Karen appears on that video setting up the dolls and toys she has brought for Jesse to play with, while the DHS personnel knit their brows as if there was something in these mundane actions that needed to be recorded and discussed to protect the child from harm.

Now DHS had total control of the visitation situation and a hostage. They had been given the right, by Judge Lindhoff, to manipulate the terms of Karen's visitation, without court oversight. They could even cancel it without a hearing, by saying that she had tried to "circumvent" their rules. They created rules that had no relationship to Jesse's best interests; they changed the rules arbitrarily, capriciously, and frequently.

Karen believes there was a link between her efforts to free Jesse and increased visitation restrictions. The more she fought, the more ferociously DHS punished her by creating additional difficulties in her visits. Finally, the day after she submitted the medical reports from Drs. Chadwick, Frazier, and Bailey, her visitation was suddenly terminated by DHS. The following letter, typed on plain paper, was written by the DHS staff member who was most hostile to Karen:

November 13, 1991

Karen,

Your caseplan says that you will be allowed one visitor per month. On 10-24 you brought Jesse's grandmother, who was the second visitor for that month.

Your caseplan says that you will wait until the visit supervisor is out of the camera direction before you take photographs. On 10-24 you took a photograph which included the supervisor, and you did it again twice on 11-7.

The court order reads, "Any attempts made by Karen Carter to circumvent the directions of this court or the rules set by the Department of Human Services shall result in the immediate cessation of all visits until further order of court."

Your visits will be canceled effective immediately.

Sincerely,

[Janet Ferguson], ACSW

Social Worker, II

This letter raises several serious questions: Why was it not written on DHS stationery? Was it typed at home by social worker Janet Ferguson, rather than through official channels? Why, if DHS did not want the grandmother at the supervised visit on October 24, did they permit her to be there? DHS hosted and totally controlled the visits, regulating them severely. They took place in a locked room at DHS headquarters, with admittance only by permission of DHS itself. Karen was required to call in advance to ask permission to bring another visitor, as if there was some reason to keep grandparents away from Jesse. Therefore, if DHS found it necessary, to protect Jesse, to refuse admittance to her grandmother, it was well within its power to do so. How could DHS conclude that Karen's photos included visitation supervisors, when DHS did not have the pictures? When Karen produced the photographs at the trial the only people in them were Jesse, Karen, and Jesse's grandmother. In one shot, part of an unidentified person's foot is visible behind a close-up of Jesse's face.

It is conceivable that these empty and untrue excuses were dreamed up in order to cancel Karen's visitation in case Jesse's problems became so serious they could not be covered up or hidden even during hour-long supervised visits with her mother. Karen says, "The only way to keep Jesse silent forever was to keep her away from me; the only two people she ever talked to were me and the therapist. And Galloway was removed by the judge at the recommendation of Jesse's own lawyer."

The State of Iowa spent more than $40,000 of taxpayers' money guarding Karen Carter's visits with her daughter between the ages of two and a half and five. After that, Karen was deprived of all contact with Jesse by

DHS, which used a peculiar double evidentiary standard: they could not "determine" whether Jesse had been molested in spite of photographs of her injured hymen; but they could "determine" that Karen had violated a visitation guideline although there were no photographs of the visitation supervisors.

Part VI. The District Court

Meanwhile, Karen litigated vigorously for the return of her daughter. She brought a petition for modification of the divorce decree in the District Court. Without giving her a hearing on temporary custody and visitation, the court awarded $475 per month temporary child support to Bob. This sum was automatically and immediately garnished from Karen's wages (the lawyers for the company she worked for were Larson & Harper, Donald Harper's firm). Now Karen was unable to pay counsel. She continued *pro se* (on her own). Barbara Clott, Bob's attorney, made a "motion in limine"—a motion to exclude certain evidence from trial. Ordinarily this strategy is used in criminal defense work, to exclude evidence procured in violation of the Constitution, such as physical evidence obtained without a search warrant or confessions obtained through force or trickery. Clott said at oral argument that the evidence of sexual abuse should be eliminated from the custody trial because the sexual abuse question had already been "buried."

Karen's legal argument was that she was being deprived of joint custody because she believed that Jesse had been molested, that she had a right to prove the reasonableness of her belief, since it related to her fitness as a parent. She also said that Bob was an unfit parent because when he was shown evidence that Jesse was molested, he chose to ignore it rather than find out who had molested his daughter—if he had not.

The trial took place in District Court, on February 3–7, 1992. Karen had asked Dr. Chadwick to testify; he could not leave California so he sent one of the other physicians who had viewed the slides. Dr. Marilyn Kaufhold flew to Iowa City to give expert testimony on Monday, the first day of the trial. At the lunch break, she stated that she felt nauseated because the proceeding was so awful, the abuse was so clear, and her sympathy for Jesse was so strong. Clott argued, and the judge ruled, that the testimony was not admissible because evidence of sexual abuse was not allowed, but Karen placed the evidence on the record on an "offer of proof," or a "proffer," so that the Court of Appeals could consider that evidentiary ruling on appeal.

The judge would not allow the slides to be shown with a rented projector, but Karen had an easel and a large pad on which Dr. Kaufhold drew pictures of the configurations of normal hymens and Jesse's damaged hymen. She described the slides as good enough to be used as teaching slides, particularly the one showing a "keyhole configuration," or a sideways figure 8. This injury can only result from penetration that tears the hymenal tissue completely to the wall of the vagina, after which it heals with insufficient tissue to allow it to regain its original shape. According to Dr. Kaufhold, on a scale of 1 to 10, the probability that Jesse was sexually abused was 8 $1/2$; the only alternative explanation was an *accidental* penetration of the child's genitals, but such an injury would have had to be massive and noticeable, and it would have caused external injuries and bleeding as well. There was no such event recorded in Jesse's medical history.

So Karen fought to get the medical evidence into court, long after her previous lawyers had failed to do so and Judge Lindhoff had allowed Donald Harper's presentation (without the slides) to rule the day. Judge Victor Scranton, looking bored as he conducted the trial, ruled against Karen over and over, but he had to allow the evidence to be proffered on the record over objections. Getting that evidence on the record met with unusual obstacles. The testimony of Dr. Kaufhold was excluded because she had seen *copies* of the slides, not the originals, and because there was "no foundation" to prove the copies were genuine. Karen had subpoenaed Dr. Overlook with the orinal slides, but the firm of Larson & Harper submitted a motion to quash that subpoena, and the judge ruled against Karen again. When Karen subpoenaed the slides without the doctor, there was another round of motion, quash, and grant, with the judge ruling against Karen. It looked as though the foundation for the crucial evidence could not be built.

However, at 9:00 A.M. on Friday of the five-day trial, the custodian of records of Holy Name Hospital (upon whom Karen had served yet a third subpoena, unbeknownst to Overlook) handed over the original slides. Barbara Clott leaped to her feet at counsel table and objected loudly that it was "inappropriate" to admit Respondents' Exhibit 29—the original slides. "We quashed that!" she stormed. Judge Scranton looked distressed and plainly overpowered. "What can I do?" he asked candidly. He was required by law to allow the slides to be placed in the record on the "offer of proof" over the vehement objections of the now-enraged counsel for the now-frightened father. At the court reporter's desk about three hours later, Karen Carter saw for the first time the slides that had been taken while she had held her screaming two-year-old prone four years earlier. They were gruesome, red, irritated, bloody-looking portraits of glistening, damaged mucosa and the oft-described sideways figure 8.

Judge Scranton did not consider the offer of proof. He denied Karen any court-ordered visitation and ordered her to continue paying $475 per month child support until Jesse turns eighteen or graduates from high school, whichever is later. He made scathing remarks about Karen's position that Bob Fulton had molested Jesse. He expressed condemnation and indignation toward Michelle Etlin, who, scandalized that two other little girls—daughters of Bob Fulton's second wife—now lived with Bob, had notified their father of the allegations against Bob and sent him copies of Jesse's medical records. The judge did not comment on the plea by psychologist Gary Brentano to reconsider the sexual abuse charges in Jesse's best interests, or Dr. Frazier's recommendation that a new sex abuse investigation be conducted. Judge Scranton was apparently more interested in the reputation of the court system than in the quality of life of a six-year-old. In his decision he stated that Karen had been critical of the court system, which he called the best court system that had ever been created in the history of the world.

The only common denominator in all parts of the cover-up of the sexual abuse of Jesse was Donald Harper, her guardian *ad litem*. He admitted that he never met or interviewed her in the nearly seven years he represented her. Karen's complaints about his conduct to the Iowa Bar and Judiciary were dismissed. He admitted under oath that he had made an independent decision that Bob had not molested Jesse, but when he was asked what he knew about child molesters, he responded only that they "need[ed] a lot of help." His firm represented Dr. Overlook, and he may have been one of the "contacts" she had when she decided not to make a mandated report of sexual abuse. Harper was the first person Bob called when the sexual abuse report came in from DHS. Harper immediately contacted Judge Somerville; he represented Jesse in the DHS investigation and in the Juvenile Court case; he opposed all Karen's appeals; his firm quashed the subpoena for the slides from Dr. Overlook; he even opposed Karen's getting her visitation back.

PRESENT STATUS OF THE COVER-UP

Karen continued to struggle even as her physical health and financial condition deteriorated. Her phone service was cut off for nonpayment of the bill, which had grown large as she tried to organize nationwide assistance for Jesse and other molested childlren. In Iowa, her leafletting and public appearances led to a combination of notoriety and censure. Many adult survivors of child sexual abuse applauded her efforts and tried to help. The Jesse Committee, formed to back Karen's cause, later changed its name to the Iowa Children's Defense Fund. These people raised money, issued press releases, copied paperwork, organized public meetings, spoke out publicly in Jesse's behalf, and produced a twenty-minute video exposé to be shown on public access cable TV. Karen's family contributed heavily to the project. Her sister Jeannie had a thousand pencils printed with the saying "I Believe Jesse." They were handed out with petitions to sign and send to the governor, the legislature, the courts, the county attorney, the President. *Amicus* briefs were sent to the Supreme Court of Iowa, but they were rejected. Petitions with hundreds of signatures were presented to government offices in Iowa, but they were ignored. Thousands of copies of a one-page brief submitted to the Iowa Supreme Court were handed out in the fifty states, engendering public shock and outrage. Karen became well known in the anti–child abuse movement and was invited to speak at conferences and seminars. Karen's voice rose, but the Iowa Justice Department was silent. Pleas came from all over the country, from feminist Gloria Steinem and from Jack Straton of the National Organization for Men Against Sexism, but were met with cool official responses, if any. Three branches of the Iowa government remained as unaffected by the public outcry against what they were doing to mother and child as they had initially been by the evidence of the rape of Jesse Fulton.

Five years after her legal battle started, Karen won one appeal: the Juvenile Court was ordered either to give Karen back her visitation or to terminate her parental rights. This move was not supported by any of the parties because it would require a complete trial, at which Karen would have constitutional protection, and her child support obligation would be cancelled if she were actually terminated. DHS, while backing off a termination petition, still opposed any visitation. Psychologist James Cunningham, who appeared to favor Bob Fulton since the early days of the custody battle, was asked by DHS to evaluate Jesse and make recommendations. At first, he tried to avoid the assignment. It may be that no other psychologist could have been used by DHS to produce such an obviously wrongful opinion as he was counted on to deliver. Cunningham's opinion was already on the record: Karen's "conflict" with Bob (not Bob's with Karen) was the cause of all the problems. Cunningham had seen, and deliberately ignored, the medical evidence of child sexual abuse that caused the "conflict."

A professor at the University of Iowa, Cunningham teaches graduate students and does "child abuse research." He has worked on two federally funded grants at Boys Town, assessing child abuse of the handicapped population for the National Institute of Mental Health, even reporting on these projects at the Tenth National Conference on Child Abuse and Neglect. His curriculum vitae shows that federally funded child abuse research is his future.

In Jesse's case, without comment on the physical evidence, Cunningham concluded that Karen should not be allowed to see her child until and unless she ceased all allegations of child sexual abuse and until Bob felt "comfortable" about such visits. In his testimony, Cunningham referred to "incest" as "sexual involvement" between an adult and a child. He apparently could not bring himself to say that Karen believed Bob had molested Jesse. He said, instead, that she believed there had been "sexual contact." He would not link the torn hymen with "contact." He, like Dr. Overlook, concentrated on problems that the mother could cause, not problems that had already been caused by sexual abuse. He said he could not predict harm to Jesse, but that she might be made the "vector of conflict" between the parents if Karen were ever allowed to see her again. Cunningham was very disturbed that Karen had raised her voice against Jesse's father.

Jesse's own voice has not been heard again on the taboo subject of incest. Her father's legal team reports that Jesse does "fine" in school, and her teacher observed that she never spills her juice or musses her dress; she is presented as the "perfect" elementary school child. Karen asked questions at trial about the "perfect child" image of well-known incest survivor Marilyn Van Derbur; the questions were overruled.

Jesse asked why she could not see Mommy any more and was told that DHS no longer had a room where they could visit. Bob testified that he had made up this excuse because he could not bear to tell his daughter the real reason that she could not see her mother: that her mother did not obey the rules.

4

The War of Attrition

Anne Weaver was a Smith College graduate in physics when she met and married musician and artist Albert Backman. She took his name, and they had two children, Tina and Al. Family photographs show a long-haired, well-built blond man with a diminutive, bespectacled woman at his side in dashikis and dirndl skirts, clung to by pudgy toddlers. When the marriage foundered, Albert Backman was content to leave without hostile litigation. He visited the children whenever he wanted, without written court orders. Anne assumed complete financial support of the children without rancor. Soon she began to date Stew Johnson, who had played on Albert's rugby team, and whose father had previously been Executive Officer of the Mississippi Supreme Court.

Anne and Stew "went together" while Anne was completing medical school and were married while she was doing her medical residency. Stew hoped to attend law school, and Anne supported that goal. Her schedule was very demanding and many nights she was on duty or at least on call at the hospital. She was grateful and delighted that Stew was attentive toward her children.

TINA'S EXPERIENCE WITH HER STEPFATHER

Anne started seriously dating Stew in 1977, when Tina was nine and Al was six. Tina did not have a relationship with her own father at the time. According to Al, Stew had told the children that Albert Backman did not care about them, and would not visit any more. According to Albert, Stew had asked him to stay away from the kids for a while, to "help them adjust to their new family." At any rate, Albert faded from the picture, and Stew obtained permission to adopt the children soon after he married Anne.

Years later, in an affidavit, Tina asserted that she had been molested by Stew Johnson even before the wedding. According to Tina, Stew took her into the shower with him on nights when her mom was working at the hospital, and then into the big double bed he and her mother shared. Tina was confused and shamed by what he did, and assumed that she had done something to provoke his behavior. She also felt distanced from her mother, separated by the existence of the secret she had inadvertently started to keep. She said that after the first time, she "never felt normal again."

In 1979 Anne noticed a drop in Tina's grades, periods of moody silence and tearfulness, and long absences in the nearby woods. But she was not overly alarmed. Everyone thought of Tina as an artistic personality who could entice wild rabbits onto her lap—a sort of St. Francis of Assisi in a young girl's body—so her mother did not assume that her quiet demeanor and solitary, pensive style indicated problems. Looking back, Anne recognized her habit of seeing all things as beautiful and mystical, rather than suspecting perversion or evil.

In 1980, Anne gave birth to another girl. Tina, then thirteen, witnessed the birth and was alarmed when her mother became cyanosed in the throes of transition labor. "I had only one parent and she was turning purple!" Tina exclaimed. By this time, she no longer regarded Stew as her father, and she had lost touch with Albert.

Anne said that as soon as the baby was born, Stew came into the delivery room, held the newborn high in the air and said, "Look what I did!" He would not let Anne participate in choosing a name for the baby, and proclaimed the infant—whom he named Renee—"his."

Within a year of the baby's birth, the couple separated. Since Stew was in law school, an endeavor that Anne had enthusiastically supported, she agreed in the divorce that they should postpone his child support obligation. Stew did not make waves about custody as long as he could have liberal visitation with any of the three children. But soon there were problems. Anne claimed that Stew often spied on her house and took pictures through the windows. Tina objected to Stew taking the baby on visits without her along, not revealing that she suspected that he might molest her baby sister. Al did not like to visit Stew either, claiming that he was sometimes dropped off at a mall to fend for himself all day while Stew took the baby off alone.

Then an incident occurred that drove a permanent wedge between Al and his stepfather. Stew took the family dog to his house and urged Al to come live with him so he could be reunited with his pet. Al refused, and Stew coldly informed him that he had been forced to have the animal "euthanased." Al was heartbroken. He began to complain of gastrointestinal distress at and after every visit, and often became ill when he learned that a visit was scheduled.

Anne went to court and got a restraining order after a violent scene surrounding a visitation squabble. Another violent scene, complete with car chase, resulted when Stew tried to take the baby alone for visitation; Tina resisted and leapt into his car as it tore off, with her feet hanging out the open door. Renee came back from another visit with bruises and blood in her urine. She reported that her Daddy had beaten her for not including his name on a nursery school list of "favorite people." Al testified in court that his little sister often got "yelled at" for not "loving" her Daddy as much as she loved her Mommy.

INCEST ON TRIAL IN MISSISSIPPI

Incidents mounted and hostility accumulated, but the boiling point was not reached until 1984, nearly four years after Stew and Anne were divorced. Pre-school Renee began to exhibit peculiar behaviors, sexually acting out in a way that Anne did not understand. Friends suggested psychotherapy, so Anne took her daughter to Calvin Nederman, a psychologist who was well respected in the community. Dr. Nederman recommended almost immediately that Renee be taken to a female therapist, for she tried to unzip his pants and act out sexually with him. He described her behavior as "eroticized." Psychologist Charlene Bender, the next professional to evaluate Renee, concluded, on the basis of behavioral symptomatology and "disclosure evidence," that the child had been molested by her father. After a few sessions, Renee had told Dr. Bender that her father and his girlfriend routinely took her into bed with them to play touching games that involved private parts.

While her mother struggled with the information that Renee had probably been molested, Tina suffered with guilt and fear about her own silence. In severe emotional pain, she consulted a priest, who told her that she was duty-bound to tell her mother about her own incest experience.

Anne was so stunned that she did not move or react. Tina sat across from her mother, frozen in horror, afraid of her reaction. What was *not* happening was more important than what had just happened: her mother was *not* throwing her arms around Tina, saying it was not her fault; her mother was *not* crying with her and saying she was sorry it happened; her mother was *not* kicking her out of the house or sending her to an orphanage or a reformatory; her mother was *not* blaming her for being a bad girl. It appeared that her mother was *not* breathing.

Anne, meanwhile, was thinking of everything she could *not* do: she could *not* react because to do so would be to overreact; she could *not* cry because she had to be strong for her child; she could *not* scream because she would never be able to stop screaming; she could *not* kill because God said thou shalt not kill; she could *not* understand because it was impossible that both of her daughters were molested and she had not known. The two women sat opposite each other, paralyzed by their victimization. When Anne regained her voice, she quietly asked Tina to tell Dr. Bender.

Tina tried to prepare herself to testify about incest in court. Dr. Bender gave the court a written report, documenting Renee's disclosures and the corroborative behavioral signs she had detected. Things were becoming more official and clinical. Anne went to see her lawyer to deal with the unacceptable problem in an acceptable, manageable fashion. (He later became a district court judge and then entered the political arena, hoping to run for Governor.)

The lawyer immediately advised Anne to maintain absolute silence about the incest. He said Mississippi judges did not want to hear about child molestation, so the best part of discretion was not to tell them about it. He warned his outraged client that she would lose custody outright if she insisted on bringing up sexual abuse. Later Anne recalled how hard he had tried to convince her to follow his advice, saying that if she "shut up about it," the children would be molested only on weekends; she could keep custody and "be there for them the rest of the time, to give them all the love and comfort they need to get over whatever they have to go through with him." She recalled his trying to educate her: plenty of children get molested; it happens all the time; it does not do them any harm, ultimately; they just get over it, as long as nobody makes it into a big issue.

Anne thought him mad. She believed it was her responsibility as a mother to protect her children and to reveal the truth. She announced that she would go to court and trust the system to do justice and protect her children. Meanwhile, Stew sued for a change in custody in response to the allegations. Anne and Tina approached the prosecutor. Several hours after they told their story, they were informed that the D.A. had decided "not to press charges against Vernon Johnson's son."

No grand jury was convened to hear Tina's story. The civil case for custody of Renee proceeded, however. Tina was seventeen years old when she testified in a Mississippi circuit court about the experiences she had endured in Stew Johnson's bed as a pre-adolescent. Both she and her mother were horrified when Judge Boston allowed Johnson's attorney to cross-examine her as if she was a seducer, asking why had she climbed into a man's bed? She tried to defend herself, "I was only 11 years old, it wasn't my fault!" but he reduced her to tears and reviled her. Clearly, Judge Boston was not disposed to rule against Stew Johnson or to restrict his access to Renee.

After the trial, but before a decision was rendered, a Christmas visit was scheduled for all three children. It did not go well. Al threatened to commit suicide if he was forced to visit Stew again. Anne became alarmed and felt that she could not insist that the children go on visits; physical force might be needed. Her attorney arranged for a sheriff's deputy to deliver the children to their next visit with Stew. The deputy picked them up from Anne but returned them shortly, refusing to deliver them and offering to tell the judge why not. True to his word, he told the judge that he watched the mother urge the children to go, assuring them they would be fine, but in the patrol car they had pleaded with him so piteously and resisted the visit so vigorously that he "just couldn't do it." He said that he did not know the man, and he did not know the woman, but he felt there was something wrong between the children and their father.

Stew Johnson did not schedule another visit for about six months. During the summer of 1985, he suddenly demanded a two-week visit with Renee alone, and he refused to specify the time or date of her return. He had moved out of Mississippi but he refused to divulge his new address to Anne's lawyer. Renee became very frightened and begged not to be sent to her father alone. The court order had not been signed, but Anne was advised by her lawyer that Stew could make terrible trouble if he demanded a visit and did not get it. She told Tina that she could not force Stew to take her along on the visit; she told Renee she could not stop the visit; and she prayed.

SISTERS ON THE RUN

On the eve of the visit, Tina went to her mother's household safe, took out all the cash she could find, and ran away from home, giving up her college career at "Ole Miss" and taking her little sister into hiding with her. She had decided that she could pretend to be a young single mother who had to work as an *au pair* to support herself and her love-child. Two weeks later Tina wrote a nostalgic, angry, still childlike letter to her mother, dotting her *i*s with little butterfly hearts. She apologized for worrying her family and for taking the cash without permission. She described her fear: "The courts won't believe us and they won't protect Renee. You're the best mother in the world. We love you."

Anne's lawyer had become a Circuit Court judge, so she hired new counsel. Judge Boston died. His replacement, Judge Wooten, declared Anne Backman a kidnapper and ordered her to report to him whenever she heard from the girls, so he could send law enforcement officers to arrest them and bring them before his court. He swore that he would keep the custody case open until he had the girls back in his courtroom, even if it took until Renee's eighteenth birthday.

Stew then admitted to having moved away, to Dallas, Texas. Soon Anne remarried, but she and her new husband found it impossible to stay in the county, where so many of Stew Johnson's friends were hostile to her. The couple reported many incidents of vandalism and random violence. The police could not determine who beat up Al, who shot at the family, who broke their windows, who tampered with their vehicles.

Anne was offered an administrative position in the U.S. Public Health Service. Renee and Tina were still on the run; Stew lived with his new wife and her adolescent daughter in Texas; and Anne moved out of Mississippi with her new husband (Hal), Al, and a new baby—born between her second and third marriages—whom she has always described as "belonging to no man, just to myself and God."

MISSISSIPPI KEEPS CONTROL

None of the parties remained in Mississippi. Anne believed that, pursuant to the federal law that determines which courts can decide child custody, Mississippi should lose jurisdiction. Accordingly, she hired lawyers in New Jersey to transfer the legal proceedings there, hoping that Tina would learn her mother's new location from contacts in Mississippi. Anne was confident that things could be worked out legally, once the case was out of the Mississippi court system, which so fiercely favored the Johnson family. In 1987, a New Jersey judge determined that he could exercise jurisdiction if he chose to, but he honored a stipulation worked out between Stew's and Anne's lawyers that first, Mississippi should close its case by making a final ruling on the record already before it, without taking further testimony. Since Judge Boston, who had held the hearings, had died, the new judge would need time to request the transcripts and read them before making his decision. After that, New Jersey or any other state where a parent or a child lived could assume jurisdiction over current custody decisions. The order allowing Mississippi to rule "on the record" and proceed to close its case was signed by the New Jersey judge in October 1987.

Five months later, the girls surfaced in Canada. Tina had been working as an *au pair* to support Renee. She had been telling people that she had been forced to leave home and make her own living after having an illegitimate child. It was a taxing life for a depressed, traumatized young woman with full responsibility for a psychologically troubled younger child. When Anne learned of her daughters' predicament, she asked Tina to take Renee to the Catholic Children's Aid Society for help.

The social worker who took Renee into custody in Toronto in 1988 firmly believed that the child had been molested by her father. She later said that she was threatened with the loss of her job and even her pension if she "made waves," and she was relieved of responsibility for the case. The social worker who took over thought very well of Stew Johnson, and was openly hostile to Anne and Tina, who said that Renee was warned that she would never be allowed to go home until she agreed to visit Stew. Renee was kept in foster care for months, hearings were postponed, and her contact with her mother and sister was strictly limited. Still Renee stubbornly refused to see her father. She said she was afraid of him.

A psychologist who evaluated Renee described her as depressed, anxious, and feeling isolated. She had also undergone a precipitous drop in measurable I.Q. The social worker suspended the psychologist's work and withheld further evaluations for nine months. Meanwhile, the social worker continued to try to convince the child, still in foster care, to visit her father. At last Renee agreed, expecting that she would be permitted to "go home" if she did so. The social worker quickly arranged for a visit between Stew and his estranged daughter, to take place in a Toronto hotel room. After that unsupervised weekend with her father, Renee never again spoke of abuse. As soon as she fell silent, the social worker sent her to a new psychologist, Dr. Marina Monkberry, who had been quickly commissioned to evaluate the entire family and make a recommendation to the Canadian court.

Tina says Dr. Monkberry verbally attacked her during the evaluation session, demanding to know why she did not feel "guilt" for having taken Stew's daughter away from him. Anne says Monkberry attacked her credibility on the issue of child sexual abuse, criticized her for having married a man younger than herself, and called her "vain." Monkberry's report claimed there was nothing wrong with Stew Johnson, but found fault with Anne and the rest of Renee's maternal family. According to Monkberry, Anne and Tina were harmful to Renee; they had made her believe she had been molested by Stew in order to alienate her from him. Monkberry recommended custody to Stew because his new marriage was stable, and Renee needed that stability. On the other hand, she insisted that Anne's new marriage was unstable because of the age difference between the spouses, and she predicted divorce. (Ironically, Anne is still married; but Stew has been divorced and has since remarried.)

Anne's Canadian lawyer wanted a full hearing on Dr. Monkberry's report concerning Renee's best interests; she especially wanted the opportunity to cross-examine Dr. Monkberry on her conclusions, which she felt she could prove erroneous. The Canadian proceeding, however, was a "child protection" case, and Catholic Children's Aid Society, the "petitioner," precipitously withdrew its request for court protection, leaving no legal foundation for evidence or hearings. In other words, the proceeding in which Dr. Monkberry's report had been produced was removed from the docket in Canada, so there was no opportunity to delve into the report or examine the psychologist's findings.

Instead, the Mississippi court suddenly reactivated itself. Over the objections of Anne's Mississippi and Canadian lawyers, and contrary to the agreement of the parties, Mississippi Circuit Court Judge Wooten took fresh testimony in the case, including telephone testimony from Dr. Monkberry, who refused to submit herself to cross-examination. When Anne's Canadian lawyer went to court to intervene and show the Canadian judge that Monkberry's testimony was not credible, she was told that Judge Wooten in Mississippi had issued an *ex parte* order in March 1989, physically handing Renee over to Stew. Neither Anne nor any of her lawyers in Texas, Mississippi, New Jersey, or Canada knows when Stew took Renee out of Canada and transported her to Dallas. *Ex parte* means that no notice is given to the other side. In other words, the Mississippi judge gave Stew Johnson's lawyers an emergency custody order for Renee for him to use in Canada, without letting Anne's Mississippi lawyer know about it. This order has never been seen by Anne or any of her lawyers and does not appear in the court files. Such orders are frowned upon because they are unconstitutional, unless there is some grave emergency that demands such precipitous action.

Canada closed its case. The last order of business for Mississippi was to punish Anne for "contempt" and to issue a "final" custody order, which it had refused to do for the two years since New Jersey had ruled. Judge Wooten set a date for a hearing, informing Anne's lawyer in no uncertain terms that he expected Anne to voluntarily place herself in his jurisdiction by traveling to Mississippi and appearing. Anne would not do it. Her Mississippi lawyer recited the serenity prayer over and over as he tried to defend her interests before Judge Wooten, who had actually threatened to jail the lawyer in place of his client should he fail to produce her. Realizing that he could not force Anne into his jurisdiction to punish her, Judge Wooten ordered a $92,000 money judgment against her for Stew Johnson's "expenses," adding a six-month jail term for her refusal to turn her daughters in to the Mississippi court. His final ruling ordered Anne to pay child support of $500 per month and included a proviso that she could not visit Renee again unless she first submitted herself to him for punishment for contempt. (Neither Mississippi, nor any other state, nor Johnson himself has ever tried to execute this jail term against Anne.)

Stew Johnson never stood trial for the sexual abuse of either Renee or Tina. Anne was labeled a kidnapper in Mississippi without a charge or a trial. Stew tried twice to get the grand jury in Mississippi to indict Tina for kidnapping, but it handed down a "no-bill" both times.

When Anne filed a notice of appeal of the Mississippi order, she was told that the transcripts still had to be typed up. Since the transcripts of hearings before the deceased Judge Boston were the only information upon which Judge Wooten could have based a custody decision, Anne insisted that the court must have had them typed up between 1987 and 1989. The clerk's flat answer was that they had never been typed, they did not exist, and Judge Wooten had never asked for or read them. The New Jersey stipulation allowing the new Mississippi judge to decide custody by reading the transcripts of a trial held years before by his deceased colleague had been disregarded completely. Judge Wooten had no idea what had transpired in that lengthy custody trial. To appeal his decision, Anne was now being asked for $4,000 to obtain transcripts that had never been considered. She filed a motion in the Mississippi Supreme Court for the appeal to proceed without the transcripts, since the Judge had made his decision without them, but the court for which Vernon Johnson had worked all his life denied her motion, dismissed her appeal, and left the case closed.

THE BATTLE BEGINS IN TEXAS

In 1990 Renee and her father were living in Texas, and Mississippi had done as much as it could to Anne. Anne began to do her own research on suing for custody in Texas, since she had run out of money for new lawyers and was still paying six lawyers for their work over the previous ten years. She read an article called "Habeas Grabbus: How to Get the Children Back in Texas." *Habeas corpus,* otherwise called "the great writ of freedom," is used in criminal procedures to free prisoners whose constitutional rights have been violated during trial. In Texas, the same writ can be used to regain custody of a child if the order under which she is being held was unconstitutional. Anne obtained copies of *habeas corpus* petitions filed in other cases, followed the general format, and created her own paperwork based on the assertion that the Mississippi custody order giving Renee to her father was unconstitutional.

The law in Texas says that a custody issue brought to court by means of a *habeas corpus* petition gives rise to a best interests hearing. That was what Anne really needed. Meanwhile, two child advocates had notified the Texas authorities of Tina's complaint against Johnson, expressing their concern about her little sister, who was now in his custody. Texas child protection service workers conducted one brief interview with Renee, failed to "obtain a disclosure," and closed the case without interviewing Tina. Anne flew to Dallas and approached the court herself, with paperwork that might have been slightly deficient in form but which definitely stated the facts of her case for a quick hearing on her plea for Renee's return.

She was ushered into chambers with a "hearing master," who looked over her papers, said he understood what she was trying to do, and told her he would do her the "favor" of *not* filing the papers. He said they were not drawn up correctly, and advised her to get a Texas lawyer to submit them. He kept a copy of her home-made paperwork, assuring her that he was helping her by preventing the filing of a faulty petition that would fail. Anne quickly hired a Texas lawyer, thinking his job would be a small one, involving form but not substance. She looked forward to soon seeing and perhaps retrieving Renee.

The first Texas lawyer she hired called the hearing officer, purportedly to set up an immediate hearing. To Anne's dismay, however, he reported to her several days later that the conversation with the hearing master did not facilitate matters, and that he would not file her *habeas corpus* petition. He had told the judge that Anne could not get the relief she wanted using *habeas corpus;* instead, he advised her to open a completely new case in Texas, not based on the fact that the Mississippi order was invalid but on a brand new petition for a modification of custody based on "changed circumstances." He insisted that this expensive and time-consuming endeavor was the only way to proceed. Almost in the same breath, he asked how much Anne—an out-of-state physician—could pay for the up-coming legal battle.

Ross Perot had helped get Elizabeth Morgan out of jail, and Anne had heard that he sympathized with mothers who were trying to protect their children from sexual abuse, so she called his office for a referral to an attorney in Texas who would behave in a more predictable and helpful way. Perot wanted her to qualify for his assistance before he committed to anything, so he referred her to a psychologist, to determine if she was "fit" to call upon his aid. She cooperated, at her own expense, and passed the test. She was then referred to another attorney, who questioned her closely on how much money Perot was willing to spend to support her litigation. Anne had no commitment from Perot. After months of fruitless phone calls, she abandoned the idea of getting help from Perot and hired a different Texas lawyer to sue for custody of Renee.

The second Texas lawyer described herself as a feminist who wanted to help. She did not set a court date. She did not press for visitation. In spite of Anne's evidence that the Mississippi court order was invalid, she insisted that she would start by actually registering that out-of-state custody order in Texas, then asking the court to modify it, as if it had been perfectly legal to start with. Anne instructed her *not* to register the Mississippi order, because that would preclude her right to challenge its validity. But the lawyer was intractable. When she was discharged, she insisted that Anne owed her more than the $2,500 retainer she had already received. In 1991 Anne replaced her with a third Texas lawyer, who described the second one as "a light-weight."

An examination of the file two years later revealed that the third Texas lawyer, the "heavy-weight" (who later went on to become a hearing master in the Dallas Courthouse, down the hall from the hearing master who initiated the delay), let the proceeding get dismissed twice for failure to prosecute. He also failed to challenge the validity of the Mississippi order. He said Anne should concentrate on convincing the court that she deserved some visitation, rather than trying to get custody back.

Time passed with Renee in the total control of Stew Johnson and his new wife, and with Anne in the control of one lawyer or another. Finally, she succeeded in obtaining paid, supervised visitation in Dallas. When Renee saw her mother for the first time in a year and a half, she threw herself into Anne's lap, crying, "I thought I'd never see you!"

Anne pressed for a trial on custody, and her current Texas lawyer pressed for more payments on account. He could not go to trial, he said, until he had a substantial addition to his retainer. Finally it became clear that the cost of supervised once-a-month visitation, together with the attorney's fees, were using up half of Anne's paycheck and actually preventing her from getting to trial. The situation threatened to become permanent, and Anne believed that Renee's sanity and grip on reality were at stake.

By that time, it appeared to Anne that Renee no longer considered herself a bright, lovable, competent child. She was self-denigrating, alternately passive and bratty, and very withdrawn, more so with each visit. She reported that she did not go to sleep until 4 or 5 A.M. and was always tired at school. Her favorite color was black. Her handwriting and mannerisms looked years younger than her chronological age, but her manner of dress and heavy make-up were those of a grown woman not a child.

Anne got a referral from the organization Justice for Children in Texas to her fourth attorney, reportedly a bright, aggressive woman who did not mind "slugging it out" in court. Anne wanted to go to court immediately demanding that Stew Johnson take a plethysmography examination to determine whether he had pedophilic tendencies. She wanted a custody trial by jury, an advantage which is available in only two states, Texas and Michigan. She felt she could prevail, with Tina's testimony and Renee's wish to go home. In fact, Renee had been asking when she could "come home," and Anne wanted to be able to answer her.

The family went to court before Judge Cynthia Williamson, who had actually reactivated the case when Anne's first trial lawyer in Texas let it slide. Judge Williamson took charge of the case and ordered steady visitation and plethysmography tests for Stew Johnson and Anne's new husband, both to be paid for by Anne. Anne's husband passed the test without a problem. The conditions of visitation were changed from what Anne characterized as "house arrest" to a more reasonable situation, to be supervised by a psychologist whose time would be paid for by Anne. After one such visit, however, there were several "no-shows" and Anne was informed that there would be no more visits until the order was signed—necessitating another hearing.

By this time, Anne had paid her $10 fee to obtain a jury trial and it was clear there would be a serious wrangle over professional opinions being offered by the various psychologists. By the time the parties got back to court, Stew's lawyer denied having agreed to visitation supervised by the psychologist, but gave no reason for her objection. The judge allowed her to pull out of the stipulation she had previously made, and another baby step toward normal visitation dissolved. Anne prevailed upon her lawyer at least to get a visitation order signed to reflect and enforce Judge Williamson's decision, intending to have Stew Johnson held in contempt unless he took his plethysmography test. But her lawyer suddenly stopped answering phone calls and responding to letters. Although visitation had been liberalized in court, the visits were denied by Johnson and no action was taken against him because Anne's own lawyer refused to ask for action. An urgent flurry of Faxes resulted in the fourth Texas lawyer withdrawing from the case in mock indignation, never having gotten the order signed. She told the court that she quit because her client had appeared on a national television news report without her permission. Anne's only verbalization on that CBS report (about mothers who lost custody because their children's disclosures of sexual abuse were not believed) had been, "I didn't see my daughter for a year and a half; it was a nightmare."

Without a lawyer, Anne proceeded *pro se,* preparing her own papers and arguing her own case.

Since Stew had still not shown up for his plethysmography test, Anne appeared in court without a lawyer and asked Judge Williamson to require it. Anne thought the motion would be fairly simple. In response, however, Stew's lawyer diverted the judge's attention from enforcement of her order onto other matters. She demanded advance payment from Anne for the forensic examination. The hearing dragged on. Finally, at the judge's suggestion, Stew Johnson's test was again scheduled. But delay had become customary. Although Judge Williamson scheduled trial for January 1992, by the end of the year the parties were still arrayed in the same position and Renee was still seeing her mother and siblings once a month in a small room under supervision, at a cost of over $2,000.

While Anne represented herself, she succeeded in getting a volunteer guardian *ad litem,* Raymond Silver, appointed from an organization called FOCAS, an analog of the National CASA (Court-appointed Special Advocates for Children) organization. Silver, who was the supervisor of the entire Dallas program, began to evaluate the case to see how he could best serve the interests of his young client. He told Michelle Etlin that he had investigated what had gone on in the Catholic Children's Aid Society in Canada and had serious misgivings about how Renee's case had been handled there. He found out that the first Canadian social worker had been threatened and removed from the case for believing Renee, who was at that time saying that she had been molested. Silver was doing an intense and independent investigation. The case began to heat up.

A NEW DIVERSION

At a supervised visit in Texas, a process server who had pushed his way into the visitation room threw papers at Anne, saying, "There, you're served," and adding a few choice words. It was a new lawsuit commenced by Stew Johnson in New Jersey to execute a Mississippi judgment of $92,000 against Anne. All states will honor and collect each others' judgments if they are constitutional. But the Mississippi money judgment was made at a time when that state lacked "personal jurisdiction" over Anne because she did not live there, had not committed any crimes there, and refused to appear there voluntarily. The effect of this new proceeding was to open a new front and cause a lot of litigation in another state. Anne quickly filed a defense to the suit in New Jersey, saying that Mississippi had lacked jurisdiction to make a money judgment against her. She located an expert in constitutional law at a nearby law school to testify as an expert at trial. At two preliminary hearings, she held her own against Stew's New Jersey lawyers. Then, without warning, there was a mysterious change in judges. The new judge denied Anne an opportunity to bring in her legal expert, instructing her to include the expert's opinion in a brief she filed. No expert, however, would contribute to a brief to be filed by a *pro se* litigant; lawyers insist upon performing and controlling their own work. Anne then hired a second set of New Jersey lawyers to oppose enforcement of the Mississippi judgment. As trial approached, Stew's New Jersey lawyers suddenly filed a gigantic motion for "summary judgment"—that is, judgment without trial. Anne's lawyers did not even prepare a written answer to it. They said they had decided not to send her a copy because it was too voluminous to photocopy. Without her witnesses, faced with a two-inch-thick document the morning of the hearing, Anne was amazed to learn that the motion was filled with information she considered totally irrelevant to the issue of jurisdiction, and slanderous as well: it called her a kidnapper; it repeated all Stew's charges about her being an immoral woman; it was obviously designed to prejudice the judge against her rather than to argue the legal issues.

The new judge found for the plaintiff, Stew Johnson, without a trial, that very day, basing his decision—he said—on the "facts" that Anne's Canadian lawyer, first New Jersey lawyer, and Mississippi lawyer had all "agreed to" Mississippi's jurisdiction. All three of those "facts" were untrue, and Anne could have proved it, given a chance. She immediately fired the New Jersey lawyers and took the decision up on appeal, *pro se*. Her brief for that appeal was filed on January 6, 1994. A year later, she had not heard from the Appellate Division about when the decision would be made. Her motions for prompt decision were ignored.

Finally Stew showed up for his plethysmography examination by a psychologist in Dallas whose practice included treatment of convicted sex offenders. He reported Stew's test "inconclusive," as a result of his having been on medication after a recent heart attack. The raw data showed a flat line, indicating a lack of sexual arousal, until a certain point in the test, at which time Stew had apparently jumped up physically, knocking the slide projector down and breaking the equipment, so the test was terminated rather than completed. The psychologist did not schedule a retesting; nor did he do a drug-screen.

Anne hired a detective to find out as much as possible about Stew. Stew and his third wife, with whom he had moved to Texas from Mississippi, were now divorced. By the end of 1992, he had changed jobs three times since he moved to Dallas. His ex-wife still worked at the nursing home that Stew ran when they first moved to Texas. His third divorce was apparently quick and surgical; all the property stayed with him, and his ex-wife was silent about the situation. Psychologist Marina Monkberry's prediction about the stability of Stew's marriage was apparently not a sound one.

At an interim visitation hearing before Judge Williamson, Stew appeared with a new female companion and brought Renee to court with him. Anne protested that her daughter should not be in the courtroom, but Judge

Williamson called the girl up to the bench. Renee, then eleven years old, was dressed in spike heels, black nylons, a short black dress that looked like "after five" wear, and heavy make-up, including eye-liner and mascara. Anne stared, shocked, hardly recognizing her child. Stew did not seem to realize that his daughter was dressed inappropriately. Judge Williamson complimented Renee on her school attendance record and dismissed her politely. Renee nodded and marched out of the room stiffly without making eye contact with her mother.

THE "NORMALIZATION" OF VISITATION

After that hearing Anne said, "The law is what they do to keep you busy while they're destroying your children." Still she followed, and paid for, every step laid down for her in the interlocking set of legalistic manipulations that continued for another two and a half years. She was forced into bankruptcy in New Jersey by the $92,000 judgment against her. The college funds for both Tina and Al were spent trying to help Renee, and both older children enlisted in the Navy to get help toward the cost of higher education and career development.

An aggressive, successful young female attorney from Dallas, Texas had meanwhile contacted the Alliance for the Rights of Children, Inc., asking them to file an *amicus* brief in an unrelated Texas Supreme Court case involving child sexual abuse and custody issues. ARCH asked Michelle Etlin to research and write the brief, almost overnight, and thus she met the Dallas lawyer she described to Anne as "dynamite." Anne retained her fifth Texas lawyer, trusting that the final stage of the Texas litigation had finally begun.

Stew married again, and a new stepmother entered the scene. Visitation was being slowly liberalized. Tina and Al entered the fray, hiring an attorney recommended by the fifth Texas lawyer, and suing for custody on their own. Their plan was that both Stew Johnson and Anne Backman could pay child support to the grown siblings to raise their sister "away from the heat." Tina was even willing to relocate to Dallas and set up housekeeping there, to become Renee's surrogate mother again. Tina remembered how she had kept hidden from her mother the fact that Stew was molesting her and suspected Renee was now doing the same. She also felt uniquely qualified to help Renee deal with the consequences of incest during her teen-age years. She had become an independent and enterprising woman of 25 in spite of the considerable difficulties in her life caused by sexual abuse, the interruption of her college career, and the interminable and demoralizing litigation.

More mysterious changes occurred in Texas. Without notice, the case was switched to a new judge. Guardian *ad litem* Raymond Silver "disappeared," according to the staff of FOCAS (which had changed to CASA), who said his file had not been forwarded to anyone else. FOCAS claimed to have "lost" the file; it was later discovered that Silver, a well-organized executive, had left it on his desk when he took a new position. He had made provisions for follow-up care in the case, even offering to continue to work on it as a volunteer, an offer that FOCAS rejected without asking the court for a ruling and without notifying Anne. On January 14, 1993, without notice, Judge Arnold R. Singleton III, from another court in another county, who had no knowledge of the case, appointed a new guardian *ad litem* without relieving the previous one of his duties. But the services of the new guardian were not free; in fact, the day she was appointed, she filed a motion for costs. She quickly followed that with a motion for a continuance, saying that Renee could not go to trial yet, but if the child had psychological counseling, the parents might "agree" rather than go to trial. She avoided the psychologist who had already supervised visits and chose a new therapist for Renee.

Anne and Tina were welcomed in some of the therapy sessions, purportedly so that their relationships with Renee could be strengthened. But the bonds seemed to weaken with each visit. Stew's newest wife accompanied Renee to her therapy sessions and remained just outside the door throughout. According to Anne, whenever Renee was asked a question for which she did not have a prepared answer, she would run to the door, consult in whispers with her stepmother, and return with a ready answer. At last, in one joint session, the therapist asked the stepmother to leave. That day, according to Anne and Tina, Renee opened up and expressed the belief that her life was unhappy but that it made her tough. She commented, "I guess my mother loves me a lot; I guess I still have a place in my family."

A NORMAL VISIT AND AN ABNORMAL REACTION

In June 1993, pursuant to a court order, the Texas psychologist who had supervised visits flew to New Jersey, at Anne's expense, to study her home in preparation for Renee's visits there. He spent the weekend and concluded that the home and family atmosphere were suitable and that there was no reason not to grant visitation in New Jersey. Renee brought a friend along on her first visit, also at Anne's expense. The weekend was pleasant and comfortable, but Anne felt there was something strange about the friend and the visit. Renee's friend got a call from her own father in Dallas, who reported that her little sister was spending the weekend with Stew Johnson in Renee's absence. Anne made no comment. Also, every few hours, Renee and her friend, after some conspiratorial whispers, would go off "for a walk." Anne observed that Renee had long nails on her pinkies, had many minor physical complaints, and sniffled constantly. Anne wondered about the meaning of these things; later, she said, "If I were a doctor and that child were in my office, I would suspect cocaine use."

Renee refused to visit her mother again, stating indignantly that she had read the interrogatories sent to her father, and was furious. "You asked questions that are none of your business!" she declared. When Anne pointed out that Stew had been ordered by the court not to involve Renee in the litigation, the therapist explained that Renee had opened her father's mail. But the child would not have understood the legal documents, nor would she think they came from her mother, because the return address was that of Tina and Al's Texas lawyer. Then Renee changed her story and insisted that she did not want to be separated from her friends even for a day or two. Anne wrote her a firm letter, saying that she could not afford to fly the whole family to Texas when visitation in New Jersey had been court-ordered. From then on, Renee was described as very angry at her mother for "not hearing her" when she criticized her, and for "making her feel guilty." Anne's response was again firm and clear. She "heard" her daughter but expected Renee to "hear" the rest of the family.

At this point, the new therapist took over and insisted that Anne go into therapy to change *her* attitudes. Visitation was stalled permanently by the guardian *ad litem* and the therapist allegedly hired to help Renee with "progress" so her parents could reach agreement.

TOUCH-TAG WRESTLING IN TWO STATES

Meanwhile, Anne was served with process in New Jersey demanding back child support from the 1989 Mississippi court order, as well as current child support, to be automatically taken out of her paycheck from the federal government. Since the issue of child support was already before the Dallas court as part of the custody suit, Anne asked that the entire case be referred back and heard immediately in Texas. But the New Jersey judge told her that he had spoken to the new judge in Texas and had been advised that he could go forward with the child support suit in New Jersey. No transcript of an interjudicial conversation is in the file, not even a memo of it. The New Jersey judge ordered that $700 per month be taken out of Anne's check and handed over to Stew Johnson. Still there was no trial scheduled in Texas and no visitation in either state. When Anne pointed out that Stew Johnson had never supported his other children, who were in Anne's custody all along, the New Jersey judge called her vindictive. "Shame on you!" he scolded. At another point, he told Anne he pitied her because she disobeyed court orders and could not understand that everything was her own fault. To prove to Anne that her attitude was wrong, he suddenly quoted from the psychological report prepared four years earlier by Dr. Marina Monkberry in Canada. Anne asked how he had gotten that document, since it was not among the papers she had been served with and it was not in the child support file when she perused it. "Mr. Johnson sent it to me," said the judge. Anne had definitely been told that the question of Stew's molesting Tina or Renee was not an issue to the New Jersey court—all it intended to do was to collect money from her paycheck. But the Canadian psychologist's report was being read into the record, without an opportunity for cross-examination.

Meanwhile, since New Jersey had ordered child support for Stew, he had no incentive to go back into court in Texas, and the stand-still in Texas stood even stiller. The interrogatories were not answered, and the trial was not scheduled. Renee returned nonrefundable airline tickets and was said to be threatening to run away if she was forced to visit her mother. Stew's New Jersey lawyers delayed Anne's appeal of the New Jersey money judgment proceeding. No order was issued by the Texas court to enforce visitation, even though a hearing had been held, because the hearing officer who told the New Jersey judge to go ahead and collect the money was delaying making his decision about enforcing visitation. Renee's Texas therapist was satisfied that there should be no contact at all between mother and child; she reported that Renee had been a "problem drinker" before—when she had visits—but now she was having less of an alcohol problem. The therapist still insisted that Anne was the one who needed to undergo therapy, although Anne had herself evaluated and produced a prominent psychiatrist's testimony that she was without mental disability. Anne complied, for the sake of doing everything that she was instructed to do, and renewed her application to visit, regain custody of, and raise her child. A board-certified psychiatrist performed an evaluation, flew to Dallas, supervised a visit between Anne and Renee, and recommended that Anne have normal visitation immediately.

Meanwhile, Stew Johnson's answers to the interrogatories that had made Renee so angry at her mother were delivered. Anne learned that the "heart attack" that had allegedly caused Stew Johnson to take medication (producing the flat line on the plethysmograph) was not described: no doctor, no hospital, no medical records, no prescriptions, no descriptions. Stew said he had been to "various" doctors over the years but he could not remember their names.

Anne pressed for a speedy trial on her daughter's best interests. She was ready to show the jury that Renee was living with a man who had perjured himself and fabricated a heart attack to explain why he might fail a pedophilia test. Anne wanted only one thing now: a Texas jury.

Renee's new guardian *ad litem* wanted only one thing: delay. So far, that is what the Texas court has granted. When Anne insisted that her fifth Texas attorney set the case for immediate trial, the lawyer threatened to quit rather than try the case. The same day, she asked, without shame, "Do you think Renee is using cocaine?" Still, she preferred to bow out of the proceeding, leaving Renee with her father in spite of the suspicion of sexual abuse and drug involvement, rather than take the case to trial knowing that neither the court nor the guardian wanted the case tried in front of a jury.

THE FINAL HOURS

When the fifth Texas lawyer withdrew from the case, so did Tina and Al's lawyer, after writing the usual self-serving letter blaming her lack of representation on the clients. When Anne moved for immediate trial, the guardian *ad litem* demanded to be paid in advance and given an extra amount for "security" to take the case to trial. In spite of the Texas law that says a trial on a child's best interests cannot be delayed because of financial considerations, the judge who had given New Jersey the go-ahead on the child support issue, without dealing with the visitation issue, now made the custody trial dependent on the financial issues. He required pre-payment of $20,000 from Anne, pre-payment of $3,500 from the children—which they did not have—and the pre-payment of $3,500 from Stew Johnson (at any time or not at all), before the jury could be scheduled to decide whether Renee should live with a man who had apparently molested her older sister.

Tina and Al said they could understand how Renee had become "brainwashed against us." Neither of them had "fronted off" their adoptive father when they were in his control; it could be dangerous. Tina remembered the beating her younger sister had received for displeasing her father. Yet none of them is willing to stop fighting Stew Johnson, the system, and even Renee herself, to get her back. Anne likens her daughter's plight to that of Patty Hearst. She says the family needs to show their daughter/sister that they will not give up—hoping more for Renee to look back and realize how important she was to them, than for the system to vindicate them.

Renee refused to go on her last two court-ordered visits with her mother and maternal family. She screamed at her mother, after a mediation session, "You're so crazy, I tell you to leave me alone and you don't leave me alone! Fuck you, get a life, leave me alone!" Her father, stepmother, and therapist smiled at her approvingly after this outburst. Her guardian *ad litem* complained that Anne's own conduct had driven her daughter to such extremes, because of "pressure" to visit. When Anne insisted that she had not pressured the child during visits, the guardian *ad litem* said Renee objected to her mother's "praying about it." Renee testified in a visitation hearing that she refused to visit her mother because her mother was a liar, but failed to give examples of the lies. She could not cite the prayers that had disturbed her. Her guardian thought it was "grace."

Before crossing herself in the familiar gesture of childhood, Anne says grace before meals as it has been recited at her family's table every day since Renee's disappearance with her sister in 1985: "Bless us Oh Lord and these thy gifts which we are about to receive from thy bounty through Christ our Lord Amen—and bring Renee home soon, Amen."

5

The Life Sentence of Sandy Moore

THE FAMILY INTO WHICH SANDY MOORE MARRIED

In the winter of 1979, Sandy Moore married into a close-knit Texas family; eleven months later she gave birth to a boy—the family heir. Third in a line of Williams (William Roderick, the grandfather, called "Big Will"; William Samuel, the father, called "Little Will"; and now William Albert, the baby, called "Willie A"), her son immediately became an infant member of the landed gentry of the southern Texas farm and ranch territory. The family history would soon tell of a father who had a lot of problems, a marriage that had a lot of problems, and a kid who had a lot of problems, including emergency room and other hospital experiences.

Little Will, a frail man with glasses, had polio at age three. At fourteen, he broke his leg and was confined to bed for six months in a body cast. At eighteen, he broke his right hand and then his collar-bone in two separate fights; at age twenty he broke his nose and the bone above his eye in a car accident. At 24 and 25, he broke his right ankle in two separate motorcycle accidents, the second requiring surgery. Suffering many serious injuries and appearing to be accident-prone, Little Will exhibited a wild, violent recklessness.

Young Willie A seemed to have inherited a tendency toward extraordinary medical problems. When he was three, his fever from an ear infection soared over 104° for several days. He also had frequent serious accidents at his paternal grandparents' ranch, several of them requiring sutures. He reportedly fell from a tractor and was knocked unconscious, fell from a tree, was stung by wasps, and needed stitches "to repair a hole in his scrotum."

Sandy, who was a nurse, described her reaction to these accidents in a form she filled out for the Texas Council on Family Violence:

> There was supposed to have been an accident where Willie fell at the farm (out of a tree). He got stung by some bees. Will [the husband] called me and I was going to leave work and come home and Will told me I had better not, that I was being silly and irrational, that all kids had accidents

and Willie was all right. Several hours later that night my mother-in-law called because she knew if she did not I would be mad. She said that . . . right before he was given his bath she had found a spot of blood on Willie's underpants and found he had a small hole in his scrotum—she said he must have done it when he fell out of the tree! It was sutured at the E.R. and I left work and came home and no Willie! Will was there and said he was at the farm and he pushed and shoved me around because even at that late hour I wanted to go get my son! Will wound up holding me down on the bed and he threatened me and told me I was overreacting and people would think I was crazy! He promised to bring [the child] home the 1st thing the next AM. He threatened again taking Willie where I could not find him! Also he said the way I was acting he would have no trouble convincing people that I was crazy! I was almost hysterical! I got to thinking about the fact that every accident Willie had ever had in his life had been when he was at the farm!

The stage was already being set for the family to call Sandy "crazy" for her concern about her son's welfare. Even something so simple and easy to prove as physical harm and sutures could be used against her.

HARD TIMES IN A TEXAS MARRIAGE

Sandy Moore had a hard time adjusting to the in-laws and the marriage itself, but she felt that it would be very difficult, or even impossible, for her to leave. Later, on a questionnaire supplied by the Texas Council on Family Violence, she answered the question on "Physical Abuse" with the short answer:

> Slapped, kicked, burned, confined against my will, shoved, choked, punched, threw things at me, prevented me from getting proper health care, used a weapon by shooting me prior to my killing him. He also tried to break my arm by bending it behind my back.

Further down on the form, she explained her use of the words "anal rape," in her terse shot-gun style:

> Sex had gotten rougher and rougher and he did not enjoy it unless he was causing me pain. His favorite sexual position was knee on chest—like to feel buttocks on his groin area. Forced me to have sex with him, only two weeks after a D and C post-miscarriage in 1981. This particular act was not excessively violet [sic], but extremely painful. Sex got rougher post Willie, [that is, after the birth of their baby] then in 1984 the anal rape occurred.

She explained why she had not reported the anal rape in 1984:

Sex became rougher and rougher and he thoroughly enjoyed it, the rougher it was. I told him it hurt and he seemed delighted . . . would not release me until I promised not to go to the police [after the anal rape]. . . . Disallowed my going to see a doctor until months after the anal rape and then he insisted upon going into the examination room with me and he would not leave the doctor and me alone so that we could discuss what really happened.

Under the column marked "Injuries," Sandy listed:

Bruises
Sprains or dislocated joints (arm)
Cuts—Lip
Other: Breakdown of repair of rectal spinchter [sic]
    Busted Lip
    Severe back pain which continues even now

Under the heading "Permanent Disability as a Result of the Physical Abuse," she added, "I have since had to have rectal muscle repair sphincteroplasty as a result of the rape."

Sandy listed a number of threats on the form. She wrote that her husband told her that if she tried to divorce him, he would send the baby out of state and never let her see him again—but he would remain to torment her. She said her calls to the police were generally met with what she described as their "standard comment," that "this was just a domestic violence and they would not interfere." She finally filed charges against her husband, but a domestic relations lawyer advised her to drop them or the divorce "would take forever." She obtained a protective order, but it "was totally ignored by my husband." In answer to the question of whether her husband had ever been arrested for abusing her, she wrote: "Yes. However, he was let out the same day and then he made additional threats about what he would do if that *ever* happened in the future!"

HARD TIMES IN A TEXAS DIVORCE

Sandy filed for divorce, represented by the same lawyer who advised her to drop all her allegations of domestic violence. She took his advice. Joint custody with liberal contact for both parents began immediately upon separation in late 1987. Since Sandy was working two jobs and her husband was unemployed, she was also letting Little Will drive Willie A back and forth to school every day. By January 1988, however, Sandy had to take Willie A to the doctor for repeated complaints of anal soreness and irritation, and even loss of bowel control, after visitation with his father. On January 19, a colon and rectal specialist reported the results of a proctological examination:

Findings:

1. History of fecal soilage, etiology unclear at present.
2. History of possible sodomy or instrumentation/manipulation of anorectum.
3. Somewhat abnormal anorectal examination, manifested by some decrease in external sphincter tone.

The doctor was careful, however, to avoid the inference that he had detected that Willie A had been sodomized. The report continued:

Disposition:

1. The above mentioned findings and their significance were discussed at some length with the patient's mother. I explained to [her] that . . . the only unequivocal evidence of the patient being sodomized would be finding sperm on an anorectal examination. [She] seemed to understand these explanations.
2. [She] indicated to me that, on advice of counsel, the patient's father will no longer be driving him to and from school.

On April 27, Sandy sought help from the local social services agency in order to limit her husband's visitation with Willie A. By this time, as a mother and as a registered nurse, she strongly suspected incest. At first she gave her reasons in lay terms, mentioning hunches and suspicions in addition to the increasing physical indicators: she had long suspected Little Will was a homosexual; she believed he was having an affair with a known homosexual pedophile in town; he had subjected her to forcible sodomy; and her son continued to have a sore anus and loss of bowel control upon his return from visits. In June, the father's response is noted in a handwritten memo in the Child Protective Services file:

[Father] called regarding interview with Willie A—He thinks [mother] needs therapy but his attorney says cannot force—[father] is upset about [mother]'s allegations; & loss of custody of child—feels she is not rational and her anger hostility is affecting [child]. 6-24-88.

Following the advice and a referral from CPS, Sandy took Willie A for an evaluation by a child psychologist with a Ph.D., who described Willie A as

occasionally uncooperative . . . psychomotor activity was retarded. . . . A depressed mood predominated . . . vacillating between temper tantrums and crying . . . suicide potential is assessed as low at this time due to a low energy level; . . . low self-esteem . . . lack of independence, loss of autonomy, and depression. . . .

She wrapped up her impressions of the child with "The essential feature is a depressed mood."

It seemed that Willie A did not even have the "get-up-and-go" to kill himself. The psychologist concluded that he needed therapy. Sandy took him to a psychologist for play therapy early in 1989 because of his continued depression and her continued concern about incest. Meanwhile, William Samuel, the father, sued for custody, saying that Sandy was mentally unbalanced for suspecting incest and that she had emotionally abused her son by making the allegations.

On March 31, 1989, at the age of six, Willie A was admitted to the children's psychiatric unit of a Texas hospital. The initial diagnosis was oppositional/defiant behavior, encopresis, and suspected child sexual abuse. Since the parents had joint legal custody, both were permitted to visit the young patient without supervision. Hospital notes say drily, "Child does some sexual acting out, but not much emphasis is placed on that." A CPS caseworker noted her "gut feelings" about the parents—no one seemed to know who was telling the truth. "[N]o one . . . has questioned the child (?)." A CPS abuse investigation initiated by the caseworker revealed that

> Child has dilated external sphincter muscle as noted when examined by proctologist. Child complains of soreness in anal area and would not lower self in bathtub. . . . Child occasionally does say daddy "does things" to him. . . . Mother . . . is trying to protect child because [Derekville] is a small town and her first lawyer told her not to mention sexual abuse to the judge.

Yet the hospital records show that Willie A was not immediately given psychological counseling even when he was hospitalized in the psychiatric ward. According to his charts, his father and his father's family continued to have a lot of unsupervised access to him there:

> I asked [the social worker] why the child is in [the hospital] if he's not getting counseling and she had no answer. I stated surely the proctologist findings would prove something. Either she is not privy to the results or no one cares because both parents continue to have visitation rights.

Meanwhile, Sandy had learned her lesson. She thought the authorities had failed to help her son because they considered her too aggressive. So she took a different approach. She spoke in guarded tones, as a mother not as a nurse, trying to let the professionals draw their own conclusions so she would not be seen as "hostile and vindictive" toward the man she felt sure was molesting her son. The result was the following report:

> Mrs. [Moore]'s allegations . . . or rather her proof is just as vague as ever. Her efforts to protect her child seem ineffectual and rather late and worker has a hard time trying to believe she is a strong, protective mother. . . . Worker considers Mrs. [Moore] to be a vague person. . . . [She] appeared very candid but after she was gone I realized she really didn't tell me anything.

The recommendation that resulted from these reports was three weeks of in-hospital observation by another Ph.D. child psychologist. Meanwhile, the CPS intake report recorded that: "Child is displaying very aggressive behavior and is defecating in his pants. . . ."

Another CPS social worker's parent profile took pot shots at Sandy for believing her son was molested:

> Several times, she described herself as approaching hysteria and threatened to run with the child rather than return him to his father. She has not previously been diagnosed as having psychological/emotional problems (as far as is known); however, Sandy did not always appear to be rational and in control of her emotions. She appeared convinced beyond doubt that her ex-husband has and is sexually abusing her son, although she could not provide a rational foundation for the inception of this belief. . . . [The mother's] ability to protect the child is uncertain. She has made death threats to her ex-husband, his lawyer, and the judge, as well as threatened to run with the child. Also, if sexual abuse has occurred over the time frame that Sandy alleges that it has, Sandy repeatedly failed to take the necessary steps to prevent sexual abuse.

Short of killing, however, there is no indication of what steps she could have taken. Her prior reports to CPS had never resulted in protection. She was ordered by the court to allow visitation, while being assured by her attorney that any interference with her husband's rights would result in her own loss of custody.

Meanwhile, the hospital reports on Willie A's condition grew more ominous and contained more and more blatant descriptions of the evidence and behavioral indicators commonly present in molested children. The child psychologist in charge noted in the psychological assessment:

> A and B in school, consistent; Baptist. Reports mother works two jobs, incompetent grandmother cares for boy, he visits father where there is possible sexual abuse and pornographic films. Paternal grandparents are reported as abusive and harsh with the patient. . . . aggressive and demanding of peers, with poor social skills. . . . history of possible sexual molestation, increased aggressive behaviors toward others, and regressive behaviors such as thumb sucking, bed wetting and soiling his pants. . . . fear of teeth . . . withdrawn and depressed . . . [reports] from neighborhood boys of him trying to kiss them and grab "their privates." . . . [Grandparents] being rough, grabbing his hair, shoving food in his mouth, and holding his hand over a hot burner were reported. In 1981, the patient's grandfather [Big Will] was committed to Physicians and Surgeons Hospital. [Sandy] believes he was diagnosed "schizophrenic."

A proctologist's diagnosis of Willie A read "Decreased external sphincter tone. History of fecal soilage . . . somewhat abnormal anorectal examination, manifested by some decrease in external sphincter tone." A psychiatrist compiled the following medical and psychological report:

> Diagnosis: Oppositional Defiant Disorder, 313.81 in DSM III (Axis I); History of dilated anus (Axis III); psychosocial stressors—7 including possible sexual abuse by parents, poor relationship and divorce of parents (Axis IV). Plan: further psychiatric evaluation because of extent of dysfunction with dangerousness to self and others.

Another physician commented that Willie A

> would often become angry and hostile . . . [alternating with] appearing depressed and sucking his thumb. One of the symptoms which was encopresis [soiling his pants] continued to appear at a lessening frequency initially about twice a week and then roughly about once a week in the last couple of weeks that he was in the hospital.

It is possible, then, that while Willie A was in the hospital, his ability to use his sphincter muscles to control his bowel movements improved. Meanwhile, his other problems were being evaluated. A hospital psychologist reported on history taken from Sandy that Willie A suffered from insomnia and frequent nightmares, which had been steadily increasing over the past year. He described the difficulty Willie A had discussing problems with him during clinical interviews:

> [Patient was] tense and . . . verbally hostile, particularly when asked personal questions. . . . At one point patient was asked if somebody ever did anything to him and told him to keep it a secret. The patient's response was a "yes" quickly followed by a denial. . . . [When I told him that] secrets are sometimes scary and that if anyone tells him to keep a secret he needs to discuss it with another grownup the patient appeared to listen intently and made direct eye contact with the examiner at that point. But again, when asked if anyone ever hurt him or made him do things that were scary or uncomfortable, he denied it.

There were serious psychological conclusions:

> evidence to suggest excessive hostility as demonstrated by argumentativeness and some unsocialized orientation which could be related to possible lying and stealing. . . . fearfulness and worry . . . distrust of others . . . multiple fears. . . . very low self-esteem . . . sad with feelings of being alienated and unacceptable to others . . . distrustful of others and anxious in relationships yet has a desire for help and affection . . . tends to see himself as helpless and hopeless and responds to this by denying any frustrations or problems directly.

A physician listed his Summary of Main Issues in the following order: "(1) possible sexual abuse; (2) encopresis; (3) extreme feelings of anger and hostility, etc." The doctor seemed to be coming to the conclusion that the probable source of the child's problems was sexual abuse. He recommended therapeutic hospitalization and, afterwards, participation in a support group for victims of sexual abuse. CPS still withheld making a finding. In fact, the CPS supervisor's report dated May 10, 1989 read "Worker believes no one knows the truth at this time, other than for sure, the parents are in a custody dispute over this child."

THE CUSTODY DISPUTE

The custody dispute was resolved with record speed. This time, Sandy did not follow her first lawyer's advice about keeping the allegations of sexual abuse to herself. Even though CPS would not support her attempts to protect her son, she thought she could prove at the trial at least significant doubt about the fitness of Little Will as a custodial parent. The offensive-defensive position of the father's family, however, was that Sandy was an unfit mother because of her "false allegations of sexual abuse," which they claimed had been labeled "invalid" by CPS. Their position prevailed, and Little Will walked out of court with custody of his son—but not with his son.

Although CPS had insisted that all that was known for sure was that there was a custody dispute, a psychologist on the case issued a report on June 23, 1989, documenting knowledge of much more than that. Willie A had disclosed to him that sexual abuse had occurred during visits to his father's house.

> Father "rubs on me," pointing to genitals, described father rubbing penis between child's buttocks. . . . Child stated always happens on the first day he visits with his father in [Derekville]. . . . seemed greatly relieved after disclosing the information. . . . Child has functional encopresis, sucks thumb. In therapy because mother suspected sexual abuse, unable to prove it because child would not talk. . . . also . . . aggressive behaviors, defiant, destructive, like a wrecking machine. . . . Child reportedly does not relate well to females, but appears to have a normal relationship with his mother.

The psychologist also noted Sandy's first act of open defiance: "Mother will refuse to relinquish custody on Monday."

The next day the CPS supervisor put a memo into the file suggesting that, after more than a year of Sandy's allegations that Willie A complained of his bottom being sore all the time, after a diagnosis of loss of sphincter muscle tone and encopresis, after a hospitalization and multiple diagnoses, she was still considering the possibility that the child had been indoctrinated with ideas of sexual abuse. She noted that past investigations were unfounded and that medical and psychological evidence was considered inconclusive. "Professionals involved would only state that sexual abuse was 'possible.'"

Two days later, on June 26, 1989, the Monday that Sandy had said she would refuse to relinquish custody, she told Willie A that he would be going to live with his father. He objected, so she asked if he was ready to say why. He said his father had done something to him, but he would only talk to a man about it, not to a woman. Sandy called CPS, who agreed to give Willie A another interview with a male social worker. They told Sandy not to discuss the issue with the boy. When Sandy and Willie A arrived at the CPS office, they were greeted by a female social worker. Sandy immediately said that Willie A had specified that he would only talk to a man. The child did not speak during the encounter, although, according to the female caseworker, he did peek at her from behind his mother. A male social worker, Antonio Valdez, was then asked to interview Willie A

In that videotaped interview, as Valdez calmly spoke to Willie A, the boy sucked his thumb, hid and covered his face, wrung his shirt, curled his slight frame up so that he appeared hunched over on the sofa, mumbled, fought tears, and managed to get words out that described his father putting a "thing" into his "back." He thought the "thing" was hard; it could have been like a triangle; it buzzed. Finally he described some sort of anal penetration, possibly with a vibrator. Valdez was satisfied that the boy had made another disclosure of sexual abuse, but he was instructed to try to get more information from the troubled child. The boy had nothing to add, other than his assurance that he had already revealed the abuse to a therapist at the hospital. He said he thought his mother "had a feeling" something was wrong. He then refused to discuss it any more.

CPS asked Sandy if there were any alternative living arrangements for Willie A. She would not be permitted to "keep" him because she had already lost custody. Sandy suggested rehospitalization, but CPS said they could not place a child in the hospital "for the sole purpose of protecting him from abuse." Meanwhile, Willie A's paternal grandparents wanted to take him, but Sandy vehemently objected, saying that they couldn't be trusted. A family rumor had it that Big Will had molested his own daughter when she was a child, but that she had shut up about it after being punished for telling. Sandy said there was also some evidence that her ex-husband had also been molested by Big Will. She did not consider the grandparents safe guardians and said there was pornography at their house. The paternal grandmother then offered to search her home for pornography and sexual paraphernalia, and to be cooperative and helpful if given control of Willie A. That suggestion was temporarily rejected, and a youth home was located.

At this juncture, with no explanation, a female caseworker, Fanny Jenkins, began to play a pivotal role in the case. She and Antonio Valdez described

Willie A's reactions that day. "Willie gave his father a wary look and refused to speak to him," they reported. Informed that he would be taken to a youth home,

> Willie seemed to cheer up a bit, but not much. He would not say why he did not want to go home with his father. . . . Willie stated he wanted to live with his mother. . . . He began hiding his eyes again and sucking his thumb. He refused to talk any more and curled up in a ball on the chair, eyes closed and thumb in his mouth. I left the office for a minute. When I returned, Willie was crying. I told [him] we were going to the Youth Home. Willie stopped crying. I gave him a kleenex to blow his nose.

By the next day, June 27, Valdez's name had become less prominent in the file. A doctor Faxed his report directly to Jenkins, who seemed to have taken over control of the case, even though Willie A had wanted to relate only to a male caseworker. The doctor noted that the prior disclosures Willie A made to him did not seem to have been coached, and he included the verbatim report of the child's "outcry" against sexual abuse to the male physician. (In Texas, a child's disclosure of sexual abuse is referred to as an "outcry" although it is usually mumbled or whispered.)

When Sandy Moore sought to visit her son in the youth home, her request was denied. While she was in the CPS office becoming "angry and impossible to talk to," a visit was quickly arranged by Jenkins for the boy to see his father and paternal grandparents instead. Jenkins included in her written report—as if it were important—that Sandy had used her phone without asking permission, without apologizing, and without thanking her for its use. She listened to part of the conversation and reported that Sandy had said, "That's a lie!" to the party she had called.

That day also, there was a "parent/grandparent/child visit" for Willie A with his father and grandparents. Although there is no record of his having been asked a question, the boy apparently spontaneously blurted out "I want to live with my dad," as soon as the visit was over. When Antonio Valdez asked him why he had changed his mind, Willie A would give no reason. The visit with his paternal family was described in choreographic detail:

> His father gave him a hug, but Willie did not appear to respond. We went to the visiting room. Willie sat curled up, leaning on his dad. He continuously sucked his thumb, despite comments [the grandparents] made trying to get him out of this habit. . . . [When] his father and grandparents said goodbye Willie responded verbally but did not leave his chair.

Jenkins was very involved in the Willie A case for the rest of the day; the next day, in a supervisory conference, she reported that Willie A had "recanted" and denied all the allegations he had made, that he now preferred to live with his father but that he refused to say why. The supervisor advised that the boy remain one more night in the youth home. She told the caseworker to ask the boy, the next day, how he would feel if CPS were to ask the judge to return custody to his mother.

Jenkins promptly told the paternal Moore family that "my supervisor was not yet ready to return Willie to his grandparents' home." The wording is interesting—Willie A had never previously been in their custody, so he would not be "returning" but, rather, "being placed." The father and grandparents operated as a single unit by this time, and were apparently being treated as such by CPS. They agreed to meet Jenkins at the youth home for another visit with Willie A the next day. When Jenkins picked the boy up from the swimming pool to visit his father, he immediately asked if he was "going home." The notes do not show whether "home" meant his mother's home or elsewhere. "When he learned he was not, he protested and became withdrawn, sucking his thumb and closing his eyes." On being delivered to his visit with father and grandparents, "His behavior was even more infantile today than yesterday. He curled up on his father's lap, head resting on his father's shoulder, thumb in mouth, and played with his father's ear with the other hand."

Little Will, the father, then informed the caseworker that he would not permit Sandy to visit his son, even under CPS supervision. It is not clear why he was regarded as having the authority to make such a decision, since Willie A was already in the legal custody of CPS and an investigation was pending against the father for sexual abuse. Valdez and Jenkins, together, made one more contact with the boy that day, after the paternal family's visit:

> Visit with Willie A, Victim. . . . He did not present any oppositional or defiant behavior and did not ask to return to the swimming pool. We invited him to . . . discuss the allegation again. He joined us without hesitation . . . answer[ed] questions without delay and he was not upset about speaking to workers about the allegations. . . . He stated that . . . his mother had told him to say this . . . while enroute to this office. . . . [We] asked him to share his feelings about going back to his mother. He stated that he preferred to live with his father. He also stated that he did not want to live with his mother. He did not give any reasons why he preferred to live with his father. He appeared to be very comfortable . . . showing less stress during this interview . . . not sucking his thumb. . . .

(We note that this interview, and apparently all interviews during the time Willie A was described as "recanting" his disclosure, involved a female interviewer. Willie had already refused to discuss sexual abuse with a female, even his mother, and had only disclosed in privacy with Antonio Valdez.)

Some time that day, Jenkins asked Willie A the specific question assigned by her supervisor: how he would feel if CPS were to ask the judge to give custody back to his mother. "[H]e said, 'I don't care where I live!' He said he hates Youth Home. Specifically, he hates the people there." It seems Willie A was prepared to say anything that day. "[He] denied ever having pain in his anal area or ever being examined by a doctor in anal area."

At this point, Willie A "recanted" an event everyone knew had taken place: the proctologist's examination had been documented. No one tried to figure out why such an obvious discrepancy occurred, or what implications it had for the veracity of the rest of the "recantation" of the child's outcry.

On that same fateful day, June 28, when Sandy asked to visit her son, she was told to wait another day. She was not informed that CPS was allowing the father to veto her visitation. A reading of the file suggests that she was being politely stalled until the youth home could obtain a paper trail of recanted allegations and quickly discharge Willie to his father, who could then handle "visitation" by himself.

On June 29, Sandy Moore went to the police to file criminal charges against her ex-husband for sexually abusing her son. The sheriff thought the case should go to CPS, not to the law. CPS notes say: "Worker, in speaking with . . . worker in charge, found out that . . . case has been twice referred and investigated by the [local] unit [presumably CPS]. . . . Both times investigation was invalidated."

CPS apparently did not admit to the police that this time, the third time allegations reached their office, disclosure validation had in fact occurred. They simply told the police about prior "unfounded" reports and about the custody case: "At the divorce . . . [father] was given custody. . . . [Father's] lawyer . . . had contacted [local] CPS." While CPS told the police how to handle the charges, Willie A was allowed "to return home with his paternal grandparents and father, with the stipulation that [the father] would not sleep at the house and that all visits with his son would be supervised by other adults." The "other adults" were never specified nor by what criteria they would be judged competent or trustworthy to supervise visitation.

The next day, the father told CPS that he and his parents would be going out of town to spend the Fourth of July holiday with his sister. Willie A would be going along on the trip. No details were gathered about supervision or the conditions at the sister's house. The CPS file for June 30 reveals:

> Sandy [Moore] became upset with this agency's decision. She hired a 4th lawyer and became insistent that the grandparents could not and would not protect her son from further abuse, that [the father] would pressure his son into silence and that the grandfather is also sexually abusing her son.

These revelations were later described by the CPS caseworker to be without foundation.

Apparently, Sandy began a personal surveillance of the paternal family farm, to see whether her son was being left alone with his father. On Saturday, July 1, she called the child abuse hot line from the father's property, leaving that number for the return call. When Jenkins called her back, Sandy said that her ex-husband's clothes were still in the grandparents' farmhouse. She was "upset and hysterical," according to Jenkins. "She would not tell me what she was doing at the ranch. She was crying and at times difficult to understand." Sandy demanded that CPS immediately remove her son from the grandparents' home, but the caseworker insisted that she had no authority to do so. (It was the same caseworker who had taken it upon herself to place the boy in his grandparents' home.) Sandy threatened to sue CPS if Willie A was not removed immediately and placed in foster care. Strangely, Jenkins reported that the father, Little Will, called her at home shortly after her conversation with Sandy, to tell her that they were at his sister's home and would return on Wednesday, July 5. She "informed [the father] that I had just called Sandy at a Derekville telephone number. He verified that this number is his home telephone number."

On July 3, Jenkins wrote to a CPS doctor, enclosing materials "compiled during the investigation now being conducted" regarding Willie's allegations of sexual abuse by his father. The doctor was about to hold a "staffing" on the case on Thursday, July 6. Also, a memo in the file, dated July 3, shows that Sandy again called Jenkins to tell her that she had watched the grandparents' house until 4 A.M. Sunday morning. "She did not state her purpose in doing this. She [said] . . . [the father] had not complied with the mutually-agreed stipulations imposed for the duration of the CPS investigation."

Sandy also reportedly told the caseworker explicitly that her son had "recanted because his father had access to him while he was in the Youth Home." Sandy renewed her attempts to get CPS to intervene. The neighboring CPS unit (in the town where Sandy lived) asked the local CPS unit (where the paternal family lived) to send a worker to the paternal home to "ascertain that stipulations of the child's return were being met." Nobody responded to that request.

Another memo says that Little Will called the caseworker on July 3, saying they were now back home (two days earlier than expected), and that his parents were at the sheriff's office pressing charges against Sandy for vandalizing their home. He said Sandy had broken in and smashed some things. He said his sister had returned with the family and would stay with the grandparents during the investigation. He inquired about the time and place of the staffing and got that information.

Sandy's description of the events of July 3 have not varied significantly since her official statement to the sheriff. The account in her own words—a nine-page, single-spaced narrative—bears a tragic simplicity:

> My inlaws were allowed by shelter to pick up my son Willie and take him even though it was documented that Willie had told them about the abuse and they had done nothing to help him! Willie had made an outcry to CPS and this was the last definse [sic] mechanism and hope I had about it not being true! (I did not want it to be true) but when he finally told the

psycholigist [sic] I told CPS that I just wanted to take him and run! (to keep him safe) and for this; CPS picked up my son!

Sandy continued to document her loss of hope and her desperation, right up to the day she and her ex-husband shot each other. Her last paragraph reads: "What followed all of this was an odessy [sic] all in itself! Or probably a better discription [sic] would be a waking nightmare!"

Sandy filled her car with the things she would need to "run." She had as much cash as she could put her hands on. She took her gun, as always, which she considered especially necessary since she was going to the grandparents' place to "pick up" her son first. She parked "a long ways off," where her car could not be spied. She alternately walked and ran to the ranch by a route where she would not be seen. She hid at first in the pig barn, intending to wait until Willie A came outside. She planned to snatch him and run, never to deal with CPS or the authorities again until her son was grown or at least big enough to take care of himself. Although she had no help, she felt confident and resolute. For the first time in years, she felt hopeful.

However, Sandy had one last hope of forcing CPS to rectify the situation, for she called the caseworker again. She told Jenkins that, contrary to CPS orders, the grandparents had allowed their son to be alone with Willie A; father and son had just come back from somewhere in the car, alone together. Asked how she knew, Sandy said she was in the pig barn at the ranch and had seen them herself. Jenkins then called the main house and informed the family that Sandy was hiding on their property. Sandy had turned to the system once too often.

Big Will came out of the house with his shotgun, but Sandy had changed locations and was hiding behind a tractor. He looked around but did not sense where she was, for she got the drop on him, coming up behind him with her own shotgun aimed. She told him plainly and bluntly that he was going to walk back to the house with her, go in, and send Willie A out to her. She said she knew that Little Will would have his shotgun sights on her every second from inside the farmhouse. Sandy directed her father-in-law toward the front door of the house in which her son and his were both waiting. As he walked back to the house, Sandy was behind him, using his body as a shield, so her ex-husband could not shoot her in cold blood.

Big Will refused to open the door, telling Sandy to do it herself. She backed up slightly, saying she would not open it because they both knew that there was a bullet waiting for her if she did. She kept her gun trained on her father-in-law's back. He kicked the door and dropped to the ground with a bullet in his spine, from which injury he has never recovered the movement in his legs. At the same moment another gun went off. The force of the bullet that entered Sandy's back and came out her arm helped spin her around fast enough to land two bullets in quick succession in Little Will, who was dead before his body hit the ground.

The coroner later testified that both bullets Sandy fired were instantly fatal—one caught Little Will between the eyes and the other entered his aorta—so it was impossible to determine which hit first. The one thing that could be said with certainty was that the bullet that hit Sandy was fired first, for even in Texas, dead men don't shoot.

Sandy said later that she "could'of taken" the combined physical attack by her mother-in-law and sister-in-law as she tried to retrieve Willie A. Escape with him "would'of been a piece of cake," were it not for the fact that she was already "woozy" from having been shot. As it was, they "took" her, beating her over the head with the telephone receiver and sitting on top of her while they called the police.

The dead man's mother and sister later reported that during the fray, Willie A came out of the bedroom and asked Sandy, "Why did you kill my father?" Sandy said her son ran out of the bedroom crying, "Stop beating up my mother!" (CPS reported, however, that three days later, when Willie A was in their custody, he still did not know that his father was dead. When they informed him, he cried.)

Sandy Moore was taken to the police station, bruised and bloody, with her arm in a make-shift sling. She was read her rights, she gave her statement, and she was booked on first-degree murder.

July 6, the day of the CPS staffing, was Sandy's third day in jail for murder. The CPS doctor reported: "Ms. [Moore] appeared to be approaching a psychotic episode" and that "her repeated allegations of sexual abuse are the result of displacement of her own fears, guilt, hostility or anger." He stated that he was inclined to believe the child was never sexually abused, "but has undoubtedly suffered emotional abuse from the custody battle over him." The same day, the caseworker concluded:

> I could make no clear determination at this time. If indeed the child was sexually abused, the question remains: by whom? Two other men, the maternal uncle and the mother's paramour, also had access to the child. Nothing is known about either man. Also it is conceivable that Sandy Moore, in her attempt to obtain "evidence," is capable of abusing her son toward this end.

According to Jenkins, at last CPS could drop the case: "[The CPS Program Director] advised that not enough information has been obtained to clearly validate the allegation of sexual abuse. She advised me to drop the investigation for the time being. . . . " Willie A was temporarily out of the custody of the paternal family, and nobody was being investigated for child sexual abuse.

A Texas personal injury attorney agreed to defend Sandy in the criminal trial *pro bono*. His first act was to try to get the case removed from Derekville, the small close-knit town where the Moore family held so much sway. He said he "proved up the best case for a change of venue anybody could have," but he lost. He felt no Derekville jury could possibly give his client a fair trial. Since the need to defend the safety of one's child is a valid basis for a self-defense plea in Texas, the lawyer showed the jury the evidence that Willie A had been molested. In spite of that, and the physical evidence that Sandy shot Little Will when she already had his bullet in her back, she was convicted of first-degree murder.

In spite of the final know-nothing finding of CPS and its doctor, members of the jury actually stated that, based on the evidence presented at the murder trial, they believed that Willie had been molested by his father and that Sandy intended to kidnap him from his abuser. But they decided that since she went to the ranch armed, she had formed an intent to kill. Sandy was sentenced to life in prison. Pleas for clemency based on an act of defense of her son have so far been unsuccessful. Sandy did not receive a governor's pardon as a victim of domestic violence, in spite of efforts on the part of many organizations.

Willie A has never made another allegation of sexual abuse against anybody. His grandfather returned home in a wheelchair after a lengthy hospitalization. Willie A was again placed in his paternal grandparents' custody and has never been allowed contact with his mother since the day of the shooting.

Looking frail and tired in an interview televised from prison, Sandy wept and said—to console herself as much as to prove anything to the world—that at least she had saved her son from sexual abuse.

PART TWO
THE
SYSTEM

6

True and False Allegations

In a December 1990 "Dear Abby" column, a lawyer wrote, "I was in court recently on a child molestation case. The judge stated that more than 80% of such cases that had come before him had been frivolous—the accusation has been made for the purpose of gaining an advantage in other actions." If that was the judge's comment, it was based on judicial fantasy, not research and reality.

—Judge Charles B. Schudson (1992:112)

THE PREVALENCE OF CHILD SEXUAL ABUSE

Those who assert that false allegations of sexual abuse in divorce are on the rise seldom take into account the fact that all types of reported cases of child abuse are on the rise and that this trend has been evident for more than a decade. The 1986 National Incidence Study estimated that one million children were demonstrably harmed as a result of child abuse each year. A total of 1.5 million were considered "at risk" or "threatened with harm." This represents a 51 percent increase over the reported numbers of children demonstrably harmed in 1980, which, the Study concluded, may be more reflective of increased recognition and reporting than of an actual increase in incidence. The majority of cases (64 percent) involved neglect. A total of 311,500 children were physically abused, or 4.9 per thousand. Another 188,100 were emotionally abused, or 3.0 per thousand. The study found that 133,600 children were sexually abused, or 2.1 per thousand.

National Incidence Study estimates are based on interviews with a range of professionals in sample counties across the country; however, not all cases known to professionals are reported, as mandated by law. Reported cases were somewhat lower—1.8 per thousand in 1985 (Thoennes and Tjaden, 1990). Though allegations have risen from 0.6 per thousand children in 1980 to 1.8 per thousand in 1985, this statistic is attributed to "educational efforts that have raised professional and public awareness of child sexual abuse and led more people to come forward." Thoennes and Tjaden point out that the apparent rise of allegations of sexual abuse in the context of custody disputes could be misleading, and may simply mirror the increase in general reporting patterns.

The largest study dealing with this issue to date was conducted by Thoennes and Tjaden in 1988 for the Association of Family and Conciliation Courts Research Unit in Denver, Colorado (ibid., 1990). The study considered 9,000 contested custody cases from twelve different states with extensive investigations, which had been conducted in eight court jurisdictions. The researchers found that only 169 cases involved allegations of child sexual abuse; thus allegations of child sexual abuse were made in under 2 percent of the 9,000 custody cases seen by the researchers. However, Thoennes and Tjaden estimated this rate as six times as high as in the general population. If we take the 1990 census figure of one million divorces a year involving children, a suggestion by Nancy Polikoff (1983) that 10 percent of all custody cases are contested, and the estimate by Thoennes and Tjaden that 2 percent of those involve child sexual abuse allegations, we come up with a figure of 2,000 custody cases annually that include allegations of child sexual abuse. This estimate may be conservative because it is based on new divorces only and does not take into account allegations which may arise years after a divorce or custody case was initially settled.

SEXUAL ABUSE ALLEGATIONS AND DIVORCE

Several studies have reported a higher incidence of child sexual abuse in families that have undergone marital dissolution (Corwin et al., 1987), and several reasons have been suggested for this phenomenon. Thoennes points out that child sexual abuse may create stress in a marriage and lead to its eventual breakdown. According to David Corwin,

> There are several reasons abused children may be more likely to disclose abuse by a parent and to be believed by the other parent following a separation or divorce. With the breakup of the parents comes diminished opportunity for the abusing parent to enforce secrecy as there is increased opportunity for the child to disclose abuse separately to the other parent. Decreased dependency and increased distrust between parents increases willingness to suspect child abuse by the other parent. [1987:102]

Kathleen Colbourn Faller (1991) created the following classification of child sexual abuse allegations in custody and divorce cases and applied it to her study of 136 cases.

1. *Abuse causes the divorce*. In most of these cases, the mother finds out about sexual abuse and reacts by deciding to divorce the husband. In Faller's experience, about half of mothers who discover sexual abuse divorce their

husbands and take the children with them. The mother may find out through a disclosure by the child, or be informed by outside agencies such as police or schools. Faller found that eleven of the 136 cases were of this type. She claims that such mothers are more likely to be perceived as bringing false allegations if they leave the marriage independently than if they do so only after authorities have addressed the abuse before the divorce action was commenced.

2. *Abuse is revealed during divorce*. According to Faller, in the classic father-daugther incest pattern, the abuse is only revealed when the daughter reaches adolescence or when the parents divorce. This pattern generally involves long-standing sexual abuse. The child finally feels safe to report the abuse to her mother when the perpetrator is out of the home and cannot punish her. In addition, the mother may have been unwilling to look critically into suggestive behavior during the marriage, choosing instead to tolerate it because marriage had beneficial aspects.

3. *Abuse is precipitated by divorce*. Fifty-two of Faller's cases were of this type. The abuser, who is usually not the instigator of the divorce, may feel tremendous emotional loss because of separation from the spouse and turns to the child for emotional support. Prior feelings of sexual attraction to children may have been held in check by the marriage or other inhibiting factors. Loss of family structure, however, dissolves upon separation, as do rules regulating where parents and children sleep and with whom they bathe. The abuser is also angry at the spouse for destroying the marriage. The child becomes a vehicle for retaliation. The intensity of these feelings may result in such overt sexual maltreatment that it produces physical injury to the child. Abusers cannot control their behavior because their feelings are so intense, even when they are under investigation; repeated offenses are likely. Some sexualized behavior toward children may have been apparent during these marriages, for example: intimate touching, tongue-kissing, and sleeping or bathing with the child. Once the separation unhinges the situation further, restraints vanish and perpetrators lose control.

4. *False allegations are made during divorce*. Nineteen of Faller's cases were judged to be false, and twelve were inconclusive. Parents may become convinced that estranged spouses are capable of anything and may overreact to suspicious circumstances. Behavior thought to be indicative of sexual abuse—such as resistance to visitation, nightmares, bed-wetting, and excessive masturbation—may be reactions to divorce or other stressors, not always to sexual abuse. Finally, parents may consciously lie. Three cases fell into this category.

FALSE ALLEGATIONS IN DIVORCE

The assumption that a large proportion of sexual abuse allegations in divorce and custody cases are false is evident in attempts to describe such allegations as part of a syndrome, or pattern of behaviors that occur together on a consistent basis. Blush and Ross (1987) were the first to attempt such a classification, referring to such allegations as SAID (Sexual Abuse In Divorce). According to Blush and Ross, the child is caught between two parents who cannot communicate, and so use the child to communicate. They force the child to become involved in their own feelings, thus preventing them from forming their own opinions and feelings. The very general problem of dysfunctional communication may occur in many divorces, while sexual abuse allegations occur in very few divorces. Though SAID is very nonspecific, it appears to be a forerunner of Parent Alienation Syndrome (PAS), a concept developed by Richard A. Gardner, a Columbia University child psychiatrist who was himself a divorced father.

SAID blames both parents for the miscommunication, whereas PAS blames only mothers. Dr. Gardner, the originator of PAS, has not conducted any clinical, epidemiological, or laboratory research, or even research based on a selected number of case studies. In his book *Sex Abuse Hysteria* he states that his comments and conclusions were derived primarily from his personal experiences in this area, especially from his private practice and professional involvement as an evaluator and expert witness in sex abuse litigations (1989a:1-2). Gardner acknowledges that incest is probably quite common. He claims, however, that sex abuse allegations made in the context of child custody disputes (especially those that are litigated viciously) have a high likelihood, *ipso facto*, of being false. Such allegations, he suggests, are indicative of PAS, which he subdivides into three categories—severe, moderate, and mild (Gardner 1989b). The severe and moderate types may involve allegations of sexual abuse.

Severe PAS mothers, he says, are fanatical and will use every means at their disposal (legal and illegal) to prevent visitation. While they are obsessed and paranoid, psychiatric deterioration often does not manifest itself until the custody dispute. Central to the paranoid mechanism is projection. They see in their husbands the noxious qualities that are actually present in themselves. When sex abuse allegations become part of the package, they may be projecting their own sexual inclinations onto their husbands. In the service of this goal they actually exaggerate and distort any comment the child makes that might justify an accusation. Given children's normal bizarre sexual fantasies, Gardner believes, this is not difficult to accomplish; he thinks children who have never been molested still normally provide such mothers with ample material.

Gardner endorses Freud's description of children as "polymorphous perverse," claiming that even normal toddlers can be expected to exhibit just about any kind of sexual behavior imaginable: heterosexual, homosexual, bisexual, and autosexual. Infants, he observes, have no problem caressing any part of an adult's body, with absolutely no concern for the gender of the possessor of the target body part. He gives the example of a three-year-old girl and her four-year-old brother taking a shower with their father. During the frolicking, says Gardner, it is quite possible for them to fantasize about putting the father's penis in their mouth, particularly being so close to a time in their lives when they put everything in sight into their mouths (1989a:11). He claims that children exhibit a wide variety of sexual behaviors and indulge in sexual fantasies which would be labeled perverted if exhibited by adults. Thus, sexual abuse allegations in divorce are a result partly of children's persistent and bizarre sexual fantasies, and the mentally impaired responses of PAS mothers who believe their children's wild "disclosures."

The children of these mothers become similarly fanatical, Gardner claims, coming to share their mothers' paranoid fantasies. They may become panic-stricken over the prospect of visiting their fathers, leading to bloodcurdling screams and panic states. If placed in the father's home, such a child may even run away or become paralyzed with morbid fear. Gardner cautions therapists not to take the continued allegations of maltreatment made by such children seriously, for this would do them a terrible disservice. Typically, over time, false allegations become elaborated and new ones arise. He advises that when such fabricated allegations come up in therapy, the therapist should tell the child: "That didn't happen! So let's go and talk about real things like your next visit with your father" (1989b:4). Gardner suggests that children in this category should be removed from their mothers' homes and, if necessary, the mothers should be sent to jail. Following this, contact with the mother, including telephone calls, should be cut off for a period of months or even years so the children may abandon their disclosures. Even monitored telephone conversations with a PAS mother may provide the opportunity to influence her children negatively.

In the moderate PAS category, Gardner thinks the "rage of the rejected woman" factor is more important than the paranoia factor. He advises a somewhat less radical treatment: the moderate PAS mother must be informed that any obstructionism on her part will be immediately reported to the judge by the therapist, the guardian *ad litem*, or a child advocate. When sex abuse allegations are brought into the dispute, these mothers can learn to distinguish between children's preposterous claims and those that may have some validity (1989b:3). Therefore, the threat of losing custody usually works with such "moderate PAS" mothers.

Another Columbia University psychiatrist, Arthur Green, (1986) appears to be in some agreement with Gardner. Although Green acknowledges that false denials are more common than false disclosures, he cites four situations in which false disclosures may occur, two of which arise in divorce/custody cases. In the first type, the child is brainwashed by a vindictive mother, while in the second, the child is influenced by a delusional mother, who projects her own unconscious fantasies onto the child. In nondivorce situations, a child's false allegation is either based on fantasy or is invented out of a desire for revenge or retaliation on the part of the child herself, because of recent punishment or deprivation by the accused parent.

Elissa Benedek and Diane Schetky (1987), who also believe there is a high proportion of false allegations in divorce cases, are somewhat less critical of mothers. Indeed, they point out that a diagnosis of hysteria, borderline personality disorder, alcoholism, or even a thought disorder on the part of an accusing mother does not automatically mean that an allegation of sex abuse she made or supported was false. They claim that many allegations of sexual abuse stem from borderline situations in which the father may have bathed or slept with a young child during visitation. Upon discovering this, anxious mothers may read more into the situation than was intended:

> What may have been sexually overstimulating to the child but not necessarily intended to sexually gratify the adult becomes abusive in the mother's eyes, and she begins interrogating the child after each visit with the father. [Ibid.:917]

They attribute more cases to honest mistakes than to malice:

> Much less common is the parent who, out of vindictiveness or wish to expunge the former spouse, consciously and deliberately concocts stories of sexual abuse, which are then repeated to the young child to the point where he or she comes to believe the parent. [Ibid.:917]

Patricia Bresee and associates attribute many false allegations in divorce to mothers overreacting to marginal evidence, reflecting overprotectiveness or an excessively suspicious attitude toward the father, while the mothers become overly invested in proving their suspicions (1986:563).

> Some of these mothers who bring allegations of abuse display behavior that damages their credibility. They may be histrionic or combative and often aggressively demand that the decision-makers act quickly against their ex-spouses. It is important to recognize that a troubled woman with vengeful motives may nevertheless have discovered genuine evidence of sexual abuse.

John Myers believes that allegations arising in custody litigation are viewed with skepticism because of the unwarranted comparison of custody litigation to criminal litigation. The evidence used in criminal cases generally seems stronger than evidence offered in custody cases, leading to the conclusion that custody cases involve a high rate of fabricated allegations. He points out, however, that in criminal litigation, charges are seldom filed unless the evidence is extremely strong, because prosecutors, with their sights set on convictions, will not take a case unless they feel they have evidence "beyond a reasonable doubt." By contrast, parents who suspect sexual abuse use whatever evidence they have, no matter how slight, in their attempt to protect their children, since—unlike the prosecutor—parents cannot simply decline to press charges in an ongoing situation that is dangerous to their children (1990:25).

STUDIES OF ALLEGATIONS IN CUSTODY DISPUTES

Two studies frequently quoted by the media as indicative of a high proportion of false allegations in divorce cases are those by Arthur Green (1986) and by Elissa Benedek and Diane Schetky (1987). Green documented false allegations in four out of eleven cases (36 percent), while Benedek and Schetky documented false allegations in ten out of eighteen cases (56 percent). These studies involved exceptionally small samples and were based on difficult cases specifically referred to forensic specialists in private practice, as Mark D. Everson and Barbara W. Boat point out (1989:230). Furthermore, many of Green's colleagues disagreed with his evaluation of the case of Barry D (which was crucial because of the minute size of the sample). Dr. David Corwin and his colleagues (1987) pointed out that two years after Green's evaluation of Barry D, a pediatrician found medical evidence of anal penetration, although Green had called the child's allegations "false."

It is also noteworthy that Green and Benedek and Schetky judged allegations "true" or "false," but did not address the issue of "unsubstantiated" allegations. John Myers makes an important distinction between unsubstantiated reports and fabricated reports. Fabricated reports are deliberately false. In unsubstantiated reports, on the other hand, there is not enough evidence to determine whether abuse occurred. There may be many reasons for this: the child may be too young to articulate what happened; witnesses may become unavailable or refuse to be interviewed. "The fact that a majority of child abuse reports are unsubstantiated says little about the incidence of child sexual abuse, and less about the rate of fabricated allegations" (Myers, 1990:23). Furthermore, deliberately false allegations should be distinguished from accidentally mischaracterized allegations. For example, parents acting in good faith may misperceive information about their child, leading to suspicion of sexual abuse when none actually occurred. The likelihood of this situation may be high among divorced couples, where there is continuing animosity and suspicion.

Several studies using larger and more reliable samples have produced very different results from the above two examples. Jan E. Paradise et al. (1988) sampled children seen at Children's Hospital of Philadelphia for alleged sexual abuse between June 1985 and March 1986. They found that 67 percent of those involving custody disputes were substantiated, as compared with 95 percent of non-custody type allegations. "Unsubstantiated included those in which the results were indeterminate." In Paradise's study, however, children involved in custody cases were significantly younger than those in non-custody cases. The younger age of these children may have contributed to the lower rate of substantiation, since histories may have been more diffi-cult to obtain from younger children.

D. P. Jones and J. M. McGraw (1987) conducted a study through the Denver Department of Social Services, using the 576 reports made to that department during the course of one year. Of this sample, 309 cases, or 53 percent, were deemed "founded" or "substantiated." The "unfounded" category consisted of 267 cases, or 47 percent. These cases were reported "without malice," that is, there was not enough evidence to substantiate the allegations fully. The researchers found that in the total sample, only 8 percent of the allegations were considered "false," which they called "ficti-tious." A large proportion of these false reports were made in the context of custody disputes, which was of concern to the researchers. They thus con-sulted the Kempe National Center for the Prevention and Treatment of Child Abuse and Neglect, finding twenty cases of child sexual abuse allegations in the context of custody disputes between 1983 and 1985. Of this sample, 70 percent were determined to be "founded," 10 percent were uncertain, and 20 percent were found to be "false" (Jones and Seig, 1988). While Jone-sand McGraw found that a large proportion of "false" allegations occurred in custody cases, their definition of "false" allegations (actually, "fictitious") included misperceptions and confused interpretations of nonsexual events, as well as deliberate falsifications. The authors did not give a breakdown of how many were considered deliberately false or why they were classified that way.

More recently, McGraw and Holly A. Smith (1993) examined eighteen cases of sexual abuse allegations involving divorce and custody disputes. Using criteria established by the Kempe institute they determined that 44 percent of the allegations were substantiated, 56 percent were unsub-stantiated; among the latter, three allegations were fictitious.

Faller (1990) conducted a study with 97 cases of allegations of sexual abuse, all in the context of custody and/or visitation disputes. These cases were referred to her via social services, guardians *ad litem*, or the joint agree-ment of both parents. She found 79, or 81 percent, to be "substantiated." Of the remaining cases that could not be "substantiated," ten were uncertain and eight were "invalid" or "false." In another study of 136 cases of sex abuse allegations in the context of custody disputes, Faller (1991) found that only three were deliberately manufactured.

Thoennes and Tjaden (1990) examined 9,000 custody-visitation cases in twelve jurisdictions over a six-month period beginning in later 1986. They found that only 2 percent—169 cases—involved sex abuse allegations. The validity of the allegations was addressed in 129 of these 169 cases: 50 per-cent were believed to involve abuse, 33 percent to involve no abuse. In the remaining 17 percent of the cases, no conclusion could be reached by the as-sessors (who included child protection workers or officials appointed by courts to assess the validity of the reports). Perhaps most interesting of all, Thoennes and Tjaden found that in only eight of the 9,000 cases were the allegations deemed deliberately false, that is, thought to have been made maliciously.

In a study with a slightly different emphasis, Mark D. Everson and Barbara W. Boat (1989) examined 1,249 cases reported to the Department of Social Services in North Carolina over a twelve-month period. They expected that a high proportion of false allegations would occur in custody and visitation disputes, but that was not borne out. Workers assigned to these cases determined that slightly less than 5 percent were false, and approximately 56 percent were actually substantiated. Only five false allegations (8 percent of all false allegations studied) occurred in the context of custody and divorce litigations.

Yet another angle to the issue of validation of sexual abuse allegations in the context of divorce and custody was adopted by Hlady and Gunter (1990). They conducted a study involving children seen at the Child Protection Service at British Columbia Children's Hospital over a one-year period. In comparing custody cases with non-custody cases, they found the presence of physical findings indicative of sexual abuse the same in both groups.

DISTINGUISHING TRUE AND FALSE ALLEGATIONS

There is no test or method of evaluation that can establish with certainty whether a child has been sexually abused or whether a child's disclosures about sexual abuse are true. Training and clinical experience provide no guarantee that a professional evaluating a child can make the correct determination about sexual abuse. The best any clinician can do is conclude that there is a greater or lesser likelihood of abuse having occurred. Either way, nothing is 100 percent certain—and this applies to the likelihood of allegations being false as well as true. Most clinicians have developed criteria for determining the likelihood that the allegations are true, since this work has treatment implications. Others have developed criteria for determining both alternatives, that is, of the allegations being true and false. Three bases for establishing such criteria are the clinician's personal experience, the pooled experience of many professionals, and criteria established by the use of accepted external validating evidence.

The first type of criteria are the ones most commonly found in the literature. No truly scientific corroborating evidence exists for this type. They arise from "common sense," "gut feelings," and, in some cases, just plain prejudice. Gardner's main criteria for determining the falsity of allegations are that they take place in the context of a custody dispute and that they occur in the presence of so-called Parent Alienation Syndrome (Gardner 1989b). Gardner's criteria not only lack scientific corroboration but also are internally inconsistent. Gardner maintains, for example, that in the case of true allegations, children exhibit fear of the alleged perpetrator. However, children who exhibit fear of alleged perpetrators may also be diagnosed as showing evidence of severe PAS, which is itself indicative of false allegations. Thus Gardner has all his bases covered. He also maintains that in the case of true allegations, the mothers are too ashamed to admit that their spouses committed such terrible acts and are therefore secretive about the abuse; thus, by definition, a mother who openly brings an allegation is making a false one!

DISAGREEMENT AMONG THE "EXPERTS"

While most clinicians have developed criteria that are at least internally consistent, there is considerable disagreement among the experts. Thus Arthur Green (1986) claims that children's verbalizations cannot be taken at face value because the children are subject to powerful distortions from within; and he maintains that in false disclosures, details of sexual activity are rather easily obtained in the initial interview. Corwin et al. (1987) disagree with this view and, following E. F. Loftus (1979), note that spontaneous reports are more accurate than those obtained after repeated questioning. They point out that details obtained after the initial interview could lead to the conclusion that the child was altering the story and therefore lying. Green claims that in false allegations, children only tell of abuse in the presence of the accusing parent, and that "brain-washed" children check with their parents before responding to questions by the interviewer. Corwin, on the other hand, notes that young children placed in an ambiguous situation will naturally try to reference a caregiver.

Consistency of reports over time is considered evidence of true allegations according to J. Conte's 212 experts (Conte et al., 1988). David C. Raskin and Phillip W. Esplin (1991), however, assert that maintaining the same basic story over time without modification is evidence of a false allegation (see Table 1). While many clinicians agree that appropriate emotional response is indicative of true allegations, there are conflicting views as to what constitutes appropriate emotional responses to sexual abuse. Criteria developed by the Kempe institute (see McGraw and Smith, 1993) include anger, depression, and guilt. Raskin and Esplin regard only guilt and self-blame as indicative of true allegations. They consider anger against the alleged abuser as a signal of false allegations.

Delayed, conflicted disclosures followed by retractions are considered by many clinicians, including Green, as consistent with true allegations. This pattern of behavior is so common that it has been described as an actual syndrome by child psychiatrist Roland Summit and accepted by many, if not by most, professionals in the field. The Child Sexual Abuse Accommodation Syndrome (CAAS) (Summit, 1986) comprises the child victim's adaptation both to the abuse itself and to the denial thereof by the child's trusted and powerful caretakers. Yet despite its widespread acceptance, symptoms consistent with CAAS are frequently interpreted as signs of false allegations. For example, Everson and Boat (1989) examined the criteria used by CPS workers to identify false allegations, as well as the workers' rationale for deciding when allegations were false. The reasons included subsequent retractions by the child, inconsistencies in the report, failure of others to corroborate the report, and absence of medical evidence. The first three of these factors are described in child sexual abuse accommodation syndrome, namely retraction, "unconvincing" disclosure, and denial by other family members.

Age-inappropriate sexual knowledge is regarded by some as indicative of abuse. McGraw and Smith, however, note that specific details may be obtained from memories of previous episodes of abuse; and John Myers (1990) points out that previously molested children may be more vulnerable to repeated sexual abuse, which may lead to situations in which the wrong person is accused.

Few studies have used the presence of external validating circumstances to evaluate the efficacy of criteria for determining sexual abuse, largely because evidence of such external validation is very hard to find. Faller used offender confessions—full, partial, or indirect—as external validators; then she cross-validated her first three criteria (see Table 1) with offender confessions, to check the accuracy, veracity, and internal consistency of her study. She found that

> [I]n almost two thirds of the cases in which there was a full confession, the child's statement contained all three characteristics deemed to be indicative of true allegations, supporting the validity of these criteria. The fact that these characteristics were missing in about a third of the cases where there was a full confession is a reminder that many children are sexually abused and do not tell a credible story. [1990:138]

In summary, then, the studies that have used the largest samples and analyzed the most data with the most careful methods have concluded that the validity of allegations of child sexual abuse in the vast majority of cases is quite probable. There is no serious objective scientific proof that this probability is lower in the case of allegations arising in the context of custody disputes than in any other circumstances. Moreover, the differences in conclusions drawn from various studies often correlate with the underlying views expressed by the professionals who have performed those studies, as well as with the methodologies adopted by those professionals in choosing whom to study, how to study them, and how to judge their results. Not surprisingly, it turns out that the mental health professionals who view children as little perverts have no problem concluding that they are also little liars. And if one refuses to believe them when they disclose sexual abuse, one can then attribute their manner of disclosure to the "signs" of false allegations, creating the ultimate circular argument from which no genuinely molested child can ever exit.

In another attempt at using external validation to evaluate criteria for true and false allegations, Raskin and Esplin (1991) developed a nineteen-item scale known as Criteria Based Content Analysis (CBCA) (see Table 1). Their basis for determining that allegations were false included lack of physical evidence, failure of the system to take judicial action, and denial on the part of the accused, including passing a polygraph. The problem with these criteria is that none of these factors can prove that an allegation is false, even though their converses may increase the likelihood of an allegation being true. All we know from the research is that these external criteria distinguish significantly between children's statements, but there may be an explanation other than the assumption that such statements were all true or all false.

Gary L. Wells and Elizabeth F. Loftus (1991) point out the existence of circular reasoning in the analysis resulting from this study. They suggest that children in the "false" group may have had deficiencies in logical reasoning or poor verbal skills that made them unconvincing witnesses, thus explaining both their scores on the CBCA and the absence of judicial action. If these children were also younger, those accused might have been less likely to admit sexual contact.

Raskin and Esplin confirmed that the children in the "false" group were significantly younger, but they deny that this influenced their results because, when they compared children of similar ages, CBCA scores still differed significantly. However, there may be another explanation for the results, namely, that the type of abuse was different. If, as the authors suggest, abuse generally begins on a scale ranging from "benign sexual activity" with very young children to frank intercourse with such children as they grow older and the abuse progresses over time, then younger children who actually disclose will, of course, be doing so at a time when the abuse is still relatively difficult to identify, unaccompanied by gross physical trauma, and—to their way of thinking at least—comparatively "benign." There will be no medical evidence; statements may sound unconvincing; prosecutions would be difficult; and offenders may pass polygraph examinations because they have truly convinced themselves that they have not done anything wrong.

SUGGESTIBILITY OF CHILDREN AND INTERVIEW TECHNIQUES

One commonly held view about false allegations is based on the notion that children are highly suggestible, and that they are influenced to make allegations by parents and professionals who communicate the belief of abuse in their mode of questioning. A series of creative studies designed and conducted by Gail Goodman, Allison Clarke-Stewart, and others, address the issue of children's suggestibility during questioning on sexual abuse, and whether or not interviewers can easily mislead children into reporting events that did not happen.

TABLE 1.

Clinicians' Criteria for Determining Truth and Falsity of Allegations of Sexual Abuse

According to Richard A. Gardner (1989b)

False Allegations: Characteristics of Child

1. Presence of custody dispute
2. Presence of Parent Alienation Syndrome
3. Child's willingness to divulge the abuse
4. Absence of specific detail in child's account
5. Child's story changes over time
6. Absence of guilt toward the alleged perpetrator
7. Child is preoccupied with sex; exhibits sexualized play or excessive masturbation

False Allegations: Characteristics of Mother

1. Presence of custody dispute
2. Mother more eager to divulge abuse than to maintain secrecy
3. Mother does not "initially deny" abuse
4. Mother seeks a "hired gun" either as a lawyer or mental health professional
5. Mother seeks to "corroborate" child's disclosure
6. Mother does not "appreciate importance of maintenance of child's relationship with the accused"
7. Mother was herself sexually abused as a child
8. Mother is "passive and/or inadequate"
9. Mother exhibits duplicity in areas unrelated to sexual abuse
10. Child will check story with mother through side glances during joint interview

False Allegations: Characteristics of Accused Father

1. Presence of custody dispute
2. Father strongly denies having molested the child
3. Father does not have a history of having been molested as a child
4. Absence of drug or alcohol abuse or "other sexual deviations"
5. Father not moralistic or controlling; does not suffer from low self-esteem or a tendency to regress under stress
6. Father has not chosen a career that brings him into frequent contact with children
7. Is not a "stepfather or other person with frequent access to child" [Interestingly, biological father is omitted from the description of this category.]

TABLE 1. (cont.)
Clinicians' Criteria

According to Arthur Green (1986)

False Allegations

1. Details of sexual activity obtained easily during the initial interview
2. Children outspoken and nondefensive without significant changes in mood or affect
3. Children use adult terminology for body parts

True Allegations

1. Genuine victims secretive about abuse; disclosures are delayed and conflicted, if made at all
2. Allegations often retracted, then restated
3. Disclosures accompanied by depressed mood and distress
4. Child uses age-appropriate terminology

According to Kathleen Faller (1990)

True Allegations

1. Child able to describe/demonstrate specific sexual acts
2. Child able to indicate context of the abuse
3. Child has appropriate emotional reactions when describing the abuse

According to 90% of Jon Conte's 212 Experts (Conte et al., 1988)

True Allegations

1. Child has age-inappropriate sexual knowledge
2. Reports consistent over time
3. Child exhibits sexualized play during interviews
4. Physical evidence
5. Description of abuse relates elements of pressure or coercion
6. Child exhibits precocious or seductive behavior
7. Excessive masturbation

According to Elissa Benedek and Diane Schetky (1987)

False Allegations

1. Child uses adult terms and the same rote phrases
2. Sexual themes absent from spontaneous play or drawings
3. Child displays inappropriate affect
4. Evidence of possible secondary gain, e.g., the need to please parent
5. Child has history of lying
6. Child's memory vague
7. No physical evidence
8. Child tells of abuse only in the presence of the accusing parent

According to Patricia Bresee et al. (1986)

True Allegations from Accusing Mothers

1. Mother expresses remorse at not having protected child sufficiently to prevent abuse
2. Mother willing to have child interviewed in her absence
3. Mother willing to consider other explanations for child's behavior
4. Mother concerned about the impact if the child has to testify
5. If allegations cannot be verified, mother willing to waive investigation as long as child can be monitored through therapy or some other process

False Allegations from Accusing Mothers

1. Mother insists on being present during the interview and prompts child
2. Mother unwilling to consider other possible explanations for the child's symptoms
3. Mother eager for child to testify
4. Mother shops for professionals who support her view
5. Mother demands that investigation continue regardless of impact on child

According to the Kempe Institute (McGraw and Smith, 1993)

True Allegations

1. Child's account includes explicit details of sexual abuse
2. Child's account includes unique distinguishing details of surroundings, e.g., smells
3. Child uses age-appropriate terminology
4. Account consistent with a child's perspective regarding abuse
5. Child's expressed emotion consistent with abuse
6. Psychological response to abuse includes anger, depression, or guilt
7. Pattern of abuse suggests increased severity over time
8. Evidence of secrecy, coercion, or threat in child's account
9. Evidence of pornographic involvement

False Allegations

1. Child's account lacks evidence of accompanying emotional abuse
2. Child's account lacks detail
3. Child's account lacks unique details within the allegation
4. Evidence that the accuser has traits suggesting a tendency to misperceive or distort

TABLE 1. (cont.)
Clinicians' Criteria

According to David Raskin and Phillip Esplin (1991)

True Allegations Based on Witnesses' Accounts

General Characteristics
1.   Structure of statement logical
2.   Descriptions unconstrained and somewhat unorganized
3.   Specific details present
Specific Content
4.   Events in spatial and temporal context
5.   Reports include reproduction of conversation/interactions
6.   Conversations reproduced in their original form
7.   Report includes unexpected complications/difficulties
Peculiarities of Content
8.   Presence of unusual yet meaningful details
9.   Presence of superfluous details that do not contribute directly to the allegation
10.   Child accurately describes object or event but interprets it incorrectly
11.   Reference to external sexual events that did not occur within the specific incident
12.   Subjective thoughts and feelings described
13.   Reference to alleged perpetrator's thoughts and feelings
Motivation
14.   Spontaneous corrections made
15.   Child admits lack of memory
16.   Child acknowledges that aspects of story seem unbelievable
17.   Child self-deprecating
18.   Child pardons or excuses perpetrator
Offense-Specific Elements
19.   Incestuous relationships typically progress over time, beginning with relatively benign sexual acts and escalating to intercourse and/or sodomy. Invalid accounts might include fully executed sexual acts during the first incident.

Many professionals have concluded from these studies that children are essentially reliable witnesses under certain circumstances. Lucy McGough (1991) concludes that children are amazingly nonsuggestible in a relatively benign interview environment, and that they can resist suggestibility if a benign interview environment is created and maintained until after their account is recorded. However, potential sources of contamination include adult actors other than the interviewer, and these interactions are rarely disclosed. John Brigham (1991) concludes that children are not easily led to making false reports of sexual abuse when interviewed once by a stranger. However, repeated "incriminating" interviews can have a strong effect on children's interpretations of what they have experienced.

The research raises the problem of "ecological validity," which is the problem of generalizing from a research context to the real world. In this vein, Raskin and Esplin (1991) are critical of studies by G. S. Goodman and colleagues (Goodman and Aman, 1987, 1990; Goodman et al., 1989, 1990; Saywitz et al., 1991; Clarke-Stewart et al., 1989), insisting that data developed about children's responses to questions in everyday circumstances cannot be applied to questions about their suggestibility in sexual abuse investigations. They claim, for instance, that questioning children on whether a doctor had her clothes on or off during an examination provides no information about children's suggestibility in sex abuse cases, because all five-year-olds know that doctors do not disrobe during examinations. Children would not expect adults to believe such statements and would be reluctant to make such absurd claims to adults in almost any circumstance. In sexual abuse investigations, on the other hand, Raskin and Esplin claim that children may have motives to misrepresent the facts and may tell the interviewer what the interviewer wants to hear. They also claim that normal children have had experience with medical examinations, situations with which they are familiar, as compared with sexual situations, with which they are not familiar. In defense of Goodman's studies, the same argument might be made for expecting children to suppress reports of incest. Every child knows that fathers do not stick their fingers into daughters' vaginas, and child victims probably feel that no mentally competent adult is likely to believe that this happened to them.

Stephen Ceci (1991) of Cornell claims that Goodman's studies are conducted in an innocent atmosphere and thus fail to pick up the web of inducements and pressures present in a real interview of a possibly molested child. Recently he provided examples of such inducements and pressures. He noted that in the Wee Care Nursery School case, most children were told by interviewers, prior to their disclosures, that their peers had already revealed that Kelly Michaels (the accused teacher) was a bad person who had hurt them (Ceci and Brook, 1993:405). It is critically important, however, to distinguish between cases arising in day-care situations and incest cases. In day-care cases, children are typically brought into interviews having made no prior disclosures, exhibiting no particular suspicious behavior, and with no discernible physical evidence. The only grounds for suspicion in setting up the interview is the fact that some other child or children in the same class made a disclosure. Quite the opposite process typically takes place in incest cases. Evidence of or even a criminal conviction for sexual abuse of one daughter by a father would not be grounds for suspicion that another child in the same household was similarly abused, as two of our cases illustrate. In incest cases, children are typically brought into interviews having made a spontaneous disclosure to a parent, baby-sitter, or teacher, or because of behavioral symptoms, sometimes accompanied by physical evidence. As we will show, the same bullying techniques used in day-care cases to get children to disclose are used in incest cases to get children to recant.

Some of the conflicting advice given by "experts" on how to interview children reflects this difference. For example, when Arthur Green recommends frequent contact with the child over a longer period of evaluation, he is referring primarily to abuse allegations arising in divorce/custody cases. Corwin et. al (1988) criticized Green, saying that contamination of information increases with the increase of time of evaluation—a fact which is borne out by research. Contamination of data, however, is precisely what many clinicians in this area are hoping to accomplish, especially those who specialize in defending accused fathers. There are cases where one questionable comment made by a tired child after multiple interviews can be used to cast doubt on the entire process. Thus a double standard exists for interviewing methods depending on whether we are dealing with a nondisclosure situation in day care or a disclosure situation in divorce/custody cases.

Perhaps the most interesting research on false allegations comes from studies conducted by Ceci himself. He found that three-year-olds who were told that it was naughty to let someone kiss them when they did not have any clothes on denied having been kissed in the bathtub by their parents the previous night, even though this had in fact happened. In another situation, children who had not been kissed were told that good parents who love their children kiss and hug them while they are in the bathtub. When asked if they had been kissed, these children replied that they had (Ceci et al., 1993). Thus, children will lie about acts perpetrated on their bodies by their parents if they think the act is something their parents should have done, that is, they will lie to make their parents look good. They will also deny such acts having happened when they are told that the acts are wrong, again, to the parents' benefit, not detriment. These results may be expected because children love their parents and are fiercely loyal to them. The same studies, however, provide no rationale for children lying about incest.

THEORY VERSUS PRACTICE

While the research community may disagree on the interpretation of these studies, one thing the studies do not indicate is how well or how poorly established protocols (of any kind) are followed by child protection workers and others in making determinations about child abuse. One study showed that protocols are followed poorly, if at all, in custody cases.

McGraw and Smith's study of eighteen cases reveals investigators' prejudices about sexual abuse allegations during divorce and shows how their feelings affect the validation process. When the study began, CPS workers in the Boulder County Colorado Sexual Abuse Team had validated only one of the eighteen cases (5 percent). McGraw and Smith found that investigators had failed in many instances to apply their own protocols for the validation process. Furthermore, when the more detailed clinical process of validation used at the Kempe Center was applied, the number of validated cases rose from 5 to 44 percent. McGraw and Smith found that the perceptions of the investigators were heavily influenced by the fact that they knew, before their evaluations began, that these particular allegations arose in custody or divorce cases. Their tendency to treat the evidence differently even caused them to overlook physical evidence if it arose in custody cases. "In many cases the simple knowledge that an allegation was made in the context of a divorce or custody proceeding led caseworkers to prejudge the allegation as false" (McGraw and Smith, 1993:60).

The research does not show how facts are interpreted or how the same type of behavior or statement may be interpreted differently using different criteria.

In one case, a teen-age girl from Virginia, reported that she had been sexually abused by her father. She said that while her mother was traveling, he came into her bedroom, got into bed with her, inserted his finger into her vagina, and "circled it around." Child protective service workers questioned her about details, asking her which finger he had used. She replied that he had used his third finger. The conclusion of the investigation was that the allegation was false because the room had been dark, so she could not have known which finger he used. This finding would have been consistent with Philip Esplin's argument that children bringing false allegations attempt to answer all questions and do not acknowledge gaps in their recollections. However, another attitude could also have led to the decision to consider the allegation false, as the following case illustrated.

A six-year-old girl from Virginia alleged that she had been sexually abused by her father; she claimed that he had put his finger in her "bottom" and "hurted" her. When asked which finger he had used, she said she did not know. This led CPS workers to conclude that the allegation was false, presumably based on the criterion that the child could not provide sufficient detail.

Other problems may arise when questions designed to elicit detail have different meanings for the child and for the CPS worker. For example, when a four-year-old boy from a southern state alleged that his father "sucked [his] pee pee," a CPS worker asked him: "What does that mean?" He answered, "I don't know." The boy thought he was being asked the meaning of having his pee pee sucked, and answered truthfully that he did not know. The CPS worker was trying to elicit detail, of course, but she asked a vague and ambiguous question. Instead of rephrasing the question to see if the child could provide more detail, the interviewer merely concluded that the allegation was false. Another child, hospitalized for three days with genital bleeding after a visit to her father, said he had injured her "down there" with his fingers. When she was asked why he did it, she could not answer. That case was marked "unfounded" because the interviewer said it was not clear that the father's purpose in touching the child had been to derive sexual gratification, and "it only counts as abuse if the person does it to get sexual enjoyment."

Do adults ever coach children to make false allegations? Of course they do. Fortunately, false allegations of this kind are few and far between, and they are easy to distinguish from allegations that are merely difficult to understand, hard to believe, or burdensome to deal with. The following is an example of an allegation that was probably false:

Cindy, a physician, and Carl, a lawyer, were separated when their son, Andy, was about two years old. Even before the separation, Carl had made claims that Cindy was a drug abuser and that she was becoming psychotic. Cindy became suspicious that Carl was trying to "build a case against her" to prove her an unfit mother, so she voluntarily submitted to weekly urine testing. By the time the custody battle began, she had solid proof of Carl's vindictiveness and lack of credibility. After the drug abuse and psychosis charges fell through, Carl became increasingly angry that he was unable to defeat Cindy in the custody battle. After a protracted and costly court case (three forensic psychiatrists found her perfectly fit), Cindy was finally awarded custody of Andy, but she agreed that Carl should have joint physical custody. By that time, Andy was over four years old and the custody battle was nearly three years old.

Then came the false allegation. Carl picked up Andy from Cindy's house and took him to his place, where he and his new girlfriend sat him down and began to "commiserate" with him about how awful it was to have to visit Mommy's relatives. By the end of the evening, Carl had written a 28-page affidavit full of dramatic detail that sounded like a soap opera. He had it notarized the next morning. Carl made the allegation that Andy's ten-year-old cousin Jason had molested him on visits to his family's farm, and that Cindy, who had been informed about the problem, refused to help her son. Carl reported in the affidavit that he and his girlfriend had comforted Andy and promised to help.

Andy was very uncomfortable about what had transpired at his father's house the night of the affidavit. The next morning he asked to speak with the director of his summer day camp, saying he had "a problem he needed to talk about," since the director had told the children they could go to him with any "problems." The director wrote a letter saying that Andy had spontaneously said that he felt bad because Carl had told him he could not see his cousin Jason anymore. He said his father had told him to say that Jason had touched his penis. He was disturbed that he would not see his cousin, and particularly by the fact that he had been required to say these bizarre and untrue things. When the camp director asked if anyone had *ever* touched his penis, Andy answered yes, that another child at nursery school had once done something like that in the context of a curiosity-motivated bathroom inquiry. By the time a social service caseworker interviewed Andy, he was most worried about the fact that his father appeared to hate Jason so much, and he denied being molested.

Andy's answers were perfectly believable, internally consistent and age-appropriate. He showed none of the behavioral signs of a molested child. He was not afraid to reveal his condition to the authorities. He was simply puzzled at this strange behavior on his father's part and upset at being unable to play with his cousin. The characteristics of this false allegation are fairly simple to identify: 1. The person who fabricates the allegation has a history of this kind of behavior, in the marriage, in the divorce, possibly in previous relationships or at work. 2. The allegation is usually made against someone (like a ten-year-old boy in another state) who cannot be evaluated or investigated and who may not be able to defend himself against the charges. 3. The allegation is made in an extremely elaborate, often dramatic, much too efficient and legalistic manner by an adult who seems to be extraordinarily well-versed in presentation. 4. The child quickly and easily denies the allegations without exhibiting guilt or fear, and still responds to other questions about sexual matters in a frank and childlike manner. 5. The child does not have behavioral symptoms otherwise consistent with a history of child sexual abuse. 6. The parent who is accused of abusing or allowing abuse is forthright, concerned, and cooperative, and does not try to intimidate anyone into dropping the investigation or to manipulate the child into changing his position.

The research indicates that while substantiated rates of sexual abuse allegations during divorce are high, there is a tendency on the part of caseworkers and professionals to treat these cases in a prejudicial fashion, neglecting to apply established protocols to such cases and applying existing criteria in a biased fashion. Furthermore, the research fails to acknowledge that there are no criteria which conclusively prove a particular allegation false, nor does it recognize that some experts' criteria for true allegations are identical to other experts' criteria for false allegations. Finally, while interview methods leading to disclosures of sexual abuse are carefully scrutinized by the clinical and research community, no similar scrutiny has been given to interview situations which lead to recanting of allegations previously made.

7

The Denial of Incest

My father molested me until I left home at age 17. . . . He forced me to sit on his lap, to cuddle with him, to play with his penis in the bathtub. . . . Incest and child abuse thrive in darkness, in secrecy. One of the great taboos about incest is talking about it, dealing with it and healing from it. I believe the more voices we hear, the braver we become. . . .

This statement was made in 1991 by actress/comedian Roseanne Arnold, one of a growing number of celebrities who have revealed that they have been victims of incest. The list includes former Miss America Marilyn Van Derbur, singer Latoya Jackson, talk-show hostess Oprah Winfrey, and publisher Frances Lear. These disclosures come at a time when society is discovering that incest and child sexual abuse are serious problems. At the same time, a backlash has developed. Aging parents accused of incest by their adult children are bonding together, denying the allegations, and claiming that they are the result of "false memories" planted in their children's minds by overzealous, misguided, or malicious therapists. While a growing body of research is demonstrating the harmful effects of child sexual abuse and its prevalence in our society, other studies describe "syndromes" that explain why an ever-increasing number of allegations by both adults and children should be considered false. These contradictory trends are played out daily in courtrooms around the nation, where children who have previously been taught not to fear revealing sexual abuse, are invalidated, disbelieved, and handed back to those they have "told on."

Why is this happening? How prevalent are incest and child sexual abuse? Why is society only now beginning to take the problem seriously? Is the occurrence of child sexual abuse solely a Western problem, or does it occur worldwide? What kinds of societies permit child sexual abuse, and why?

Sexual abuse of children has not always been regarded as a crime, as a sign of mental illness, or as potentially harmful to the victim. These views of the problem are relatively recent and specific to our culture. Some cultures regard child sexual abuse as mildly unacceptable or embarrassing, but certainly not punishable; while others even regard it as socially acceptable within certain unspoken protocols. There are even societies where specific kinds of child sexual abuse are socially mandated.

DEFINITIONS

Researchers and professionals can use a confusing array of terms. While the terms "child sexual abuse" and "incest" overlap, they are not identical. Anthropologists have traditionally limited the term "incest" to sex between biologically related, consenting adults. However, it has come to imply exploitive sex involving adult perpetrators and child victims within the family.

Diana Russell distinguishes between incestuous abuse and extra-familial child sexual abuse. She defines the former as "any kind of exploitive sexual contact or attempted contact that occurred between relatives, no matter how distant the relationship, before the victim turned eighteen years old" (1986:41). Russell notes complications in distinguishing between exploitive and non-exploitive incestuous experience and cites as examples of non-exploitive experiences siblings or cousins of approximately the same age engaging in sexual experimentation whose effects were regarded as positive or neutral. Children less than five years apart are commonly considered peers, though even peers can sexually abuse one another. Typically, however, researchers use the five-year age difference as one criterion for determining the exploitive nature of the sexual contact, even in cases where the younger child reported the experience as positive. Russell includes sexual contact between peers as abusive if it caused distress to the child who was not the initiator, even if the distress was not felt at the time of the incident.

Russell defines extra-familial child sexual abuse more narrowly as

> unwanted sexual experience with persons unrelated by blood or marriage, ranging from attempted petting (touching breasts or genitals or attempts at such touching) to rape, before the victim turned fourteen years, and completed or attempted forcible rape experience from the age of fourteen to seventeen years (inclusive).

For Russell, the five-year age difference between victim and perpetrator does not apply in extra-familial sexual abuse, yet she apparently sought to exclude from this category unwanted petting or intercourse in dating situations, what is commonly referred to as date rape. Russell's definitions of both extra-familial and incestuous abuse exclude non-contact forms of exploitation such as exhibitionism and exposure to pornography. Only cases involving contact or attempted contact were defined as abusive for the purposes of her study.

David Finkelhor believes that there is an unnecessary emphasis on the distinction between intra-familial and other forms of child sexual maltreatment. Within the general category of child sexual maltreatment, he distinguishes three forms: 1. the sexual exploitation of children for adult sexual gratification; 2. the mortification of children's sexuality, including genital mutilation, and the vilification and repression of children's normal sexual interest; and 3. the eroticization of children and creation of environments where inappropriate stimulation interferes with their mastery of other developmental tasks (1991:218).

Definitions thus vary in terms of the age of the victim in relation to the age of the offender, the nature of the activity, the feelings and responses of the victim, and the relationships between victim and perpetrator. As this field of research expands, definitions of incest and sexual abuse will have to take into account whether they are culturally sanctioned activities, as in child marriage or genital mutilation during organized initiation rituals. For our purposes, it is necessary to distinguish between incestuous abuse and other forms of child sexual abuse, especially when the perpetrator and the victim live or have lived in the same household. It is important not only from the perspective of vastly increased opportunity to harm the victim, but more particularly with regard to our society's response to the victimization and to attempts to stop further incidences of such victimization by anyone but the perpetrator.

Our society is more willing to accept the concept of a stranger as a loathsome molester than to suspect a father figure of such behavior. It is therefore more eager to protect children from abuse at the hands of strangers than to prevent such risk if it interferes with familial relationships, when a child accuses a father, a stepfather, or an older relative. According to Judith Herman,

> The relationship between father and daughter, adult male and female child, is one of the most unequal relationships imaginable. It is no accident that incest occurs most often precisely in the relationship where the female is most powerless. [1981:4]

This is the form of sexual abuse that our society is most unwilling to identify, address, admit, and give up.

HISTORICAL EVIDENCE OF CHILD SEXUAL ABUSE

The sexual maltreatment of children in historical times must be seen against the background of their unprotected status (see Sommerville, 1990; Fraad, 1991; De Mause, 1974). As David Finkelhor points out, in the past children have been sold or indentured, married off at an early age for economic gain, or forced to do dangerous and difficult work (1984:6). It is therefore plausible that they were subjected to other abuses, including sexual. While numerous written records attest to sexually abusive practices toward children throughout history, historians, like other scholars, have avoided dealing with the topic.

> Although we have ample evidence to document the existence of incestu-ous behavior and other forms of child sexual abuse throughout the last three thousand years, this subject has received scant attention from the historical profession. . . . Perhaps it is less painful for some people to re-search Corinthian columns or other architectural phenomena in antiquity, rather than cruelty to children; and so generations of historians have ne-glected the seemingly universal heritage of child abuse. [Kahr, 1991:195]

In ancient Greece, children were treated with notorious cruelty, and accounts by Greek and Roman historians of ritual slaughter have been cor-roborated by a Harvard archeologist who unearthed the remains of children at special burial sites (Stager and Wolff, 1984; quoted by Kahr, 1991:197). In this context, the openly accepted sexual use of children should come as no surprise. Kahr notes that in Greece most prepubescent boys became victims of sexual abuse by older men, a cycle which they perpetuated when they became adults. Though little is written about the rape of girls or infants, it is likely, says Kahr, that it occurred as well (ibid.).

The Romans adopted the sexual proclivities of their predecessors, and many of their historical writings contain references to incest and the sexual exploitation of children. Certain Roman leaders—notably Emperors Tiberius and Caligula—were notorious for their sexual abuse of children and incestu-ous behavior. Kahr writes:

> I hold firmly to the belief that the Greek and Roman endorsements of sexual abuse have provided us with a horrendous heritage that has had a profound impact on the nature of child abuse today and our responses to such crimes against children. . . . [Ibid.:201]

And he concludes that the Greeks and Romans bequeathed "an historical trauma of monumental proportions."

Burton and Myers (1992) point out that from ancient Greece to the Middle Ages children were viewed as property, and thus the sexual "use" of one's children—as opposed to "abuse"—was not a matter of debate. This view of children as property is also evident in the Bible. Referring to Talmudic sources, Florence Rush notes that "marriage was the purchase of a daughter from her father, prostitution was a selling and reselling of a female by her master for sexual service, and rape was the theft of a girl's virginity which could be compensated for by payment to her father" (1980:19). In the list of forbidden sexual liaisons set forth in Deuteronomy, father-daughter incest is not included among the "Thou Shalt Nots"; technically child rape did not exist unless an outsider had "taken" a child's virginity without her father's permission. If the accused paid the bride-price and entered into marriage with the victim-child, the "rape" become a valid legal marriage and the girl was no longer "dishonored," or raped at all (ibid.:21).

The openly licentious practices of the Roman period became replaced with "fanatical prudery" during the Middle Ages (Kahr, 1991:201), and Christian writings of the time strongly discouraged parents from "seducing" their own children (ibid.:202). Laws did emerge in Great Britain prohibiting the sexual use of children during the Middle Ages, but they were enforced weakly if at all because of the continued perception of children as their parents' property (Rush, 1980:34–35). The Middle Ages saw a trend toward the projection of adult sexual wishes onto children, which culminated in the witch frenzies of the sixteenth and seventeenth centuries. During this period numerous little girls were imprisoned, tortured, even burned at the stake because they were alleged to have fornicated with the Devil (Kahr, 1991:202). Though the sexual use of children who were destitute, orphaned, neglected, or homeless was probably common throughout history, the widespread recruitment of such children into the prostitution industry, known as "white slavery," reached a peak in the nineteenth century. During this period, unsuspecting children were recruited from the ranks of the poor, the homeless, and newly arrived immigrants by predatory sex merchants with huge networks of employees trained to approach them, ensnare them, and "break them in" (Rush, 1980:64–65).

Child pornography was another industry that burgeoned around this time, spurred by the growth of technology and sexual interest in little girls (ibid.:60). In Victorian England, the production of kiddie porn began with the invention of the camera, and the pornographic literature of those times indicates an obsession with "defloration mania" and the infliction of graphic pain on young children (ibid.:61). The Victorian populace "repressed their shameful lust, enacting their abuses only in darkened bedrooms and writing about their sexual deeds only in the most reviled pornographic literature of the time" (Kahr, 1991:203); and there was a large and lucrative market for such pornography.

Toward the end of the nineteenth century, the sexual victimization of children attracted the attention of activists and reformers. One of the first was Josephine Butler, who crusaded for the abolition of the sexual slavery of women in England (Rush, 1980:68–69). She was followed by John Stuart Mill and others in England, and in America her cause was taken up by a number of reformers, including Lucy Stone, Elizabeth Cady Stanton, and Susan B. Anthony. The National Society for the Prevention of Cruelty to Children and other such societies were founded in an effort to suppress the traffic in child prostitution. Linda Gordon notes that although these societies recognized incest as a problem, and were ostensibly dedicated to protecting children even from their own parents, they tended to redefine incest victims as sexually perverse delinquents and "wayward girls," and their mothers as neglectful or promiscuous themselves. Finally, this reconceptualization focused on the stranger as molester, not on the father as perpetrator (Gordon, 1988:215).

For the most part, the history of child sexual abuse and incest is marked by a failure to recognize the sexual use of children as abusive or to regard it as wrong or harmful. A major change came in the late nineteenth and early twentieth centuries by way of the newly developing field of psychoanalysis and the theories of Sigmund Freud. Judith L. Herman and L. Hirschman (1981) remark that the history of incest and child sexual abuse over the past hundred years is marked by both the new "discovery" of the problem and then the almost immediate suppression of it.

THE LEGACY OF FREUD

Freud has been accused of scientific deception. He discovered the incest phenomenon in his clinical practice, and at first he described his findings. Faced with opposition and outrage, he promptly buried his conclusions and proceeded to develop a theory which instead influenced generations of psychiatrists to dismiss their patients' stories of child sexual abuse as mere fantasy (Rush, 1980; Herman and Hirschman, 1981; Masson, 1984).

Freud's discovery of the incest problem began when several of his patients—women from conventional, respectable, prosperous families—complained of vague pains, hallucinations, anxiety, and uncontrollable impulses. He recognized the similarities of their symptoms and called the disorder "hysteria." These "hysterical" women reported to Freud that, as children, they had been sexually abused by their fathers, their fathers' friends, or other adult male relatives (Sack, 1990:19–20). At first Freud was stunned by these revelations. The men being accused were highly respected members of society, considered fine, upstanding citizens. However, he recognized that these revelations were an integral part of his patients' symptomatology, and he initially believed that they had indeed suffered sexual molestation as children. This led him to assert, in several learned and original papers, that the origins of hysteria could be found in early childhood sexual trauma.

His revelations were greeted as preposterous, rather than scientifically analyzed and appreciated for their valuable research and insight. After coming under severe criticism by his fellow professionals, Freud finally gave up his seduction theory, even though that required a public apology. Apparently he was relieved to absolve himself of the responsibility for discovering the source of his patients' problems, and he redesigned his own beliefs to accommodate his new position. His willingness to adopt the new-found belief that all his patients' reports were untrue was also apparently tied to his own uncomfortable desires toward his daughter and suspicions about his own father (Herman and Hirschman, 1981:10).

Freud therefore reconsidered his evidence with an eye toward understanding why so many of his patients would "lie" to him about having been molested by trusted individuals. The answer, he believed, lay in the sexual desires and fantasies of the child. Freud developed what has become the famous "Oedipal Theory"—that every child goes through a stage when he or she sexually desires the parent of the opposite sex (Russell, 1986:5). Freud now had a theoretical model for analyzing the disclosures of his "hysterical" female patients—they were afflicted by their uncontrollable fantasies and desires to have sex with their fathers. Thus their stories were an outpouring of their sexual fantasies, in which their fathers or other male relatives played aggressive sexual roles. In the cases where it was clear that a sexual encounter of some kind had indeed taken place, the women had clearly been the seducers, playing out their own desires, seducing their helpless fathers and relatives.

Thus Freud's scenario was complete. Most of the allegations made by his patients were delusion fantasies. Freud was unable to accept the idea that so many fine, upstanding citizens had actually molested their daughters or stepdaughters. Further "proof" of the fantasy was the commonness of the disclosures: they represented to him female fantasies, created by the patients' uncontrollable urges, the expression of which needed outlets in neurotic manifestations and behavior. "The Freudian legacy, then, is to discount the reality of incestuous abuse and, where discounting is impossible, to blame the child for being the one who wanted the sexual contact in the first place" (Russell, 1986:6).

This legacy is apparent in the position of the next group of experts who came across the incest phenomenon, the Kinsey group. While Kinsey did not deny the reality of child sexual abuse, he did much to deny the damaging effects it had on the subjects of his surveys. Despite the fact that those who reported sexual abuse asserted that the event had been frightening and upsetting, "Kinsey cavalierly belittled these reports" (Herman and Hirschman, 1981). He attempted instead to assert that any trauma suffered by a child-victim was attributable not to incest itself but to the regrettable emotional reactions of other adults (such as angry, prudish parents and ignorant educators) who learned of the abuse. Children were not naturally negatively affected by sexual abuse, but by the "hysterical" reactions of their parents and/or the authorities involved in the issue after the fact.

Incest as a widespread social problem with serious consequences for the mental health of the child-victims was brought to public awareness beginning in the mid-1970s. The new reform movement began with an exploration of the problem by feminist mental health professionals such as Judith Herman and Florence Rush. It was catapulted into public awareness by such groundbreaking works as Armstrong's *Kiss Daddy Goodnight* (1979), Butler's *Conspiracy of Silence* (1978), Herman and Hirschman's *Father-Daughter*

Incest (1981), and Rush's *The Best Kept Secret* (1980). Within a few years, self-help books for survivors of incest became available (Bass and Davis, 1988), support groups for incest survivors emerged, and in 1991 several well-known celebrities went public with their own incest experiences (Roseanne Arnold, Marilyn Van Derbur, and Montel Williams).

In recent years the unprecedented and sustained attention to the incest problem by professionals, the media, and survivors has given impetus to a new backlash movement. Some critics have argued that child abuse is over-reported (Besharov, 1985, 1990; Schetky, 1986; Wakefield and Underwager, 1988). Others argue that overzealous investigators can lead suggestible children into making false allegations (Benedek and Schetky, 1987; Coleman, 1986). Erna Olafsen, David L. Corwin, and Ronald C. Summit (1993), in charting the cycles of discovery and suppression of child sexual abuse awareness over the past hundred years, caution that the current backlash may be part of a social cycle of resuppressing awareness, returning us to what Jean Goodwin called the "shared negative hallucination" (1985:14).

CURRENT EPIDEMIOLOGY OF INCEST AND CHILD SEXUAL ABUSE

One of the first studies to present findings on incest was conducted by Kinsey and associates in 1953. Kinsey obtained information from 4,441 women regarding sexual contacts with adult males before the age of fourteen. Fourteen percent of his sample reported such contacts, of which more than half had been with strangers, around 30 percent with friends or acquaintances, and about 22 percent with family members. Using recalculations of Kinsey's data, Russell (1986:63) estimates that around 3 percent of the women reported incestuous abuse—1.2 percent by an uncle, 0.5 percent by a father, 0.4 percent by a brother, 0.3 percent by a grandfather, and 0.7 percent by some other relative. It has been suggested that the incidence of incest has been underreported in Kinsey's data for a number of reasons: His interviewers were male, and some of the female respondents may have felt uncomfortable discussing their experiences with them. The sampling may have been flawed by the use of group samples (for example, members of a church) as compared with population samples, and the exclusion of women from lower educational backgrounds, those who had served penal sentences, and minorities (Leventhal, 1988). Perhaps most significant was the use of researchers who had a bias against recognizing the abusiveness of incest, which may have discouraged many victims from revealing their experiences (Russell, 1986:65).

The next significant study on the prevalence of sexual abuse appeared 25 years after Kinsey's publication. In David Finkelhor's (1978) study of

530 female college students, 19 percent had been victims of sexual abuse by age seventeen; 10 percent of the total had been victims of incest, 1.3 percent having been abused by a father.

The best designed of the prevalence studies to date was conducted by Diana Russell (1983), who interviewed 930 women from a random sample in San Francisco. She found that 38 percent had been sexually abused by an adult by the time they reached age eighteen; 152, or 16 percent of the total sample, had been victims of incestuous abuse, with 4.5 percent having been abused by fathers and 4.9 percent by uncles. When noncontact sexual abuse was included in the statistics, the proportion of incestuous abuse victims increased to 19 percent.

In a similarly well-designed study conducted in Los Angeles County in 1985, Gail Wyatt found that 45 percent of the women she interviewed reported sexual abuse before the age of eighteen. Twenty-one percent of the cases were incestuous, including 8.1 percent involving fathers. When noncontact sexual abuse was included, 52 percent of Russell's sample and 62 percent of Wyatt's sample reported such experiences before age eighteen.

Russell's questions were quite specific about the nature of the abuse, and thus the details are more clearly delineated in her study than in those that preceded it. She found

> that stepfather-daughter incest is far more prevalent and severe than biological father-daughter incest . . . for those stepfathers who become a primary parent in their stepdaughters' lives, [the] . . . data suggest a one-in-six risk factor. . . .

Thus Russell's data illustrate that incest and sexual abuse are far more prevalent than was previously thought, and that the intra-familial abuse in 64 percent of the cases was classified as very serious (for example, vaginal intercourse or oral sex; Russell, 1986, in Leventhal, 1988). While there is no question that reporting and detection have increased in the last few decades, Russell's data show that sexual abuse has also increased. In general, the older the informant, the less abuse suffered as a child, while the youngest victims suffered the highest rate of abuse (1986:79–80).

Leventhal (1988) compares Kinsey's study to Russell's to determine not only the differences in their methodologies and results but whether such differences indicate an actual change in prevalence during the three decades between the two. He found that there has probably been a decrease in stranger-perpetrated sexual abuse but an increase in incest and nonstranger-perpetrated abuse. While Leventhal attributes some of these differences to the fact that Kinsey interviewers asked less-pointed or less-specific questions, he concludes that "it is likely that some of these differences are true ones" (1988:773). Thus, studies suggest that the prevalence of incestuous sexual abuse is not only higher than was once thought by researchers but also appears to be increasing in the United States.

ANTHROPOLOGY AND
CROSS-CULTURAL COMPARISONS

Historically, anthropologists have been more interested in the incest taboo than in the occurrence of incestuous practices. Until recently, anthropologists believed that incest was rare and hardly of consequence when it did occur (Fox, 1962, 1980). In the late nineteenth century some anthropologists thought that the incest taboo originated for biological reasons: consanguineous marriages and intercourse were thought to be outlawed because of the potential for genetic damage to offspring (Meiselman, 1986:5). Later theories focused on the relationship between the incest taboo and exogamy— a rule forbidding marriage among certain groups of relatives, and requiring that people marry outside their kinship group, whether it be the nuclear family, the lineage, or the clan. Robin Fox (1980) asserted that the evolution of the ability to control "incestuous" impulses could well be at the root of humankind's ability to play the "exogamy game." For Fox, the incest taboo provides a reason for the practice of exogamy, which in turn forms the basis for elaborate systems of social exchange creating interdependency and co-operation among larger human groups.

Unfortunately, most anthropologists missed the point about incest and have regarded it as an activity between consenting adults, even when that is obviously not the case. Fox's book *The Red Lamp of Incest* (1980) begins with Jacques Prevert's poem about a young woman who commits suicide after being raped and impregnated by her father. Fox uses this example to demonstrate the vague unease or bemusement society feels about incest. That it created enough pain and horror to the young woman to cause her to take her own life does not seem to impress Fox.

More recently, anthropologists have taken a different approach to incest and child sexual abuse. Researchers such as Jean La Fontaine (1990) are more willing to study incest as a real phenomenon and to recognize its damaging consequences for victims. Anthropologists have also recently begun to recognize the traumatic impact on children of initiation rituals which involve such practices as genital mutilation and homosexual fellatio (Tuzin, 1982; Herdt, 1981, 1982; Rosen, 1988). They ask whether these culturally prescribed traumas may induce behavioral changes or lead to the development of psychological traits that are culture-appropriate and therefore adaptive.

The cross-cultural study of child sexual abuse has been spurred recently by the emerging field of psychohistory—the study of the political effects of adult treatment of children (Sommerville, 1990:xi). While prevalence data on child sexual abuse in contemporary non-Western and preliterate societies are not yet available, psychohistorian Lloyd deMause provides ample evidence that such practices are recognized and even approved of in some cultures. He notes that sexual abuse of children by family members has been documented in Latin America by Oscar Lewis (1965), E. N. Padilla (1951), Romon Fernandez-Marina (1961), and J. M. Carrier (1985). According to deMause, "[c]hildhood in much of India begins with the young child being regularly masturbated by the mother" (1991:142–143), a practice also observed in Latin America, the Middle East, and Japan (ibid.:140, 154, 158).

The literature on attitudes and beliefs about children and sexuality in India shows that familial incest has traditionally been quite prevalent in that country. DeMause notes, for example, that child marriage was previously justified on the grounds that female children were so oversexed that child marriage was their only salvation (ibid.:145). He quotes an old Indian proverb which claims that for a girl to be a virgin at ten years old, "she must have neither brothers nor cousin, nor father" and thus concludes that Indian girls moved from familial incest to sex with older men chosen by the family.

In Japan, where the occurrence of incest is denied, experts were surprised to find that newly installed child abuse hot lines were flooded with calls. One of deMause's major findings in Japan was that, in addition to the usual father-daughter incest found in the West, 29 percent of such calls involved complaints about mother-son incest (ibid.:156).

DeMause cites several studies which document both sexual abuse and ritual abuse of Middle Eastern girls. For example, a survey of childhood seduction by a female Arab physician, Nawal el Saadawi (1980), concluded that most girls are subjected to sexual assault in their early years. A recent survey of Egyptian girls and women showed that 97 percent of uneducated families and 66 percent of educated families still practice the rite of clitoridectomy, and sociologist Frank P. Hosken (1979) estimates that there are approximately 74 million mutilated girls and women in countries where documentation of the practice exists. According to Lightfoot Klein (1989), as quoted by deMause, the rationalization for clitoridectomy is that little girls are naturally so sexual that it is necessary to release them from the bondage of sex to stop them from masturbating. DeMause writes:

> Clitoridectomy—like all genital mutilations of children—is, of course, an act of incest motivated by the perversions of the adults who perform the mutilation. Although we are not used to thinking of it in this way, in fact mothers who attack their daughters' genitals with knives are as incestuous as the fathers who rape them. [1991:163]

THE MENTAL HEALTH CONSEQUENCES OF SEXUAL ABUSE

The mental health profession has until very recently ignored or denied the role of child sexual abuse in the etiology of mental disorders. This was part of the legacy of Freud. Writing in 1963, a psychiatrist described his training:

> I was taught in my . . . early years in psychiatry, as most of us were, to look very skeptically upon the incestuous sexual material described by my patients. . . . Any inclination on my part or that of my colleagues in the

training situation, to look upon these productions of patients as having some reality basis was scoffed at and was seen as evidence of our naivete. [Bernard C. Glueck, quoted in deMause, 1991:123]

Changing attitudes and more data, however, have caused researchers to take a closer look at the mental health consequences of child sexual abuse. Reviewing the literature in 1986, A. Browne and D. Finkelhor reported that the long-term effects of sexual abuse included suicidal tendencies, low self-esteem, substance abuse, sexual dysfunction, and promiscuity, as well as a tendency to experience revictimization. There have been several recent studies of the effects of child sexual abuse on both the normal population and adult psychiatric inpatients. John Briere and Marsha Runtz's study of 278 female college students (representing a nonclinical sample) revealed that approximately 15 percent "reported a history of sexual abuse" (1988:53). The sexually abused group suffered more anxiety than the non-abused group, as well as greater tendencies toward dissociation and somatization, which could be defined as fear or anxiety in connection with bodily dysfunction (ibid.:55). Their study allowed Briere and Ruutz to

> hypothesize that sexual victimization is not only relatively common but often traumagenic as well. The persistence of such potential effects into adulthood, even in as high functioning a group as the current sample [of college students], suggests that therapists should seriously consider the possibility of unresolved sexual abuse trauma in clinical groups, especially when client complaints include dissociation, somatization, and dysphoria. [Ibid.:56–57]

Many other studies, primarily of non-clinical samples, essentially confirm a relationship between a history of childhood sexual abuse and adult psychological symptoms (Jumper, 1995).

Further corroboration comes from clinical samples. Elizabeth F. Pribor and Stephen H. Dinwiddie investigated the relationship between adult psychiatric illness and childhood incest experiences. They administered the Diagnostic Interview Schedule, which measures various forms of psychiatric illness, to 52 adult women who had experienced childhood incest and to 23 age- and race-matched controls referred from self-help agencies. They found that

> the incest victims had markedly higher lifetime prevalence of most major psychiatric disorders, . . . [demonstrating] a substantially higher lifetime prevalence of agoraphobia, alcohol abuse or dependence, depression, panic disorder, post-traumatic stress disorder (PTSD), simple phobia, and social phobia. [1992:54]

The subjects under discussion constituted a treatment group, not a randomly selected group; however, most of the victims in the study did not approach the treatment agencies with complaints of past abuse. In fact, "many of the women volunteered that they had never told their psychiatrists about the abuse, nor were they ever asked" (ibid.:55). Pribor and Dinwiddie found an association between abuse and psychiatric disorder but could not explain it.

Two mental disorders that have been particularly strongly associated with a childhood history of sexual abuse are borderline personality disorder and multiple personality disorder. Though the former has for some time been of great theoretical interest to the post-Freudian ego psychologists and their followers, it is only relatively recently that studies have linked it to sexual abuse (Herman et al., 1989). Multiple personality disorder (MPD), once thought to be extremely rare, has gained increasing attention from clinicians and researchers in the past decade. Although little solid information is known about this disorder, researchers are discovering that in many if not most cases, the occurrence of MPD can be correlated with childhood abuse, often sexual abuse (Ross et al., 1989, in Pribor and Dinwiddie, 1992). Richard Kluft (1987) has reported that more than 90 percent of patients suffering from MPD had histories of child abuse. There is also evidence that the consequences of childhood sexual abuse are physiological as well as psychological. One group of scientists has demonstrated abnormal brain-wave patterns in sexually abused children (Teischer et al., 1994). Other scientists have found that sexually abused girls show impairment of the hormonal system responsible for mediating environmental stress (DeBellis et al., 1994). This study showed that children who suffer sexual abuse experience long-term changes in cortisol and other hormones that have major effects on behavior, physical growth, and development. As there is strong correlation between cortisol level and psychopathology, especially dissociative symptoms, this effect of sexual abuse on hormones may be the link researchers are seeking in the association of adult psychiatric illness and child sexual abuse. While it is too early to tell, these studies may lead to proof that incest and sexual abuse of children have damaging effects.

While the group Herman and Hirschman (1981) have labeled the "pro-incest" lobby (borrowing the term from culture critic Benjamin DeMott) continues to assert that incest and the sexual use of children by adults are consensual and even enjoyable activities for such children (for example, the North American Man/Boy Love Association [NAMBLA]; see Hechler, 1988), current research reveals that incest and child sexual abuse are rarely "consensual" (even if that term is used in the common rather than the legal definition), rarely desired or enjoyed by the child-victims, and often seriously damaging for those victims (Russell, 1986). It is generally agreed that the extent of such damage is not yet known.

WHY IS INCEST PRACTICED? WHY IS THERE A TABOO?

If sexual abuse is harmful, why is it practiced? Current research has focused on the psychology of the individual abusers, addressing their particular psychopathology and circumstances of the abuse. Jean La Fontaine, who traces the evolution of thought on this subject, asserts that early thought led some researchers to adopt the Freudian attitude that "all individuals are initially attracted to children but are weaned away from these feelings by social conditioning and repression" (1990:99). More-recent examinations of the issue have led researchers, especially feminists, to assert that "sexual domination is an expression of men's power over women" (Russell, 1986:100). This hypothesis suggests that abusers feel threatened by adult women and thus turn their sexual impulses toward children, who are weaker and more vulnerable.

Russell offers several explanations for the increased occurrence of sexual abuse and incest. She suggests that the "sexual revolution" may have encouraged the attitude that any kind of sex is permissible and should be encouraged, giving credence to NAMBLA's self-interested assertions that children should be allowed to explore their own developing sexuality. Russell also cites as possible factors the need of some men to dominate weaker women or children, the possibility that some men were themselves abused, and the weaker incest taboo for stepfather-daughter relationships.

The focus of these explanations for the occurrence of incest moves away from the individual and addresses the issue from a more sociological angle. Our focus, too, is more sociological, addressing not only actual incest but the incest taboo. Earlier we mentioned Fox's (1980) theory that incest prohibitions provide a mental construct for the practice of exogamy. Fox, however, has difficulty explaining the universal taboo on incest within the nuclear family, even though the rules of exogamy vary widely. If we adopt a position that incest always involves sex between children and adults, then the incest taboo is a prohibition on the sexual use of children by their adult caretakers. Since the sexual use of children interferes with their ability to master certain developmental tasks and has long-term negative mental health consequences, the value of such a taboo to society should be immediately apparent.

If incest and sexual abuse are so damaging, why do they occur at all? The answer is that the positive physical or mental health of every member of a society is not always considered a contribution to the best interests of that society. Many oppressive and abusive cultures have thrived on the notion that individuals must sacrifice their own well-being for the good of more powerful others or for the good of the whole. Some damage to certain members in culturally prescribed ways may be necessary for the continuity of valued institutions. Sociological and anthropological literatures are filled with examples of abusive or even sadistic practices toward children which are defended as a necessary way of life for particular cultures. For example, the practice of clitoridectomy (so-called female circumcision) in Egypt and the Sudan is viewed as an important rite of passage for young women, who are seen to be moving from the status of children to women in cultures where the ritual is practiced. While some argue that female circumcision is indicative of fear of female sexuality, the ritual is maintained most strongly by the women themselves within those cultures (Gordon, 1991). The argument for defending a practice that is painful and dangerous to individuals is that, as a ritual, it maintains the continuity of the culture, and to devalue it puts a stress on the entire culture.

To a certain extent, incest in the United States today can be viewed as a child-rearing ritual. It is practiced in secret, and there is widespread pretense that it does not exist, but this is true of many rituals and cultural practices. According to Russell, the facts that

> incestuous abuse is so much more widespread then heretofore thought possible and that there is a strong relationship between experiences of such abuse in childhood and adolescence and later experiences of victimization . . . suggest that millions of American girls are being socialized into victim roles. [1986:12]

If one accepts that incest is a strong force that socializes some women into victim roles, it could be argued that certain segments of society maintain a strong interest in cementing, rather than alleviating, the status of that group of victims. Children who suffer incest become available for further misuse in later life and can be exploited in numerous ways—as rape victims, battered wives, prostitutes, "collaborators," and models for pornography. There are some people for whom incest is extremely profitable and who would stand to suffer, certainly economically if not otherwise, if the victimization were to end.

The sexual use of children was not considered abusive in prior centuries because children were viewed as property. In the last century, researchers and professionals have recognized the issue of incest, but unfortunately the attitude that incest was fantasy pervaded the medical community for many decades. More recently, professionals have made tremendous progress in understanding both the prevalence and the effects of child sexual abuse and incest. Although there is no consensus as to why incest occurs or has been allowed to continue, it could be postulated that by helping to foster a group of victims who will be vulnerable to continued victimization later in life, incest remains an integral part of society. The refusal of many people to recognize incest, and the refusal of many segments of our society to protect children from incest may be seen as ways of maintaining a profitable commodity—exploitable victims.

8

Anti-Mother Bias

Although traditional American culture glorifies the concept of motherhood, it also has a history of blaming mothers for a variety of social ills. But even contradictory images of mothers in American folklore cannot explain the current situation in which mothers trying to protect their children are vilified. This is particularly strange in view of the fact that mothers in the past have been blamed for failing to protect their children from incest. We still come across reports of the stereotypic "incest mother," who is collusive and pretends not to know what is going on, or even the frigid mother, who prefers exposing her daughters to incest to satisfying her husband's sexual needs herself. Is this concept of the "incest mother" now being replaced with a new stereotype of the "false allegation mother"—a vindictive woman making charges of sexual abuse?

MOTHERS AS ABUSERS

Some activists have objected to the conclusion that protective mothers face an anti-mother bias in our courts. The refusal to acknowledge the seriousness of child sexual abuse is not an anti-mother issue, they say, because some mothers are abusers too. The organizers of the White Ribbon Campaign against child sexual abuse have received protests from angry incest survivors who object to the Annual March on Washington held on Mother's Day, claiming that their mothers had either abused them or failed to protect them.

Epidemiological studies have found that sexual abuse by mothers is rare, but researchers and clinicians point out that such abuse may be underreported. Cultures in which mothers openly sexually abuse their children, even torture them, are known to be extremely patriarchal and misogynist. In these cultures cruelty to women is not only tolerated but institutionalized, and woman-to-woman cruelty is sometimes also the norm. For example, in some Middle Eastern societies, it is the older women, including the mother, who mutilate young girls through ritual clitoridectomy. Women in patriarchal societies are not punished for such abuse if it is performed in the interest and support of patriarchal institutions. In India, in many families, the only socially acceptable way for a woman to exercise power was by dominating, even abusing, her daughters-in-law (Miller, 1992).

Margaret Mead has proposed that while mothering in women is deeply rooted in biological conditions, nurturing in men—the basis of social fatherhood—is learned behavior, which can easily be destroyed. It is more difficult, but not impossible, to destroy mothering behavior, according to Mead:

> The mother's nurturing tie to her child is apparently so deeply rooted in the actual biological conditions of conception and gestation, birth and suckling, that only fairly complicated social arrangements can break it down entirely. Where human beings have learned to value rank more than anything else in life and where attaining rank is valued more than anything else, women may strangle their children with their own hands. Where society has so overdone the rituals of legitimacy that men are kept good providers only at the cost of social ostracism of the unmarried mother, the mother of an illegitimate child may kill or abandon it. . . . [T]he evidence suggests . . . that men have to learn to want to provide for others, and this behavior, being learned, is fragile and can disappear rather easily under social conditions that no longer teach it effectively. Women may be said to be mothers unless they are taught to deny their child-bearing qualities. Society must distort their sense of themselves, pervert their inherent growth-pattern, perpetrate a series of learning outrages upon them, before they will cease to want to provide, at least for a few years, for the child they have already nourished for nine months within the safe circle of their own bodies. [1950:191–192]

Mead's point can be carried a step further. Society may go to extraordinary lengths to pervert the mother's natural protective instincts toward her child, and if that fails, as sometimes happens, society may actually take the child away from the mother. But why would society want to interfere with the mother-child relationship? The reasons may vary with the social structure. In patriarchal societies, for example, excessive closeness between mother and son could be detrimental to patriarchal law and order. In some patriarchies, boys are forcibly removed from their mothers at a certain age and subjected to painful rituals designed to establish a strong paternal identification (Rosen, 1988). In other cultures, in which mothers mutilate their own daughters in comparable rituals, their instincts to protect their children are prevented for a "higher social good." In such social conditions, protective mothers may be punished when other efforts to thwart their protective instincts have failed. This may partly explain why American mothers are currently being punished for bringing or supporting their children's allegations of sexual abuse against ex-husbands.

Three interrelated principles pertaining to sex roles and gender discrimination contribute to the present problem facing mothers of incest victims:

1. Our society is, and has historically been, partriarchal. Contrary to popular belief, mothers' rights to their children have always been tenuous at best, and nonexistent at worst.

2. Despite gains made for women's rights, feminists did not adequately address the issue of mother's rights, leaving mothers—the most vulnerable of women—to bear the brunt of the backlash virtually unrepresented.

3. Nevertheless, the gains in women's independence spurred by the feminist movement empowered women to exercise their natural protective instincts toward their children, relatively uninhibited by deference to male domination. This meant that fewer girls and boys would be socialized into victim roles, and society, threatened with a loss of its victim supply, adapted by taking children away from protective mothers.

HISTORICAL PERSPECTIVE ON CHILD CUSTODY

While we have seen a few cases in which protective fathers have been mistreated in the courts when bringing allegations of sexual abuse against mothers' boyfriends or even child-care providers, these cases are much less frequent than situations in which protective mothers lose custody and visitation rights. This flies in the face of the commonly held belief that courts generally prefer mothers as custodial parents, and that in the family court system gender bias is exercised against men, not women. There is a widespread public misperception that a mother who loses custody must have something terribly wrong with her.

In patriarchal cultures such as our own, women do not really have rights over their children. They may be assigned or allowed to care for their children physically, at least while they are young, because they are thought to be better able to do so than others. In the book *The Custody Revolution: The Father Factor and the Motherhood Mystique*, R. E. Warshak argues that fathers deserve as much of an opportunity to raise their children as do mothers. Without employing studies of custody disputes or even custody assignments, Warshak asserts that

> the legacy of the tender-years presumption has continued to influence custody decisions, so that the best-interests standard, despite its literal meaning, has come to be interpreted primarily as a justification for the mother's preferential claim in custody disputes. [1992:32]

What evidence is there to support this statement?

In our society, from the Colonial period until after the First World War, fathers automatically gained custody of their children in divorce cases (Little,

1982; Chesler, 1986). Unless they were found to be "unfit" parents, fathers received custody as a legal right as heads of the household. This principle derived from Roman law and was carried over into English law, which did not deviate from it until 1839, when a statute called Justice Talfourd's Act was passed (Little, 1982). Though rights of the father were still dominant, the act provided that he also had to maintain certain marital obligations toward his wife and address the needs of his children (Schouler and Blakemore, 1921, in Little, 1982). American law followed much the same principles, and legal commentators at the beginning of the twentieth century asserted that "if all other things were equal, the father would still be preferred as the custodial parent" (Little, 1982:5). If both parents were equally entitled to custody, the father had the right to take the child without being considered a kidnapper. As the idea of the child having legal rights was not yet developed, the father's rights superseded those of both his wife and his children. A man's children were essentially his property.

Around the turn of the twentieth century, the courts began to take into consideration such factors as the age, sex, and health of the child in custody matters (Little, 1982). This concern shaped itself into what is now called the Doctrine of Tender Years (this period has never been defined), which indicates that mothers are the more suitable and "capable" parents during a child's early years. After 1927, the tendency to prefer the mother for custody of pre-school children spread quickly, the rhetoric being that children of "tender years" or "delicate condition" were better cared for by the "loving and devoted" ministrations of the natural mother (ibid.:8). In practice, it usually meant that while the children were cared for in the home and needed a lot of attention, they were allowed to stay with their mothers, but that as soon as they were in school and required very little actual care, they were "returned" to their paternal "owners."

However, Chesler points out that even when the Tender Years doctrine was in effect, it was not perceived as a maternal right but implied a concern for the best interests of the child. It applied only to the custody of younger children, and no history of care given by a mother would vest in her any maternal rights once her care was no longer needed (1986:254). The question of parental "fitness" was also an issue, but a strong double standard existed: A woman's adultery was evidence of immoral behavior and was grounds for removing or denying custody, while a man's adultery was not sufficient grounds to affect a custody decision (Little, 1982).

After several decades, the concept of the Best Interests of the Child evolved from the Tender Years doctrine, and the courts began to focus on the welfare of the child in a social and economic sense, rather than on the parents' sex as a measure of their respective abilities to care for the child. While this changing focus was couched in gender-neutral language, it actually heralded a shift toward preferring fathers as custodial parents. This shift was influenced by three important and interdependent factors: the rising divorce rate and changing demographics of the American family, the changing image of the father as opposed to the changing image of the mother, and gender bias in the courts.

The divorce rate began to rise in the 1950s and peaked in the 1970s, when one in every three or four marriages ended in divorce. This led to an increase in single-parent families and problems for both mothers and fathers (Drakich, 1989). Divorced mothers had the double burden of raising their children alone while fending for themselves economically; their chief complaint was fathers' decreasing participation in financial support and child care after divorce. Fathers complained of their children's absence from their lives and the "greed" of ex-wives. The idea of participant fathering was further nurtured by the media and an outpouring of social science literature, which, when interpreted uncritically, gave the impression "that if a child has an active father he or she does not really need a mother" (Drakich, 1989:75). More careful examination of the research showed that the much-louted image of the caregiving father was largely a myth. As late as 1987, only one percent of primary care-givers in the country were fathers, regardless of the fact that both parents worked full-time in a large number of American households. One study found that fathers who claimed to spend an average of fifteen to twenty minutes a day with their one-year-olds actually spent an average of fifteen seconds per day.

> The image of the nurturing father is a double-edged sword. On the one hand, images of fathers as nurturers provide masculine role models of parenting that promote the feminist vision of co-parenting and challenge rigid male gender roles. On the other hand, the image of the nurturing father has taken on a reality of its own that misrepresents the reality that mothers are still the primary caregivers of children. [Ibid.:83]

The new fatherhood ideology was not a good-faith effort to encourage fathers to participate more in child care, but a fiction developed to make it easier for judges to award them custody. This fiction was necessary to enable fathers to regain control over their families—control which had been threatened by the rising divorce rate and the economic feasibility of mother-headed households.

> What the fatherhood ideology does do is provide judges with a plausible explanation for awarding custody to fathers and acceptable justification for their decisions. The ideology of fatherhood is a smokescreen for men's entrenched privileges and rights to their children. [Ibid.:86]

The effects of this smokescreen soon became apparent. Perhaps the first significant case heralding the era of "custodial rape" of mothers involved one of America's most beloved folk singers of the 1960s and 70s—Judy Collins. While estranged from her husband, Peter Taylor, Collins took ill and was hospitalized for a long period with tuberculosis. Taylor and his family had vowed that in the event of a divorce they would obtain custody of pre-schooler Clarke, the couple's only child. While Collins was in the hospital, the Taylors took physical possession of Clarke and refused to return him to his mother after her discharge. Taylor then insisted that the divorce be final-ized before the custody decision.

Collins and her attorneys, unaware of the dangers that lay ahead, agreed to this arrangement, assuming that judges would award custody to a mother unless she was found unfit. Immediately upon divorce, Taylor remarried, thus providing Clarke with a politically correct mother substitute. During the cus-tody evaluation which followed, a social worker visiting Collins at her home in Greenwich Village, asked, "How can your son adapt to living here, Miss Collins? His friends and all his activities are in Storrs [Connecticut]?" (Collins, 1987:103). Judy Collins lost custody of Clarke in 1965. Writing in 1987, she continued to berate herself for what she still perceived to be her failure as a mother: "'Most women are given custody as a matter of course' my lawyer had said to me. I was the exception; I must be a monster. My revulsion at myself was complete" (ibid.:104). Whether he knew it or not, Peter Taylor was a significant pioneer in the fledgling fathers' rights movement, which caught the imagination of the nation a decade later. Some of the legal maneuvers he used—perhaps unheard-of at the time—became so common-place that they are now included in published advice to fathers on how to get custody and illustrated in task force reports on gender bias in the courts. However, it was not until 1975 that landmark decisions signaled a major turnaround in child custody decisions nationwide. In that year a New York State judge awarded custody of two children to Dr. Lee Salk, a child psychologist, on the grounds that he could provide a more enriching environment for them than his ex-wife, Kersten, who had only been a home-maker. The judge did not find Kersten unfit, only "uninteresting" (Chesler, 1986:256). Curiously, the reason the judge gave for depriving Kersten Salk of custody was the opposite of what Collins perceived to be the basis of her own custodial deprivation a decade earlier. Because her career was more suc-cessful and interesting than Taylor's, Collins blamed herself for the custodial rape she had endured.

Despite these high-profile cases, it still appeared that most divorcing mothers did retain custody of their children. In 1982, Nancy Polikoff pointed out that only around 10 percent of divorcing fathers gained custody, but this statistic tells only part of the story. In the majority of divorces, children remain with their mothers because their fathers do not seek custody. The court's rubber-stamping of arrangements made by the parties themselves does not reflect bias, because it plays only a passive role in the proceedings. Examination of those cases in which custody is contested reveals a different picture. In 1968, 35 percent of fathers won custody in contested cases; in 1972, 37 percent. In California, by 1977, 63 percent of fathers who sued for custody were successful (Weitzman and Dixon, 1979). In 1979, in a study conducted in North Carolina, 50 percent of the fathers who sought custody prevailed (Orthner and Lewis, 1979).

THE GENDER-BIAS TASK FORCES

By the decade of the 1980s there was a growing awareness that something had gone seriously wrong. While mothers were losing custody without being considered unfit, fathers were gaining custody even in cases where there had been domestic violence. The unequal treatment of women in the courts became a major concern throughout the country and spurred the establishment of task forces to study gender bias in the courts. The first one was in the State of New Jersey; it was followed by task forces in New York, Maryland, California, Massachusetts, and Rhode Island. By 1991, 30 states had supreme court task forces working to document gender bias, and thirteen task forces had issued their reports (Wibler and Schafran, 1991).

The New Jersey Task Force found that

> although the law as written is for the most part gender neutral, stereotyped myths, beliefs and biases were found to sometimes affect decision-making in the areas investigated: damages, domestic violence, juvenile justice, matrimonial and sentencing. [Quoted in Schafran, 1987:283]

The New York Task Force was more gender-specific in its condemnation of the attitudes of the courts:

> The Task Force has concluded that gender bias against women litigants, attorneys and court personnel is a pervasive problem with grave consequences. Women are often denied equal justice, equal treatment and equal opportunity. Cultural stereotypes of women's role in marriage and in society daily distort courts' application of substantive law. Women uniquely, disproportionately, and with unacceptable frequency must endure a climate of condescension, indifference, and hostility. [Ibid.]

The task forces for both states found that with respect to issues of domestic violence, even though legislation was strong and should be sufficient to provide victims with the means to protect themselves, judicial enforcement of the legislation was "often influenced by a common law heritage and cultural stereotypes which treat wives as the property of their husbands, sanction wife abuse and assume that women provoke the attacks and enjoy the pain" (ibid.). Both task forces found that judges were not adequately informed about the psychology of batterers and victims, or about the economic influences and coercive techniques batterers use to get complaints of domestic violence withdrawn (ibid.) A social worker appearing before the New York

Task Force testified that one judge started the proceedings in a domestic violence case with "Well, well, well, we had a little domestic squabble, did we? Naughty, naughty. Let's kiss and make up, and get out of my court" (Cook, 1986:30). Such insensitivity and disregard for the victims of domestic violence and wife-battering were regarded as unacceptable by the task forces, which made various recommendations to improve the situation.

The task forces found that treatment of custody disputes was influenced by gender stereotyping of both men and women. One attorney testified in New York that some judges were unable to accept that a father could be an effective primary caretaker for a young child. However, the stereotype that mothers are more natural parents is a double-edged sword; it reinforces unrealistic expectations of mothers and encourages highly negative views toward those who cannot meet those ideals. When a woman works or seeks assistance with child-care responsibilities, for instance, she is viewed as unwilling or unable to fulfill her natural maternal role. Indeed,

> The cultural stereotype that a good mother is the one who is home full-time still influences custody decisions. Both task forces noted the irony of cases in which a homemaker mother is awarded custody but not enough spousal or child support to remain a homemaker, then loses custody when the father remarries and tells the judge that his new wife is at home and can be a *proper* mother to the child. [Emphasis added; Schafran, 1987:286]

A female attorney in New York, responding to the task force survey, pointed out that a less-than-perfect mother is criticized for any imperfection and may lose custody because of it, while fathers are exempt from examination for blame and are applauded by the courts merely for expressing the desire to love and care for their children. The fact that a father has engaged in very little of the labor of raising the children is viewed as immaterial; he may be awarded custody because he loves his children and is financially more able to support them (ibid.).

Studies also found that women were vulnerable not only to situations of domestic violence but also to judicial unwillingness to acknowledge or comprehend those situations. A New York attorney described the difficulties faced by some battered women seeking custody:

> Battered women are penalized by the courts for a lifestyle which is a direct result of the physical abuse. Many battered women may have to move frequently in an attempt to escape the batterer. They may try to keep their home addresses or phone numbers unknown, and [as a result] be accused of limiting access between father and the children. The courts are likely to view this as evidence of instability [on the part of the mother]. [New York Task Force, 1986, quoted in Schafran, 1987:286]

In other words, when a battered wife seeks to protect herself from abuse (as the courts remain unwilling to help her), she is viewed as unwilling to share access to her children with her abusive husband. Her punishment then is to lose custody to the abusive father, who in the court's eyes is a better parent than one who cannot protect her children.

More-recent studies have presented an increasingly gloomy picture for mothers. Chesler found that 70 percent of custodially challenged "good enough" mothers lost custody to fathers, some of whom were frank wife-batterers or child abusers. In her study of sixty cases Chesler found:

> 70 percent of these custodially challenged and "good enough" mothers lost custody, both in courtrooms and privately, to challenging fathers, 83 percent of whom had not previously been involved in primary child care, 67 percent of whom had paid no child support, 62 percent of whom had physically abused their wives during marriage or divorce, . . . and 37 percent of whom had kidnapped their children. [1986:66]

Chesler contends that one of the strongest forces assisting fathers in custody battles is money: the fathers' financial superiority was considered in the children's "best interests"; the fathers were better able to sustain expensive and protracted legal battles; and they were financially able, in effect, to kidnap their children in preemptive strikes. Women in the study lost custody most frequently because judges upheld the fathers' views that the mothers were "uppity" and punishably "sexual." Mothers who wanted to move, or even needed to move, were prevented by the courts from doing so or deprived of custody (ibid.:83). These trends progressed unabated.

A study conducted in Orange County, North Carolina, from 1983 to 1987, found that in 84 percent of contested custody cases, fathers obtained either sole custody or mandated joint custody (at their request) regardless of a history of wife-battering or physical child abuse (Committee for Justice for Women . . . , 1991). In cases where child sexual abuse was alleged against the fathers who sought custody, the figures changed—in the opposite way from what one would expect: 100 percent of fathers accused of sexual abuse were granted custody. Can the current climate for mothers get much worse? Contrary to the popular myth that child sexual abuse allegations are "the atom bomb of custody disputes," such allegations virtually guarantee the mother's loss of custody and often of visitation. In that climate, women's advocates have asked whether the metaphor is being misapplied: is it possible that for some unscrupulous persons, sexual abuse of children during a divorce or custody dispute can be a calculated act of litigious warfare, prompting an understandably explosive reaction that is, in our legal system, almost guaranteed to backfire?

HAS THE FEMINIST MOVEMENT HELPED?

Linda Gordon has noted that "Concern with family violence usually grew when feminism was strong and ebbed when feminism was weak" (1988:4).

Thus the current trend, which effectively refuses protection to children whose mothers allege sexual abuse and punishes their mothers, may be seen as part of the backlash against feminism, which reached its peak in the 1980s. Susan Faludi, in her book *Backlash* (1991), has shown that despite the fanfare trumpeting women's equality, women are still no better off than they were twenty years ago in certain fundamental areas. At the same time, the anti-feminists are blaming women's present unhappiness on their alleged equality, which Faludi has argued does not really exist. Indeed, with regard to sexual violence, women are actually worse off than they were twenty years ago. Yet there is more to this story than the backlash against feminism. Mothers' rights had been deteriorating for some time before the main backlash received the movement's attention. However, this earlier trend went almost unnoticed and is only now beginning to appear as an issue on some feminist agendas, probably because of the movement's almost exclusive focus on economic and political gains for women. Children have been seen primarily as a factor preventing women from entering the work force, while the question of the parental rights of women has never been adequately addressed.

Traditional feminists took a traditional patriarchal view of motherhood, which led them to the conclusion that motherhood was a form of slavery. In order to become free and equal, women must liberate themselves from the prison of caring for children, go out to work, and become economically powerful and equal to men. Simone de Beauvoir in *The Second Sex* (1953) and Shulamith Firestone in *The Dialectic of Sex* (1970) attributed women's inequality to "biologically given unequal distribution of reproductive labor" (Webster, 1975:150). Because of reproduction and child-care responsibilities and burdens, "woman has always been restricted to maintaining a nurturing role, while man has appropriated the creative, and for de Beauvoir transcendent role" (ibid.). The feminist solution was to get women out of the home and liberate them from the need to bear and care for children. There has never been a significant feminist attempt to address or even recognize the rights of mothers, let alone defend or bolster these rights.

American feminism's ignoring of women's parental rights paved the way for successful attacks by the anti-mother father's rights lobby, which has also supported many alleged molesters in custody battles. American feminism has had an uneasy relationship with the concept of motherhood. While it was seen as an impediment to equality, there was no way of evading the fact that most women were also mothers, or would become mothers. Leaders of the backlash against feminism have accused the feminists of an "anti-mother crusade." Sylvia Ann Hewlett, author of *A Lesser Life: The Myth of Women's Liberation in America* (1986), accuses the women's movement of "reviling" and "raging" at mothers and claims that this stance has discredited the movement in the eyes of today's women. Faludi, however, defends the position of the women's movement on motherhood:

> While the women's liberation movement certainly, and rightfully, criticized American society for offering mothers hollow Hallmark sentiments as a substitute for legal rights and genuine respect, its leaders also pressed for a wide range of rights that would benefit mothers. In the early 70's feminists campaigned for five day care bills in Congress. Three of the eight points of NOW's original 1967 "Bill of Rights for Women" dealt specifically with child care, maternity leave, and other benefits. In the following years, NOW and other women's groups repeatedly lobbied Congress, staged national protests, and filed class action suits to combat discrimination against pregnant women and mothers. [1991:316]

Faludi correctly argues that while the movement has been blamed for destroying women's happiness by securing their equality, women have not actually gained true equality. The irony of crediting feminism with the discontent of newly "liberated" women is that such women are still underrepresented in business, politics, and many areas of culture-shaping institutions.

Faludi has carefully scrutinized many commonly held beliefs regarding the failure of the feminist movement to make women "happy" and has not found evidence to support these assumptions; yet there is abundant evidence that discrimination continues on many fronts. One area that Faludi does not address is discrimination in the courtroom, especially in judicial decisions involving child custody. She touches on gender bias in the courts in connection with alimony decisions and the resulting financial problems of divorced women who were previously homemakers. She denies allegations that these financial inequities resulted from feminist-backed legislation, saying, "The real source of divorced women's woes can be found not in the fine print of divorce legislation, but in the behavior of ex-husbands and judges" (ibid.:24). While she agrees that the unfair treatment of women in the courts is part of the backlash against feminism, Faludi's solution is to correct pay inequities between the sexes: "if the wage gap were wiped out between the sexes . . . one half of female-headed households would be instantly lifted out of poverty" (ibid.:25).

Certainly, financial independence has given women much more leverage, allowing them to assert themselves and seek their rights. But the converse is not necessarily true, that further improvements in women's economic status will make any difference in custody court. Nor is it clear that having more professional women in decision-making roles vis-à-vis child custody proceedings would help. There are, proportionately, as many female professionals—doctors, lawyers, and judges—as males who have made inexplicable anti-mother decisions.

Economic and political equality do not measurably increase a mother's likelihood of retaining custody of her children, and such factors may even become the rationale for custodial deprivations. In Oklahoma, District Court Judge Eleanor MacIntyre, who had the power to make decisions about child custody for other mothers—the same power as any male judge—lost custody of her own child for believing and supporting her daughter's disclosure of sexual abuse. Although the court-appointed psychologist agreed that the child might well have been molested by the father, as MacIntyre claimed, the judge in the case found her the less fit parent because the alleged molester father was able to turn his attention *away* from the problem and "get on" with the business of raising the child, whereas the mother *focused* on the problem. MacIntyre, a conservative and previously powerful woman, found herself on the run—a fugitve from the law, like so many other mothers before and since. She was apprehended in a foreign country and jailed for months without trial while her daughter was returned to the alleged abuser. As a judge, MacIntyre was as powerful as any man; as a mother she was as powerless as any woman.

Elizabeth Morgan was a plastic surgeon at the top of her profession and a best-selling author when her custody battle reduced her and her entire family to penury. She fared no better in court than any of the mothers with much less money or status. And there are many more examples of professional women, powerful women, well-connected women, rich women, and even women skilled in the art of patriarchal warfare, whose stories end up much the same. A phrase we have coined, "an anti-mother pogrom," is the most vicious aspect of the anti-feminist backlash.

Robin Fox, a leading theoretist on the anthropology of the family, has asserted that American feminism has confused the role of the patrilinealist's "wife/incubator" with the genuine role of mother:

> In starting up their cooperative movements and asserting that as women they have interests to be protected from male exploitation, they are returning to normal. Where they get confused, because of the close established link by recent history, is to think that their protest is against the role of mother. Since this has been defined as part of the role of wife in a monogamous nuclear family, they lump the whole lot together and attack it all. They imagine that what they really want . . . is dominating male jobs in a male world. What they do not realize is that this is playing right into male hands, just as the so-called sexual revolution presented male chauvinists with a nirvana of sexually available women for whom they had to assume no responsibility. This is suicidal for women. True "sisterhood" is the sisterhood of comothers, and mothers and daughters. . . . The only solid anchor for female solidarity is in *the protection of their rights as mothers against males, against the "family," and against the state and religious apparatus that threatens the absolute sanctity of the mother-child bond.*
>
> Rather than truly transforming society to bring it back closer to the basic pattern in which, in my opinion, women were equal and important, the militants are simply demanding to play male roles in a capitalist con-

sumer society that both physically and mentally exploits men and women. [1980:210, 211; emphasis added]

Fox's warning that feminism was failing to protect mothers' rights was apparently correct. However, most women do not know that their rights as mothers have been eroded until they face the court system, and then it is often too late.

9

The Failure of the Child Protection System

A parent who is concerned that his or her child may have been sexually abused is likely to get the following message when calling for help:

"If you suspect sexual abuse, call this number. Someone will take your report and interview your child. If she discloses sexual abuse, they may schedule a medical evaluation to collect evidence. Then there will be an administrative finding in our agency. The case may also be referred to law enforcement for prosecution. In any case, if there has been abuse, a petition will be filed in court and you will get an order of protection or other appropriate relief to protect the child. Perhaps you should consult your lawyer."

This advice, or something similar, is offered to protective parents to show them that they will have every opportunity to obtain help for their children. Many social workers seem to believe that such a boiler-plate recitation of procedures exonerates them for the fact that the end result—protection for the child at risk—is often never reached. See Table 2, below, for the various pitfalls that make the system inoperable.

The system starts with the "invitation in," which can take many forms. Children are being bombarded with public service announcements on television and programs in their schools telling them that sexual abuse is not permitted and that they should "tell" if anything suspicious is done to them. Parents are also being invited into the system by television, news reports, and announcements of a toll-free number to call if they suspect child abuse. That 800 number in turn gives out a local agency's number.

SOCIAL OR "HUMAN" SERVICES, THE FIRST STOP

The first telephone call a protective adult makes on behalf of a child is to the local social service agency that is a part of county government. It may be called Welfare Department, Child Protective Services, Social Services, Family Services, Human Resources, or some similar name. (State laws require social workers, health care providers, teachers, and other professionals who work with children to report to state child protection agencies any suspicions of abuse they form from their contact with children. These are called "mandated" reports.) The telephone call is answered by an intake worker or caseworker, who has wide discretion in deciding what to do: whether to give advice, write a report and open an investigation, or unilaterally determine that there is no problem and ignore the call. If the report survives this first capricious contact, it becomes a "case" and is subjected to whatever procedures the particular agency uses to determine whether the case is valid.

Most agencies make administrative findings—within unspecified periods of time, which can drag on for months or years—and which fall into one of three categories: "founded" (meaning they believe it), "unfounded" (meaning they do not believe it), or the very dangerous "undetermined" (meaning they do not know and seemingly do not care). The agency in the Carter case (which started with definite physical evidence) only reached the level of "undetermined." Social service agencies intervene only in cases labeled "founded"; and intervention means that the agency takes the case to court. There, a single judge can decide whether or not to believe the administrative finding. A judge who disbelieves the finding can rule that there is "no credible evidence," and that case is as good as "unfounded."

What steps lead to the agency finding? There is no standard answer to this question. Usually, the child is interviewed by agency personnel. The child's own therapist, mother, doctor, and other trusted significant adults may be completely ignored; the child is usually expected to repeat her disclosures to a stranger interviewing her on behalf of the agency. The interviewer does not need to follow any particular procedure. Social workers are subjected to rigorous cross-examination about their conclusions only if they do in fact believe a child and go to court to support the allegations. If, however, they disbelieve the allegations—regardless of the reason—their conclusion is automatically accepted as the basis for an unfounded case and their rationale is not challenged. If one worker believes an allegation, the child is sometimes interviewed by other workers. Some children have been subjected to as many as fourteen interviews. As long as they continue to disclose, they stay on the treadmill; but the first time they fail to disclose, the case is marked as a "recant" and considered unfounded. If, after a recant, a child returns to the original story, the disclosure is considered "inconsistent" and thus unfounded. In the face of multiple interviews, most molested children will recant at some point because the sheer volume of interrogation leads them to feel that their disclosures are not being believed. Molested children, who are especially insecure, are very vulnerable to such tactics and may recant at some point because they feel threatened in general.

FORENSICS, THE SECOND STOP

If an interviewer believes the child's disclosure, there will generally be a search for physical evidence. In 80 percent of all real cases of sexual abuse, however, there is no physical evidence of the act. Only the presence of semen in a child's body, or unhealed evidence of forcible penetration of the genitals of a girl whose hymen was previously proven to be intact, can rise to the level of "solid evidence," and there are very few such cases. Research shows that the sexual abuse of young children usually consists of acts that do not leave clear physical signs: oral sex, "fondling," partial penetration, sodomy, forced fellatio, digital penetration. A multitude of such acts can be perpetrated upon a child many times and leave nothing for physicians to identify. Even if a child is afflicted with a sexually transmitted disease, it is rarely possible to identify its origin because the perpetrator may have sought treatment before the child's symptoms are identified. More often than not, then, the results of the search for forensic evidence results in a lack of findings or, at most, a finding that is called "consistent with but not conclusive of" sexual abuse. Unfortunately, the translation from medical to legal terms subtly changes the semantics of this kind of finding. What a doctor calls "consistent" but "not conclusive" is often described by the lawyers as "inconclusive" and leads judges to conclude illogically that the finding really means "no abuse."

LAW ENFORCEMENT, THE THIRD STOP

If medical findings firmly support the conclusion that the child has been molested, the agency generally involves the police and/or prosecutor. Unfortunately, that can create more problems than it solves. Police do not look at a case in terms of child protection; that is someone else's job. They are interested in whether their prosecutor will take the case to court, and so they look at the potential weaknesses of a case not at the evidence. They may ask, for instance, whether the child has ever masturbated, in case the defense lawyer tries to explain away physical evidence by suggesting that she penetrated herself. Such questions frighten many children and cause them to become "not a good witness," which would be fatal to a prosecution. Prosecutors determine whether to press charges by measuring their chances of winning, not on whether they believe the crime has been committed. Since criminal proceedings require "proof beyond a reasonable doubt," and since most prosecutors are not eager to add losing cases to their balance sheets, they refuse to prosecute incest cases if they have any of the following weaknesses: victim under ten years old; "conflicting information" developed in the multiple interviews; a perpetrator who is already accusing the protective parent of "false allegations in a custody dispute." Prosecutors can refuse to take a case for any reason or for no reason at all and are under no obligation to prosecute.

Most prosecutors prefer cases against stepfathers or mothers' boyfriends to those against biological fathers. The odds against a successful prosecution of a biological father for incest are almost unsurmountable unless he admits guilt.

The fact that a prosecutor decides not to prosecute is often flaunted as evidence that the allegations were "false." Time after time, social workers who have supported children's disclosures have been pressured to change their positions after prosecutions have been dropped because of "insufficient evidence." Of course, this confuses law enforcement purposes (convictions) with social service purposes (child protection), but the reality is that a failed or abandoned prosecution usually results in a rebound that drives the social services agency off the case forever.

COURT ADJUDICATION, THE FOURTH STOP

Lay persons often assume that a judicial decision to protect a child from the risk of sexual abuse is equivalent to finding a defendant guilty as charged, while a decision against protecting a child is the same as finding a defendant innocent. A few years ago, a man at a Free Elizabeth Morgan rally loudly insisted that the judge had "found the father innocent." That was not true. Eric Foretich was never tried for sexual abuse of his daughter in either a criminal court or a child-abuse proceeding; the District of Columbia court ruled only on the custody issue. The judge had not found Foretich "innocent"; he had simply granted the father's request for visitation. People frequently misunderstand the differences between criminal and civil proceedings as well as whose rights and which rights are at stake if the wrong decision is made. Advocates for alleged molesters mention with horror the idea that lengthy prison sentences can be imposed on the basis of flimsy evidence or children's lies. But seldom do we hear about the standards of evidence required to ensure a child's right to protection from possible rape, even when the alleged molester is not being criminally charged. A certain circular reasoning is involved: if the alleged molester is not charged with or not found guilty of a crime, he is innocent; and if he is innocent, the child needs no protection. That analysis fails to take into account the possibility that a child needs protection even when there is not enough evidence to put an alleged molester in jail—which is most often the case. The confusion is compounded by the fact that in the three different kinds of possible proceedings (criminal, child abuse, and custody), there are three different standards of proof.

Criminal Proceedings. Child sexual abuse is a crime. Cases involving incest by a biological father are rarely prosecuted. The social service agency may decide that it would be harmful for the child to testify or that a trial would not help the family. If there is prosecution, the standard of evidence is proof beyond a reasonable doubt—a very heavy evidentiary standard.

Civil Proceedings: Child Abuse. The county attorney, not the prosecutor, usually decides whether an alleged molester will be charged with child abuse, child neglect, or something called "endangerment" in a civil proceeding. The county attorney also represents another powerful client, the social service agency. In an abuse hearing, the standard before a family court judge—not a jury—is "clear and convincing evidence" that abuse did occur, at a particular time, in a particular way. A judge may call the evidence "not convincing" merely because *he* is not convinced. Judge Gordon Mitchell of Dade County, Florida stated on TV that he was upset by being asked to rule against a father who was a professor of political science at Miami University. He characterized his problem as being asked to "say that somebody put his penis . . . in somebody else's tush!" For that, he said, "the evidence has to be conclusive, and I looked at it, and it was not conclusive." The evidence that he "looked at" included a boy's disclosure that his father had molested him; statements from two psychologists that they believed he had been molested; a police officer who believed the boy had been sexually assaulted; the Children's Services Division, which believed the boy had been sexually assaulted; and the opinion of the medical director of the Miami rape treatment center, who had examined a tear to the child's anus and concluded that the boy had been sodomized. But Judge Mitchell was not convinced. Obviously, there is no definition of what constitutes "clear and convincing" evidence.

Civil Proceedings: Custody. In a custody case, the standard is not "clear and convincing" evidence but a "preponderance of the evidence," meaning 51 percent. In the Morgan-Foretich case, Judge Herbert Dixon ordered Morgan to send her daughter on a six-week unsupervised visit with her father while the evidence that the child had been raped by her father was "in equipoise." Equipoise is 50/50—one percentage point short of tipping the scale for a preponderance. In other words, Judge Dixon, believing there was a 50 percent chance that the child Hilary had been raped on a previous visit, ordered that the 50 percent risk of rape be repeated for six weeks. If she and her mother had not left the country, the judge could have decided custody on the 50/50 line he had mentally drawn between protection of the child and the right of the father to have unsupervised access to her.

Who Is the Defendant? When William Kennedy Smith was acquitted of charges of rape, constitutional law expert Alan Dershowitz said on television that the complaining witness should be charged with perjury for making false allegations against the accused rapist. If "reasonable doubt" can be expressed as 10 percent doubt, Smith might have been acquitted because a jury could not conclude, with 90 percent certainty, that he had raped the witness. It does not mean that the alleged victim was 90 percent wrong about being raped. And if there was a 10 percent chance that she had perjured herself, that would not even rise to what is called a *prima facie* case (enough evidence for a prosecution to go forward). Yet one of the nation's most highly respected criminal lawyers made the illogical suggestion, which was accepted by many Americans as a reasonable and rational idea, that something had been proven false by failing to have been proven true.

With regard to incest allegations, the system sets up an unreasonable standard of proof. When it is not met, the same system maintains no standard to presume wrong-doing on the part of the protective parent or complaining child witness and creates confusion as to who is the actual defendant in a child sexual abuse case. The confusion is not merely the result of a leap of logic; it is also the result of failure to realize who should have the lion's share of constitutional protection. Although the child is not a defendant in the traditional legal sense, the position of any child at risk of incest is equivalent to that of a defendant in terms of loss of liberty if the judge errs on the side of the alleged molester. If one is not sure, beyond a reasonable doubt, that a child's disclosure of incest is invalid, it should be presumed valid, the child should be presumed innocent of making a false allegation, and the child should be protected.

The Criminal/Civil Abuse/Custody Court Shuffle. With or without prosecution, a social services agency will go to court for a protective parent and child only if it has firmly made, and continues to support, a founded case of sexual abuse against the named perpetrator. If it has chosen to call the case "undetermined" or "unfounded," it is just as likely to go to court against the protective parent, either in a "disposition" hearing in the abuse case or in a custody case, and testify that the parent tried to get them to substantiate sexual abuse—as if that were a crime or evidence of parental unfitness.

This point in the process is the most dangerous to the protective parent, even if travel through the social service maze has been successful so far. If one court is empowered to hear abuse and another is empowered to hear custody, the case may be transferred; then evidence of abuse may not be admissible because the case is not in the right court to hear about it. As though abuse were not relevant to custody determinations, judges often rule that if a prior court proceeding hearing abuse was transferred or consolidated into the custody forum, the transfer effectively prevents the "contestants for custody" from using evidence of abuse developed in the other court. Therefore, by the simple expedient of suing for custody in the midst of a child-abuse trial, an alleged molester can whisk the evidence into no-man's-land, as the custody judge will not hear it and the abuse judge has given up jurisdiction to hear it. Without cooperation from the social service agency or the county attorney (who represents the social service agency), the protective parent cannot prevent this kind of legalistic sleight of hand from destroying a perfectly valid child-protection proceeding.

Worse yet, the fact that the protective parent believed that there was sexual abuse can now be used against her in a custody proceeding (called "interference with visitation" or "anti-spousal behavior"), whereas the valid reasons for her belief are excluded from the proceedings. Since she cannot adduce the evidence that would show she had a sound reason to believe her child was molested, she is left without a defense against the charge that she deliberately tried to alienate the child from the father, against whom, by now—at least in this court—there is "no evidence."

DISPOSITION AND PUNISHMENT OF THE VICTIMS, THE FINAL STOP

After a case has been examined by social services, bounced around through county government, examined by professionals, subjected to the vagaries of prosecutors and courts, and handled and mishandled by lawyers, it is almost impossible to pinpoint where in the system things went wrong. Even narrating and documenting such a case becomes nearly insurmountable because at any juncture there can be half a dozen twists. It would take a person of enormous strength to get through this maze and still remain calm and in control at all times, especially if her child is at risk or, worse yet, still being abused. As a result, "mistakes" pile up that are later charged against the protective parent: she should not have said this, she should not have done that, she should have gone to a different doctor, hired a different lawyer, made sure a certain subpoena was issued, made a particular call, not made that call, etc., etc., *ad nauseam.*

At the end of this travail, most victimized mothers and their advocates mistakenly identify one piece of the puzzle as "the problem," often picking the moment when they were the most shocked or astounded. One mother insists that interviews should be videotaped because children are often intimidated; another thinks that medical examinations should always be done with colposcopes so photographs can record the results; another wants judges hearing custody cases to be required to consider certain kinds of evidence; another believes that prosecutors should be legally required to issue whatever subpoenas the complaining witnesses demand. Although all these arguments can lead to attempts to change the law or pass new ones designed to make the system work, the impassioned and fragmented responses of victims and their bedraggled advocates have never changed the big picture.

We argue that the system is in fact working—in the way it has chosen to work. No matter which adjustment we support, it will continue to do what it chooses in response. The political and practical reality is that the goal of the system is to perpetuate itself and the policies, written and unwritten, by which it has already chosen to operate. Table 2 summarizes the steps involved in traversing the system as well as the possible pitfalls that may arise at each step.

The system as we have outlined it appears capricious at best and unreliable at worst. This does not mean, however, that children are never protected from sexual abuse. It is important to remember that our overview is applicable primarily to incest cases, or cases of intra-familial sexual abuse. A somewhat different set of principles applies in cases involving stranger molesters. Some steps in the system are the same for both kinds of cases, but others differ, depending on the identity and legal rights of the named perpetrators. Strangers do not have inalienable rights over a child and cannot sue for custody. Even in criminal court, different procedures are used, and these, in turn, affect civil proceedings. For example, a biological father accused of molesting his own child is usually given an exculpatory polygraph by the prosecutor's office. If he doesn't want to submit to the test, or if he takes it and fails, that is not used against him, since the test is not admissible as evidence. However, if he passes the test the charges against him are usually dismissed immediately. Strangers accused of molesting children are not given the same courtesy. Table 3 shows the difference between the system's approach to familial and non-familial sexual abuse cases.

The bottom line is that a child is more likely to be protected by the system from a stranger-molester (from whom his own parents can protect him) than from an incest perpetrator.

WHY DOES THE SYSTEM WORK THIS WAY?

A major theory that backlash was responsible for the failure of the child protection system was advanced by David Hechler in *The Battle and the Backlash* (1988). In the early 1980s the highly publicized McMartin Preschool trial in California and similar sensational prosecutions created the impression that the system designed to protect children from sexual abuse had generated a witch hunt. After an expensive two-year trial, with hundreds of witnesses, ended in acquittal, it was easy for the public to believe that the "child-savers" were overreacting and that sexual abuse allegations were often groundless.

In our view, the backlash theory does not apply to incest, a special subgroup of child sexual abuse. It confuses allegedly overzealous prosecutions of day-care cases with age-old passive reactions to incest cases, although they are vastly different. The media continue to use a different standard when covering incest or reporting stories of stranger, day-care, and clergy sexual abuse. Prosecutors have learned from their early mistakes and have achieved many successful prosecutions of non-family child molesters, some resulting in lengthy prison sentences. The cries of "witch hunt," however, include and even focus on incest cases, which were never regularly and vigorously prosecuted, and in which the press took very little interest.

TABLE 2.
The Child Protection System and Its Pitfalls

Step in Process	What Should Occur	What Can Go Wrong
Initial call for help	If the call is a mandated report, CPS should investigate by taking detailed information from the mandated reporter, then from the child and others.	CPS can choose to ignore information from the mandated reporter and can even obtain a new "expert" to contradict the report.
	If the call is not a mandated report, intake worker should record details and arrange contact with the child while the child is away from the alleged perpetrator.	Intake worker can ignore call by making a discretionary decision that it is not valid. Or he can interview the child in the presence of the alleged perpetrator.
Initial CPS investigation	Child should be contacted in a way that encourages trust, allows disclosure, and discourages abuse of the system by any party.	Child can be deprived of contact with protective parent in a way that causes her to fear CPS intervention and results in failure to disclose and even recanting.
Validation	One highly qualified professional should perform an in-depth validation interview with the child, taking time to gain the child's trust so child will feel comfortable disclosing.	One person can, by her own disbelief, "invalidate" a disclosure; if one person validates, repeated procedures can be ordered, resulting in a later "invalidation" that allows the alleged perpetrator's lawyer to attack the credibility of any prior "validations." The process can cause a child to recant.

What Can Fix It	New Problems Arising from "Fix"	Comparison of Status Quo and "Solution"
A requirement that mandated reporter making a call be involved in the final administrative and adjudicative process.	Mandated reporters will not wish to be involved in the entire process; future mandated reports will be chilled.	Now, mandated reporters may overcome their reluctance to get involved if their involvement can end peacably once the information is reported. The specter of intense involvement in litigation may chill reports.
A requirement that the intake worker report every contact; that CPS investigate every report by interviewing child away from the alleged perpetrator.	Will encourage defensive cross-reports by alleged perpetrators to make it seem that just as much suspicion falls upon protective parent; and child would be subjected to repeated interviews, at least half of them depriving her of the supportive contact of her protective parent, possibly causing her to "recant" in self-defense.	Adding technical requirements to the system without making fundamental changes may proliferate opportunities to manipulate the system. It will become even more unwieldy and unresponsive and will generate an even greater sense of frustration and mistrust.
Nearly impossible to fix. With the present system subject to adversary court proceedings, interviews with children are distorted by legalistic demands.		
Training validators to be more effective; give validations more weight; prevent "invalidations" from being ordered to follow validations.	Wide discretion in whether a validator "believes" a child's disclosure and the lack of a standard method for conducting validation interviews can lead to new difficulties.	System of validation will remain dependent on the personal reactions of the individual validator, whether he be the first, second, or sixth to interact with the child. No amount of training will prevent dangerous error. Belief is subjective and will remain so.

TABLE 2. (cont.)
The Child Protection System and Its Pitfalls

Step in Process	What Should Occur	What Can Go Wrong
Collection of Forensic Evidence to Corroborate Disclosure	If a child discloses the kind of sexual abuse that would normally be expected to produce physical findings, such as repeated vigorous vaginal or anal penetration, there should be a medical evaluation.	In 80 percent of cases of actual child sexual abuse, the medical finding is "normal," indicating no medical evidence consistent with a history of sexual abuse. This can be misinterpreted to mean that there was no abuse. If medical findings are consistent with abuse, the medical examination cannot identify a particular perpetrator, except when semen is present in the child's body and that semen is DNA-tested.
Law enforcement authorities are brought into the case for possible prosecution of the perpetrator	Police who are trained to handle child sexual abuse cases work together with the CPS personnel to present to the prosecutor a *prima facie* case. Prosecutor gathers the evidence and prosecutes, or presents the alleged perpetrator with the situation and obtains a plea bargain.	Police can misinterpret and contaminate disclosure or behavioral evidence. Prosecutors can choose not to prosecute. Acquittal can be referred to as "evidence of no abuse." Defendant can use an exculpatory polygraph to undo the case, but a failed polygraph cannot be used to convict. Evidence of the protective parent cooperating with the prosecution can be turned against her and used to show in a later civil proceeding that she was vindictive, hurting chances of protecting the child from further abuse.

What Can Fix It

There is no way to make forensic evidence gathering more predictable, reliable, and useful. Because all medical evidence will ultimately be subjected to adversarial attack on its credibility, it is just as well not collected since it traumatizes the victim and does not identify the perpetrator, except in cases of rape reported within hours. Then undeniable evidence can be collected immediately with minimal harm to the victim. Otherwise, this phase is extremely resistant to improvement of any kind.

Train police to be sensitive and skilled in their contacts with children so as not to cause confusion and "conflict" in the evidence; encourage prosecutors to devote attention and care to child sexual abuse cases. Provide prosecutors with technical assistance on reaching successful results in child sexual abuse cases; allocate more resources to making incest prosecutions feasible.

New Problems Arising from "Fix"

New procedures or laws will cause more problems than they can solve. Insisting that all examinations be performed with a colposcope will give rise to "broken equipment" cases. Insisting on corroborative examinations will cause conflicts among professionals. Insisting that findings of "consistent with history of sexual abuse" be treated as positive for abuse will give rise to legal pressure against professionals making such findings.

Problems caused by enhanced prosecution cannot be overcome. Because of the need to protect constitutional rights of criminal defendants, every movement toward more effective prosecution will have an opposite reaction by the defense, which is already deadly effective in incest cases. Child-friendly police interviews in New Jersey gave rise to appellate upset of a child sexual abuse case because the police had allegedly "bribed" children into disclosing; prosecutorial zeal has caused backlash activity; the more

Comparison of Status Quo and "Solution"

No comparison is possible. In Rockland County, New York, an assistant county attorney reported that she lost a case in which a DNA test of a fetus in a pregnant teenager proved that the biological father was the man accused of molesting the girl. Since the problem in child protection is not the lack of forensic evidence, the problem cannot be solved by improving the process of collecting that evidence.

No improvement can be expected from concentrating on prosecution of incest offenders. When there is a conviction, the sentence does not necessarily protect the child, and the danger of violating constitutional rights of the alleged perpetrator far outweigh the benefits of trying to improve this phase of the process.

TABLE 2. (cont.)
The Child Protection System and Its Pitfalls

Step in Process	What Should Occur	What Can Go Wrong
Adjudication in a child abuse proceeding	CPS takes the case to court and county attorney proves to the judge by clear and convincing evidence that the child has been abused by the named perpetrator; resulting in protection for the child.	Alleged perpetrator can institute custody proceedings, short-circuiting the entire process; or the child-abuse proceeding itself can become a custody case in disguise, with a finding of "no abuse" causing the court to make a "dispositional decision" giving custody to the alleged abuser.

What Can Fix It	New Problems Arising from "Fix"	Comparison of Status Quo and "Solution"
	(cont.) attention is devoted to prosecution, the more formidable becomes the focus on the rights of the alleged perpetrators, not the protection of the child.	
Separate child-abuse proceedings from custody proceedings; put a stay on custody proceedings while child-abuse proceedings are pending; new laws to educate judges.	If custody and child abuse were required to remain separate, judges could find "no abuse" first and then change custody in an "unrelated decision."	Real changes cannot be effected as long as judges use the standard "best interests" to decide a child's fate. A finding of "no abuse" is possible regardless of the evidence and regardless of the law; changes here are academic.

INCEST VERSUS SEXUAL ABUSE
BY A NON-FAMILY PERPETRATOR

According to a study conducted by Ellen Gray in 1993, child molesters convicted of sexual abuse are treated differently in the criminal justice system
depending on whether the victims were their own or other people's children.
For incest, the accused is likely to be "sentenced" to psychotherapy, while
for molesting someone else's child, he is more likely to go to jail.

In the early 1970s, in Atlanta, Faye Yager alleged incest against her estranged husband. The evidence included the fact that her toddler had
gonorrhea, as did the father. Yet he was awarded custody, and Faye was deprived of visitation and contact. Years later, the father was arrested on an
unrelated child pornography charge and was finally prosecuted—but only for
sexual offenses against other people's children, not against his own daughter.

In response to the treatment she and her daughter had received in the
courts, Yager became director of the Mothers' Underground Railroad. She
boldly declared on national television that she had created and ran a network
to hide mothers of abused children from the courts, the FBI, and sexual and
satanic ritual abusers.

Why does the system operate in such different ways for a molester-father
and a molester-stranger? Society is obviously uncomfortable with the idea
of sexual abuse, even more so when the abuser is the biological father. It is
possible to accept the image of the stranger in a trench coat on a park bench
lusting after little girls playing hopscotch, but it is nearly impossible in our culture to accept the image of a doctor, lawyer, teacher, preacher, psychologist,
judge, or singer bathing his toddler daughter in the evening, penetrating her
genitals with his soapy fingers, and orally sodomizing her. We just cannot
afford such images in the American tableau.

The image of the American family must be kept paramount. The child
protective system is really a family protective system, as the name often tac-
itly admits. Children must be removed from danger, but they must not be
removed from families, for families are presumed to be protective units for
their own members. We cannot as a society give up this impression any
more than a molested child can give up her impression of her parents as
loving protectors, regardless of the facts. Removing children from danger,
then, fits into two categories: protecting children from the danger of *anti-
child* behaviors, which includes prosecution of non-family molesters such as
day-care workers; and protecting children from *anti-family* behaviors, which
includes punishment of any conduct perceived as attacks on the acceptable
image of the family.

Ironically, it is the second category which is invoked by those who wish to
demonstrate how unfairly the system treats accused parents for relatively
minor infractions. For example, a set of intact parents who are public drunks,
who allow their children to become unsightly and to annoy neighbors, stand

a very good chance of losing those children—not because of specific findings of abuse, but because they damage the public idea of how a family should look to the outside world. In a case which reached the Supreme Court, a couple were deprived of their six children for no crimes more serious than having created disturbances in the neighborhood. Children have been removed from parents who were bi-racial, who were homosexual, who were living in communal situations outside the accepted norm of their neighborhoods, or who otherwise differed from the public perception of the way families should appear. No showing of abuse by clear and convincing evidence, no grueling series of interrogations and interviews of the children, no proof of irreparable harm, no testimony of experts was considered necessary. The social workers "knew" and the judges confirmed that it was in the children's best interests—particularly if they were healthy, attractive children—to be removed from the unsightly or politically incorrect environment they were born into, and placed in foster care or put up for adoption by "good" families instead.

THE TWO SYSTEMS: A CASE OF DOUBLE BOOKKEEPING

We say that the system is failing if social workers do not adequately investigate cases, but rely on prejudices to make decisions that endanger children and punish innocent mothers. But in our view the system is *not* failing; it is working the way it was meant to work. In fact, there are two systems—the overt and the covert. The overt aspect comprises all the structures set in place for child protection: CPS, professionals, courts, and judges. The covert system involves the same structures but its goals are different; namely, to preserve the father-headed family and to protect the overt system from the complaints that inevitably occur when cases are mishandled. Outside authorities are rarely aware of these complaints because the covert system operates under a cloak of secrecy.

Since it has never been stated that there are two systems, ordinary people naturally believe that the system functions in a straight-forward manner, until they experience the duplicity themselves. Their first response is usually disbelief. People are willing to accept the fact that overworked officials can make honest mistakes, or that poorly screened foster families may turn out to be abusive. They are not prepared, however, for officials who deliberately invalidate children's disclosures, call them liars, vilify their mothers for supporting their allegations, and conspire to take children away from protective parents and hand them over to molesters.

Our system of child protection incorporates contradictory principles: on the one hand, of protecting children from harm; and on the other, of preserving the image of the family, which requires that it not interfere with the victimization of children within the family. It reviles child sexual abuse at the

TABLE 3.
Incest Offender vs. Non-Family Molester

Step in Process	Treatment of Incest Offender	Treatment of Non-Family Molester
Initial Call	CPS process invoked if the call is considered "valid" by the intake worker.	Parents are directed to notify police at once.
CPS Investigation	Even if initial protection is arranged, the child is required to visit the alleged perpetrator under supervision almost immediately, and her conduct with him in supervised visitation is recorded to be used as "evidence" either that she gets along with him or that her protective mother is turning her against him.	Child is immediately protected from contact with the molester; usually the police clearly tell the accused that he may not try to contact the child, who will presumably be a witness against him. Parents are supported, not blamed, for their actions in protecting their child from contact with the accused.
Forensics	No matter what the findings from the first forensic examination, the accused incest offender is permitted to challenge them and to have the child subjected to further testing; even positive results are disregarded and considered useless in identifying the perpetrator.	CPS will usually believe the child about the identity of the molester, so if there is physical evidence, the forensic expert is considered an ally and not attacked for his inability to identify the perpetrator. Defendant is not allowed to order "second opinions."
Police Investigation	Police tend to avoid incest cases and detailed investigations; they rarely issue search warrants, and they look for improper motives on the part of complaining witnesses.	Police are usually very aggressive and efficient; they tend to issue search warrants, develop evidence in the neighborhood, and even stake out the alleged perpetrator.

Step in Process	Treatment of Incest Offender	Treatment of Non-Family Molester
Prosecution	Prosecutors usually give the alleged incest offender a chance to take an exculpatory polygraph test; if he passes, all charges are dropped. If he fails, he can repeat the test, get a voice-stress test, or get his own polygraph. If the prosecution goes forward, the accused is usually allowed to plead out to "child endangerment" and accept therapy as a sentence. If there is a plea bargain that does not admit actual incest, or if there is an acquittal, that can form the basis of a new custody case as if he were "proved innocent."	Prosecutors may become extremely blood-thirsty with non-family sex offenders, and may even try to get the press involved to show how tough they are on them. The stranger molester cannot evade prosecution by taking a polygraph test. He can rarely plead out to lesser crimes. He is likely to go to jail, especially to be made an example before election time. If he forces the proceeding to a jury trial, the prosecution often works very hard and the media often cover the case. Even if the accused is acquitted, the child is rarely allowed to see him again, and other children are often kept away.

same time as it protects incest. The following are some of the ploys the covert system uses to deal with the paradox of the incest taboo.

"IT'S O.K. TO TELL"

Social service agency offices are often plastered with signs urging children to "tell" if they are molested, but paradoxically, their employees often call the children liars and urge them to recant once they do "tell." In one such office, two Maryland girls were looking at a pamphlet from an organization fighting child abuse. The cover had a drawing of a child's face with tears pouring down her cheeks; the caption read: "Keep Telling and Telling till Someone Listens." The older girl turned to the mother and said, "That's exactly what we've been doing but no one is listening."

The campaign to encourage children to "tell if someone touched [them] with a bad touch instead of a good touch" or touched them "where their bathing suit covered" gained momentum in the 1980s and continues unabated with promises of understanding and sensitivity toward the victims, help through counseling, and assurances that what happened was not the children's fault. But what really happens when children "tell" is very different from what is promised, as the two Maryland girls learned. They are often treated cruelly and blamed for the problem by the very authorities who urged them to "tell."

The organization that produced the pamphlet described above had on its advisory board Jane R., a mental health professional who was frequently appointed by the courts to evaluate incest cases. One of her cases involved six-year-old Wendy, whose mother had left her marriage after, and as a result of, Wendy's disclosure of incest by her father. Wendy's mother reported that after several therapy sessions, the child complained bitterly that "Miss Jane" did not believe her. Indeed, Jane R. told Wendy's mother she did not believe the allegations because this was "a divorce case." A few days after a therapy session with Jane R., we spoke to Wendy.

Q: Wendy, did you see Miss Jane the other day?

W: [Nods in the affirmative.]

Q: OK. Did you like that?

W: [Shakes her head emphatically in the negative.]

Q: Oh. How come? What did you talk about?

W: [Hangs her head silently, reaches for her mother.]

Q: Did you talk about your mommy?

W: [Nods] She said my mommy lied to me, but I told her, *no* [shakes her head vigorously to demonstrate] because my mommy didn't lie!

Q: Oh. OK. Did you talk about your daddy?

W: [Hangs her head silently.]

Q: Did she tell you anything about your daddy?

W: [Emphatically, loudly] She said my *daddy didn't ever hurt me* but he *did*!

This incident is a good example of the contradictory principles being expressed within an organization purporting to combat child abuse. We reported Wendy's case to the organization, asking it to mediate with Jane R. on the child's behalf. Instead they defended not the child but Jane R., noting that the judge who appointed her had recently sentenced a stranger-molester to a long prison term. The instruction "It's OK to tell" preserves the impression that children are being protected from sexual abuse, and they may in fact be protected, but only from sexual abuse by strangers. It preserves the sanctity of the father-headed nuclear family, by defending children whose fathers are willing to help protect them from stranger-molesters; but it simultaneously condemns as "lies" any allegations children make about incest by their own fathers.

THE CRAZY MOTHER, A SELF-FULFILLING PROPHECY

The "crazy mother" was invented by the lawyers who specialize in defending men against allegations of sexual abuse of their own children or stepchildren. Many articles and books have been published advising such fathers or stepfathers to sue immediately for divorce and custody of the children who made such allegations, and to divert the focus of the investigation from those allegations to the mother's "vindictive" or "psychologically impaired" behavior. In fact, advice given to trial lawyers in these cases is to question the mother as to why she believes the child was molested. The mother's belief is actually used as a negative diagnostic device: if she firmly believes the child, she is deemed "crazy" and the allegations are then considered false because of her craziness.

In May 1994, New York State Senator David A. Paterson conducted hearings on a high-profile sexual abuse–custody case. The prosecutor had dropped sexual assault charges against the father in spite of enough evidence to constitute a *prima facie* case. Paterson was astounded to learn that the prosecutor had dropped the case because he had been told that the victim's mother was crazy. Paterson said, "I am sure that many accused criminal defendants in this state would be delighted to learn that the charges against them could be dropped if the victims' mothers were considered crazy!"

There is, unfortunately, a certain self-fulfilling prophecy to the "crazy mother" myth. Mothers who try to advocate for and protect their children (which is what mothers are normally expected to do) are subjected to court proceedings where the evidence relating to the real issue of sexual abuse is completely ignored. They are threatened, belittled, mistreated, and bullied by their own lawyers; abandoned in frustrated desperation by their own families; and blamed and betrayed by many professionals whom they formerly trusted. Often they become so stressed that they suffer from a variety of serious reactions, including acute attacks of anxiety and depression. One mother said pathetically, "If I were not driven crazy by what they have done to me, I really would be nuts!" After two or three years in this system, most normal people would become suspicious and hostile and would suffer from feelings of depression and guilt. The following refrains are often heard: "I should have done it differently"; "I should never have told"; "I should have run away"; "I should never have tried to run"; "I should have stayed with him"; "I should never have married him"; "I should never have had children"; "I should have killed him when I found out."

SEARCHING FOR THE SCUTTLE FISH

The scuttle fish has devised a clever way to evade capture by its natural enemies. When under attack, it exudes an inky black substance which darkens the water around it so that it cannot be found. In sexual abuse cases, there is an analogous defense, "We will never really know what happened." It begins when a mother enters the system, bearing whatever data she has. She is interviewed at length. Notes are made. She is advised to bring in papers and evidence. A dizzying series of fits and starts stresses even the sanest and calmest of mothers, adding layer upon layer of persons who advise and control her while the abuse allegations are investigated. Calls and contacts proliferate. The mother is told by one how to deal with the other, by the other how to deal with the first, and all the while they consult with one another on how to deal with the mother. In many cases, at the outset, the mother is advised to get a lawyer. This is not a logical first step, and should perhaps tip her off that something is wrong. After all, if she is seeking the help of a public agency designed to protect children, why should she need a lawyer? But the addition of a lawyer complicates rather than simplifies. More copies, more explanations. Finally, from the rat's nest of communications there arises the summation that "This is an extremely complicated case and no one can tell what happened, whether the child was abused or not, whether the mother is crazy or not." Searching for the scuttle fish thus involves the deliberate creation of confusion in order to obscure the truth, leading to the conclusion that the truth will never be found—because of the volume of the confusion—and that conclusion is considered an end in itself.

SOLUTIONIZING

In the midst of this appalling social disease, responsible journalists and professionals have brought the problem to the attention of politicians, jurists, officials, and legislators. In order to appear to their constituents and the press that they are concerned about child sexual abuse, these persons have created their own formula for dealing with the problem; the word we have coined for this process is "solutionizing."

Solutionizing probably developed from a related but less elaborate device that has long been used to deal with such problems: the "rhetorical response." Rhetorical responses can take care of ordinary citizens and activists, giving them a feeling that they have done something positive, after which they can go home. It consists mainly of appreciative commentary, public relations gestures, meetings, seminars, and assurances that the concerns are being addressed. Solutionizing is a more aggressive activity aimed at the more persistent and energetic advocates. Since it often involves funding, experts have raised solutionizing itself to an art. Extreme examples of institutional solutionizing are geared to satisfying the "new breed" of advocates and members of the public who demand action. Solutionizing channels frustration and rage away from the causes and causers—of the problem by creating intermediate "solutions" which are not solutions at all, but which use up money, energy, and time to create the illusion that they are really addressing the problem. Serious solutionizing almost always achieves its goals.

For example, one may approach a legislative panel and show that the Department of Human Resources deliberately covered up sexual abuse. The panel may pass a resolution, appoint a task force on child sexual abuse, fund it, and assign it to work for two years, putting the advocates through their paces, making and meeting deadlines, compiling and analyzing, after which it will report that one in three girls and one in five boys are molested before the age of eighteen. Neither the original problem nor the cases used for examples will have been affected in the least. The budgets will have been used up and the advocates are either satisfied and gratified or exhausted and embittered.

Until we have a structure that can stop a person molesting a child, we have solutionizing rather than solutions. The immediate problem is not seen as "a child being molested" but as "a person complaining about a child being molested." Taking care of the person who is saying that the child is being molested is considered a solution to the problem. If the complaining does not stop, then another solutionizing response is always available, but no action is taken to stop the molestation.

Solutionizing involves several established roles that are acted out, consciously or unconsciously, in prescribed ways. These roles are taken by professionals whose presumed function in the overt system is contradicted by their actual behavior in the covert system. The players include mothers' attorneys, children's guardians *ad litem,* health care professionals, government or court-appointed specialists, and judges.

Guardians ad litem. There may be confusion about this term and the role of guardians *ad litem.* Under recently developed programs, lay persons— often dedicated volunteers—may testify on behalf of children in court proceedings. We have not observed pervasive problems with such persons or programs. On the other hand, attorneys hired or appointed by the courts to represent children have often generated or aggravated problems in child abuse cases and have frequently ignored the rights and interests of their child clients. In some unfortunate instances, they do not meet the children they represent, as in the Carter case (see Chapter 3). Some court-appointed lawyers openly advocate for the rights of alleged molesters. In Wendy's case, the court-appointed guardian *ad litem* told the mother's attorney, "I don't care what [the father] did to [the child]; he has a right to visitation." The true role of the guardian *ad litem* is to make it seem that the child was ably and fairly represented.

Mothers' Attorneys. It is often said that mothers fare worse than fathers in these proceedings because they have less money and cannot afford good attorneys. This is only partly true, for even mothers who are wealthy have not been well served.

Mothers' attorneys often try to get their clients to be compliant and cooperative, and to go along with whatever the system wants, even when they believe sexual abuse occurred or detect procedural irregularities or illegalities. The lawyer representing Wendy's mother did not object to the guardian *ad litem* openly advocating for the father. One of the attorneys for Anne Backman advised her to teach her children to accept sexual abuse. Another attorney for a mother prevented the issuance of a warrant against the alleged perpetrator and actually advised her client not to try to retrieve her children. Mothers' attorneys, contrary to their overt role, often do not advocate vigorously for the mothers, do not object to damaging motions brought by the opposing side, do not appeal erroneous rulings, do not depose relevant witnesses—all the things that fathers' attorneys can be expected to do. As a result, the written law reflects the overt system, with reported cases showing the system working well and fairly, since the mothers' attorneys have not, in general, created appellate records of its persistent and inexplicable failure. The mother's attorney's role in the covert system is to help control the mother and keep her from becoming a problem by recognizing the realities too early.

Health Care Professionals and Service Providers. The role of CPS workers and health professionals in the covert system is to create sufficient confusion so that the scuttle fish cannot be found. They then take the position that the mother should stop worrying about sexual abuse because nobody can figure out whether or not it happened; thus it is unhealthy to "focus" on it. If the mother continues to be concerned, she is accused of psychologically abusing her children. This argument may be used even in the presence of a finding of sexual abuse. In the MacIntyre case in Oklahoma, a psychologist actually said that, although the five-year-old had probably been molested by her father, the child would repress the abuse as long as her mother did not "focus" on it. He said the healthy response was the father's response—to forget about it. In the H case, a Maryland psychologist found Mary psychologically impaired because of her continued fear about the safety of her child with a convicted child molester; since he had been in therapy for six months and was declared "rehabilitated," she was considered overly anxious.

Physical evidence is disposed of in a number of ways by professionals who operate simultaneously in the overt and covert systems: 1. Torn hymenal tissue has been attributed to causes other than sexual abuse, such as birth defects or diaper cream, even if those alternative explanations are extremely implausible or downright ridiculous. 2. The physical findings can be acknowledged but the abuse can be attributed to an unknown molester, not the named perpetrator, even if the child insists she knows who did it. 3. A new professional sympathetic to the perpetrator can be asked to repeat a physical examination weeks or months later and will find "no corroboration" of the evidence of abuse. Professionals asked to deliver a second opinion are immune to attack on cross-examination: no findings, no evidence, no way to contradict them. The covert-system role of such health-care professionals is to create an impression of genuine effort to establish the facts, while exonerating the rest of the system for its own incompetence and inaction.

Judges. Family court proceedings do not involve juries. Ordinarily a single family court judge conducts a trial, and his or her prejudices rule the proceedings absolutely. The only way to overturn a decision is to purchase expensive transcripts of the entire trial and appeal, citing frank and clear legal error or "abuse of discretion." But in a custody–abuse case, the judge's discretion is nearly absolute, there is little accountability, and appeals are rarely successful. Some judges do not concern themselves scrupulously with the "weight of the evidence." They make decisions for a variety of reasons, including personal misogyny and indignation at the actions of disobedient women; some actually identify with accused molesters. In a Florida case where the protective mother of an abused child was herself a lawyer, a judge admitted under oath that his custody decision was not based on the best interests of the child but on the fact that the mother had disobeyed a court order.

The cornerstone of legal proceedings in custody cases is the "sacred court order principle." It is not unusual for judges to consider obedience to their orders for unsupervised visitation with alleged molesters more important than avoiding the possible rape of a child. Such judges do not try to hide their positions, and in only one case that we know of—that of Mary H—was there an appellate decision that gave legal consideration to a mother's right to protect her child from incest in violation of the "sacred court order."

"Abuse of discretion" is extremely hard to prove because a judge is the sole arbiter of the credibility of the evidence. Thus a solid case with expert testimony can be dismissed if the judge simply says (s)he does not believe it. Even legal error is difficult to prove. Judges sometimes create evidence they wish to rely upon in making their decisions. For example, Judge John Kastengood of Annapolis, Maryland, who casually describes incest cases as "follow[ing] an all too familiar pattern," discovered experts who express opinions that are wondrously consonant with his own beliefs. He wanted those therapists to evaluate two girls who had alleged abuse, expecting in advance that their opinion would support his intent to "decide" that there was none. He faced a problem, however: these experts were in Philadelphia and he, a Maryland judge, lacked the authority to order the mother to take her children out of state for the evaluation. When she resisted, he issued an order—illegal on its face—directing a Maryland sheriff to take the children by force to Philadelphia and deliver them to the therapist. Faced with this threat, the mother capitulated, to protect her daughters from the trauma of being seized by police officers, driven over state lines, handed over to hostile "therapists," and forced to spend the night in a hotel with armed law enforcement officers. No appeal or civil rights lawsuit after the fact would help her children; thus Judge Kastengood remains untouched and, as a practical matter, untouchable, even after breaking the law so blatantly.

A judge, furthermore, can control the evidence, making it very hard to identify what is really happening in the overt and covert systems. He can call frank physical evidence "not a scintilla of evidence" if he disbelieves it; he can rule that a psychologist is not credible because he does not believe his testimony; he can pronounce an alleged molester a perfectly fit parent by using his own subjective standards; he can decide that allegations of incest were all the fault of a mother who was vindictive; and he can prevent the underlying facts from getting out.

Family court judges are rarely held accountable by the public because they operate in secrecy. They can issue "gag orders" to prevent litigants from turning to the public and activist organizations for help. They can seal files so evidence never sees the light of day or the limelight of media. The media, meanwhile, insist upon the production of documentation—which is unavailable to the victims—to prove the validity of the horror stories they hear. Even when testifying before Congress, citizens may be denied the right to divulge information from the family courts. Senator Joseph Biden once warned protective mother Annette Garner, in public Judiciary Committee hearings held on May 16, 1989, that she could not reveal "gagged" information from her own case because he did not want to share a jail cell with her! A judge in a sex-abuse custody case can gag the parties and even restrain the press by suggesting that knowledge of the molestation would be harmful to the child. Thus judges routinely protect themselves from exposure and opprobrium by seeming protective of children's anonymity. These cases are never exposed to public censure; thus, evidence of the existence of the covert system is within control of the system itself, not its victims.

The role of judges in the covert system is to protect its operation by rewriting history in their decisions. Their orders are legal press releases that tell the story the system wants told; as a result, the outside world cannot prove that the realities are any different from the reportable events.

CONVINCING THE NON-BELIEVER

The public activist trying to break through the solutionizing network of the nonprofit and governmental worlds generally meets two kinds of people: those who believe the system is working because they cannot afford to believe otherwise; and those who know it is not working but who feel powerless to change it. Since those in the first group cannot give up their beliefs, they must find alternative explanations. They may adopt the position that the mother (or even the child advocates) caused the system to fail by being "too zealous." They may feel that caseworkers made mistakes because they were overworked and underpaid. They may feel that the judge "didn't believe" the allegations because the father's lawyer was so convincing or political. They can never be convinced that the system is designed to perform what they regard as a series of truly imponderable acts.

The "non-believer," however, knows that the system is not working, usually from first-hand experience, but generally reacts with helplessness and, in self-defense, avoids future involvement. In 1990 a prominent child psychiatrist refused to help a mother in order to avoid "sharing her helplessness." He stated that his colleagues would refuse for the same reason; they did not fear legal processes, retribution from the abuser, or hostility from CPS workers: they feared helplessness.

Helplessness is the real American taboo. Doctors who doubt that their testimony on behalf of abused children will be respected feel helpless, so they decline to testify. Lawyers who anticipate that a case will generate endless trouble for little or no money feel helpless, so they avoid those cases. Judges who expect to be overturned on appeal avoid bringing the gavel down on their own careers. Throughout the system, the helplessness of the child facing incest is mirrored in adults who can keep out of it by feigned disbelief or refusal to get involved.

A New Jersey journalist who had written several stories about corruption and ineptness in local government was asked to write about an ongoing incest case which was being mishandled in the same system. She said, "You are asking me to take on the entire system and change it—I can't do that!" A New York emergency room physician presented with a four-year-old girl who seemed to have venereal disease refused to keep the child in protective custody and report suspected abuse until the cultures came back from the laboratory. Since previous medical evidence of abuse had been disregarded, she concluded, "If all these people failed already, what can I do? I can't fix the system!" Therapists, physicians, professionals, journalists, even chaplains often recognize and avoid requests to share the helplessness of protectors of sexually victimized children. They don't want to be criticized, scorned, sued, labeled as "zealots," or forced to bear the negative consequences that accrue in these cases, and they recognize that their chances of protecting children from incest in this system are often slim.

PROFESSIONALS WHO REFUSE TO PLAY THE GAME

Some professionals, of course, do get involved and stand by their belief that children they have treated need protection. The common response of the system is to disbelieve them, call them "hired guns," and explain away their findings. Other professionals are appointed to reevaluate their cases and present different findings. Judges can then exercise their discretion to believe the opposing professionals. Mary Froning, the therapist who supported the child's disclosures in the Morgan-Foretich case, was attacked in the press and was sued. Professionals who refuse to play the roles assigned in the covert system are criticized, ridiculed, ostracized, threatened and punished with lawsuits, subjected to professional complaints, and publicly defamed for believing and supporting children and for reporting incest.

Adults are in control of the entire system. They tend to empathize with other adults not with children. They tend to empathize with those who represent the system not with those who criticize it. They also tend to empathize with the accused not with the victim, and to adopt the indignant position that it is socially disruptive to accuse upstanding citizens of disgusting acts. They have a hard time empathizing with powerless people such as battered women and molested children. Powerful adults know how to maintain the *status quo* and how to use the system, even to manipulate it—skills not shared by children or disadvantaged women.

"Children often lie" is the rallying cry of the person defending the conduct of the system. But adults lie to children, and most egregiously when they tempt those children to "tell" about incest, when, in fact, they will not be believed and protected and may be viciously punished for doing so. The system fails because it is working so well in its all-pervasive failure mode. This does not have to continue, if our society decides to discontinue it. If social workers were held responsible for damage to children who were molested after disclosing prior abuse, if judges lost their positions on the bench for exposing children to risk, if doctors were paying huge malpractice claims for failing to detect and report evidence of child sexual abuse, if funding for public agencies depended upon proper performance of their mandates according to overt and recognized standards, if there were any down side at all to system "failure," the pattern would quickly change.

10

The Failure of the Law

The right of a child "not to be abused" is a fluid concept and, strictly speaking, not a defensible legal principle. The language we have for talking about fundamental fairness is a difficult one in general, even more so with respect to children's rights. The child is always on adult turf in the law. For instance, if an adult who comes into your home, as a guest or on business, sits on the wrong sofa or behaves in a manner you dislike, and you scream at him, curse him, and hit him, you will probably be subjected to criminal penalties. At a minimum, he may demand payment for damages, claiming he has suffered outrage, humiliation, headaches, loss of self-esteem, panic attacks, sleeplessness. Tort law is replete with the sufferings an adult may incur if you treat him poorly, even for a few minutes. But if a child—your own child, a relative, a child who is playing in your home, even a child for whom you babysit—displeases you, and you scold him, curse him, humiliate him, scream at him, even slap him (as slong as you do not leave visible scars or marks), the law does not recognize injury.

The law was put in place to protect adult property rights. It applies to the groups (nations, states, organized governments) in which people have agreed to give up some areas of their power in order to protect other areas. People accept law for the protection it offers in controlling their resources. It would be impossible to increase their holdings if they had to devote their time protecting their past accumulations. The law was made by and for people who already had some share in the resources being protected.

In the original score of the opera *Porgy and Bess,* the penniless hero sings:

> Oh, I got plenty o' nuttin'
> An' nuttin's plenty fo' me.
> I got no car, got no mule, I got no misery.
> De folks wid plenty o' plenty got a lock on dey door,
> 'Fraid somebody's agoin' to rob 'em
> While dey's out a makin' more.

The law is the lock on the door of the people with plenty of plenty. Historically, when the men who control the most plenty (the most land, wealth, currency, women, and children) become dissatisfied with the law, that is when the law is changed.

The family is within the "lock on the door" that was designed and placed there by the law. It is the area over which men have been most reluctant to give up power. Until the twentieth century, there had been no serious need for men to protect their rights within the home; nobody had power to challenge them, for women and children had no independent access to resources. The man, as "king within his own castle," was the only person with a key to the lock the law had placed on his door. With the increase in women's independence and the rise in divorce rates, men now need the help of law inside that locked area—within the family—to enforce their previously unchallenged rights.

However, while many women have extricated themselves from male domination, their children have not. Mothers, whose welfare and mobility are constrained by attachments to their children, are often subject to the same lack of freedom that afflicts their children. As men have seen their control over women slipping away, they have reacted by asserting their control over children and over the women bonded to their children more vigorously than ever. Witness the burgeoning Fathers' Rights Movement and the increasing numbers of fathers seeking custody of children. When a child's rights clash with a father's rights, the law has a historical bias in favor of the latter.

We cannot "fix the system" to protect children from sexual abuse by making the law more protective of rights those children do not already have. Several national organizations have assembled petitions in support of a bill of rights for sexually abused children. The idea that children who have been sexually abused are entitled to certain rights they did not previously enjoy is a flawed concept. There is no basis for the abused child's rights if, before being abused, that child did not have the right to avoid or defend against the abuse.

At a meeting of the National Organization of Women (51st State NOW, Washington, D.C.) in Fall 1989, Dr. Elizabeth Morgan made several proposals for legislation regarding child sexual abuse. They would require judges to consider certain kinds of evidence before deciding the custody of children alleging abuse; for example, evidence from an older sibling, if it related to the same alleged perpetrator.

Representatives of the American Bar Association were considering these and similar suggestions when Michelle Etlin objected, characterizing these efforts as "moving the bricks around in a building that has been condemned." Her position, six years before this book was written, was that no amount of adjustment in the requirements for judicial consideration would change the fact that a family court or divorce court judge is permitted to "decide" whether a child had been molested, and whether that child should be forced, against her will, to visit a parent she feared and resisted. In 1990 Etlin proposed an analogy that she felt would be more easily understood:

> If Abraham Lincoln had insisted that slaves had the right to administrative hearing before being whipped, if he had supported a new law that said a slave could apply for medical treatment if irreparable harm could be proven, if he had insisted that owners should not be allowed to rape their slaves, and that if a salve could prove rape she could change owners, would that change the fact that slavery was tolerated in this country, side-by-side with the Constitution and the Bill of Rights? I don't think so! What if we had ameliorated the lot of the slaves so that everyone felt a little better about it? Would that have removed the blight of slavery from this land or would it have merely put a salve on the wounded conscience of the powerful who were willing to tolerate the abomination in the name of law? Just as it is true that slaves could not be free from abuse until they were free, because slavery is itself abuse, just so, children will not be free from sexual abuse until they are free—until they have their rights, including the right not to be raped. The right not to be raped is simply a human right, part and parcel of the right to be human. While children do not have the right to be human, they do not yet enjoy the right not to be raped, and no adjustment in their condition, no number of procedural requirements we place on judges mediating their fate, can or will ever change that.

In our present situation, the right of a child to protection from incest depends on whether the legal environment itself wants to consider the child previously sexually abused. By a mere pronouncement that the child has not been molested, all right to protection vanishes. As long as that determination rests with persons and agencies that have no mandate or accountability for their conduct, it will be impossible to protect children. It would be like trying to protect slaves from abuse while refusing to emancipate them, but saying that they were free to sue their masters.

THE DRED SCOTT DECISION

In the 1840s, a slave known only by the name Rachel sued her master for her freedom and won. He had taken her from a slave state to a "free" one, and then forcibly returned her to the original state. The basis of her lawsuit was that she had become free geographically, under the new state's jurisdiction. On her return to the slave state, she was no longer a slave, since there was no legal method for selling or otherwise enslaving a free person living in a free state. However, she could not sue for emancipation in the slave state, for as a slave there, she had no "standing" to sue. She had to sue her master for assault and battery, which could legally be practiced upon a slave but not upon a free person. Therefore, the court would have to make a preliminary determination on her condition of slavery or freedom—if she had a "standing to sue"—before it could declare the case worthy of the jurisdiction of the court. This strategy had been devised in the South, decades before the Emancipation Proclamation, to protect and free individual black persons.

Rachel's lawyer succeeded in securing her freedom, but that had no implications for another slave, Dred Scott, who sued his master in similar circumstances a few years later. Each case depended on its own "proof" and the individual judge's determinations of its credibility. Dred Scott, a slave in Missouri, sued his owner for assault and battery in 1846. For political reasons, a complex series of lawsuits ultimately involved the federal judiciary, the Congress, and the national and international press. The suit ended in the shameful Dred Scott Decision, in which the United States Supreme Court ruled that black persons had no rights for which they could sue, regardless of the jurisdictional niceties. According to the highest court in the land, interpreting the Constitution long after passage of the Bill of Rights, a white person, as the owner of Dred Scott, could sue for his property rights, but Dred Scott could not sue for his own right to liberty.

In a similar fashion, the law has failed to protect children, who started out, like Dred Scott, with no standing to access protection of their rights unless certain extremely unlikely circumstances and coincidences happened to work in their favor.

THE RIGHT NOT TO BE ABUSED: DISCOVERY AND INSTITUTION

In 1874, eight-year-old Mary Ellen Wilson lived with her stepmother in a New York City apartment. She was horribly abused—starved, beaten, and kept in chains. Neighbors, hearing her screams, complained to the police, who said they could not intervene in "a family matter." A creative social worker wanted to help the child, in spite of the fact that there were no laws empowering her to do so. She extricated Mary Ellen from her misery using a law passed the previous year for the protection of animals. (Gill, 1991:545). This case was widely reported in the press and led to the founding of the New York Society for the Prevention of Cruelty to Children.

In early 1988, hundreds of New Yorkers flocked to the funeral of six-year-old Lisa Steinberg. Flowers and letters poured into the funeral parlor from strangers. The coroner confirmed what the police had instantly guessed—the child had been beaten to death. Private adoption attorney Joel Steinberg and his common-law battered wife, Hedda Nussbaum, were arrested for the crime. A younger child, found tied to a table leg, bruised and starved, was retrieved from the squalor and misery of their locked house. More than a century after the Mary Ellen case, our society is confronting another child abuse crisis, making responses that are strangely different. While Mary Ellen's screams brought a vigorous response from a clever social worker, who found a way to help her despite the absence of laws protecting children, in Lisa's case, the many blatant signs of gross physical abuse were ignored by state-designated social workers who were already legally empowered to intervene. Though they received calls from neighbors and reports of suspected abuse, they ignored and mishandled these complaints until after her death.

Mary Ellen Wilson and Lisa Steinberg are not just two highly unusual cases separated by a century of legal reform and social development. They are hallmarks of their times. The lesson of these two cases is a chilling one for people who would rely on "new laws" to protect children from abuse. The legislature has passed laws for the executive branch to enforce, but the judiciary has shown that no adverse consequences ensue from disregarding them. When Mary Ellen lived, there was no law to protect her from abuse; a hundred years later, when Lisa died, there was a veritable armory of such laws in place, but the system did not choose to utilize them.

THE RIGHT TO PROTECTION FROM ABUSE

Melodie and Randy DeShaney were separated when their son, Joshua, was still an infant. Melodie claimed that her husband was violent and had beaten her horribly. Unable to afford an attorney, she lost the legal battle for Joshua's custody. A Wyoming judge placed Joshua with his father, who promptly moved to Wisconsin and remarried, depriving his ex-wife of visitation opportunities.

Less than two years later, Randy DeShaney's second wife left him, but she went to the police first and reported that her husband had been beating the child severely. The police passed the information to the Department of Social Services (DSS), who interviewed the father, recorded his general denial, and took no further action. DSS apparently considered the charges a sign of vindictiveness on the part of a wife who was leaving her husband, so they discounted her credibility.

A year later, when Joshua was not quite four years old, he was brought to a hospital emergency room by his father's new girlfriend, Marie, who reported that Joshua might have been beaten up by another child. His injuries were so extensive that the emergency room physicians made a mandated report of suspected abuse and extended protective custody over him. Three days later, DSS convened a child protection team, who decided that there was "insufficient evidence" to hold the boy, so the hospital was forced to return him to his father in spite of the doctors' warning. It is apparent, however, that DSS did not believe that another child had beaten Joshua. Randy DeShaney suggested that Marie might have abused the boy, so DSS "encouraged" him to have her move out of the house. They also enrolled Joshua in a nursery school and gave Randy "counseling," in all of which the father agreed to cooperate.

One month later the emergency room made another mandated report about more serious injuries, but a caseworker concluded that there was "no basis for action." Within the next six months, the same caseworker visited the home repeatedly and noted "a number of suspicious injuries on Joshua's head." In November 1983, the emergency room made its third mandated report. Caseworker Ann Kemmeter again visited the DeShaney home and noted that Marie was still there. On many of her visits, Kemmeter came away without seeing Joshua. Once, she was told that he had the flu; another time, that he had fainted in the bathroom, but she did not ask why. She made nearly twenty visits to the home and documented those instances when she was asked to leave without seeing the child. On other occasions she dutifully noted and described "bumps on the head" (she was told he had fallen off his bicycle), scratched cornea, more "bumps on the head," cigarette burn on the chin, cut forehead, bloody nose, swollen ear, bruises on both shoulders—a long list of traumas whose source was never explored. The file shows that social service investigators accepted one implausible reason after another to explain why Joshua was always hurt and often hospitalized. Still DSS did not make a move to protect him.

They finally intervened and referred the case to the police in March 1984, the day Joshua DeShaney was beaten so severely by his father that "he fell into a life-threatening coma." The report was made from the hospital, where he lay, insensate, with a prognosis that he might never regain consciousness, never be able to tell the social workers who had hit him, broken his skull, bruised his brain tissue, and destroyed his ability to grow and recover. Only then was Joshua DeShaney's father charged with child abuse and convicted, but he was out of prison before Joshua was out of the hospital. In fact, Joshua will never be able to live outside a total care institution. The neurosurgeon who saved his life made a detailed medical record of many older head injuries—those "bumps" on his head were telling a story that the child could no longer tell. Although Joshua eventually came out of his coma and became "viable," he suffered permanent brain damage and is profoundly retarded. He will never be able to speak, walk, feed himself, tell his own story, access his own rights, or defend himself.

Joshua's mother sued the Winnebago County DSS for failing to protect her child under the federal Civil Rights Act, 42 USC 1983, which says that anyone who deprives another of his civil rights "under color of state law" is liable to him for damages. Pro bono attorney Donald J. Sullivan of Wyoming and guardian ad litem Curry First of Milwaukee, Wisconsin, took the case forward for the still-impoverished Melodie DeShaney, who had finally achieved visitation with her brain-damaged, hospitalized child. The theory under which she sued was that DSS was the public agency responsible for protecting Joshua from damage to his bodily integrity, after receiving reports of the danger he was facing in his father's house. The attorney general of Wisconsin, acting as counsel for DSS, claimed that DSS had no responsibility to protect Joshua since it had "no special relationship" with him. He argued that the state agency had no duty to protect Joshua's right not to be beaten unconscious by a third party, his father, who was not an employee of the state or otherwise "a state actor." If DSS had placed Joshua in foster care to protect him, and he had been injured there by a violent foster parent, DSS would be responsible, because it would have established a "special relationship" with him.

The suit was initially brought in the federal district court, which ruled against Joshua and his mother on a motion for summary judgment, a procedure whereby the court makes a decision before the matter even gets to trial by jury. Both mother and guardian *ad litem* noted an appeal to the U.S. Court of Appeals for the Seventh Circuit. Justice Richard Posner, writing for that court, affirmed the district court's decision, saying that DSS did not have a special relationship with Joshua that would give rise to liability. The father's position was upheld, even in light of his conviction for child abuse:

> The concept of special relationship . . . makes it more costly for a state to provide protective services for an individual in need, since by doing so it may be buying itself a lawsuit should its efforts fail. . . . Balancing the rights of parents with those of their children is a task as difficult as it is delicate, and we doubt that it will be performed better under the eyes of federal courts administering constitutional law than by the state judicial and administrative authorities. [*DeShaney* v. *Winnebago Department of Social Services*, 812 F. 2d 298, at p. 304]

Judge Posner not only "balanced" the rights of the father and child but also considered the rights of state agencies:

> To place every state welfare department on the razor's edge, where if it terminates parental rights it is exposed to a Section 1983 suit (as well as a state-law suit) by the parent and if it fails to terminate those rights it is exposed to a Section 1983 suit by the child, it is unlikely to improve the welfare of American families, and it is not grounded in constitutional text or principle. [Ibid.]

(Judge Posner was evading the issue here, for there was no need to terminate Randy DeShaney's parental rights in order to protect Joshua in the way contemplated by the state law applicable to child protection proceedings. Joshua could have been placed in foster care if his mother and other relatives were unable or unwilling to care for him. His father could have been given supervised visitation until and unless he learned to control his violent temper. Many solutions were possible, all well established and well funded as a result of precedent such as the Mary Ellen case, none of which would have exposed DSS to danger of damages or Joshua to danger of damage.)

The pro bono lawyers would not let go. Supported by *amicus curiae* briefs from the ACLU Children's Rights Project and the Massachusetts Committee for Children and Youth, they approached the U.S. Supreme Court, applying for a writ of *certiorari* on this critical issue. Immediately, other states' attorneys offices around the country joined, to support the Wisconsin attorney general with their *amicus curiae* briefs, urging the Supreme Court to affirm the decision against Joshua.

The U.S. Supreme Court decision, written by Chief Justice Rehnquist, held that DSS was not liable because it had "no special relationship" with Joshua DeShaney. Six to three, the justices decided that the departments of social services of the several states, supported by state and federal tax dollars, have no responsibility to protect children from their parents, even if neighbors, parents, teachers, doctors, and hospitals warn them that the children are in danger. Rehnquist observed that the "due process" argument made by the mother could not succeed, but had she proven that Joshua was denied the protection given to other children because he was from a minority (an "equal protection" argument), she might have prevailed.

Joshua DeShaney is a Medicaid and welfare recipient and a charge upon the American taxpayers for the rest of his life because the Department of Social Services of Winnebago County, Wisconsin, also supported by tax dollars, was held not liable for refusing to protect him from harm at the hands of his father, Randy DeShaney. Justices Brennan, Marshall, and Blackmun, in stirring emotional dissents, decried the pile of abuse reports that accumulated in the DSS files as Joshua was exposed to the violence that nearly killed him. They thought that DSS and the caseworker, Ann Kemmeter, should have been held responsible for Joshua's injuries:

> The evidence [of abuse] stayed within the Department—chronicled by the social worker in detail that seems almost eerie in light of her failure to act upon it. As to the social worker's involvement in and knowledge of Joshua's predicament, her reaction to the news of Joshua's last and most devastating injuries is illuminating: "I just knew the phone would ring some day and Joshua would be dead."

As to the majority opinion that the Constitution remained aloof, Justice Brennan, author of the dissenting Supreme Court opinion, wrote: "I cannot agree that our Constitution is indifferent to such indifference" (*DeShaney, a Minor, by his Guardian ad Litem, et al.* versus *Winnebago County DSS, et al.*, 489 U.S. 189, 212 [1988]).

"Poor Joshua!" Justice Blackmun called the child who had no special relationship with the government and no legal recourse, according to the majority opinion. Blackmun compared the "sterile formalism" of the Court to the rigid antebellum decisions regarding slaves. Still, the Supreme Court justices who dissented did not point out that responsibility to "an individual" is different from responsibility to "a child," who cannot choose to leave the home in which he is abused, and who can only obtain shelter through the action of the state, especially if private actors who would protect him (such as his mother, the doctors, the neighbors, and the persons who called in hot line reports) are prevented, *by law,* from doing so on their own.

THE RIGHT TO SUE FOR REDRESS

In 1987, Chrissy Foxworth's mother, Dorrie Singley, faced Mississippi Judge Sebe Dale, trying to obtain protection for her five-year-old daughter from alleged sexual abuse by her father, Timothy Foxworth, who did not want his visitation hampered by supervision. Judge Dale was already notorious for refusing to believe that children were molested by their fathers. Dr. Rebecca Russell, of Children's Hospital in New Orleans, performed a colposcopic examination of Chrissy and reported "conclusive evidence of sexual molestation," but Judge Dale refused to consider the medical report. Dr. Sylvia Strickland, a national expert in the field of diagnostic procedures relating to child sexual abuse, later reviewed the films and confirmed Dr. Russell's findings. The D.A. refused to prosecute, and Judge Dale would not revise his conclusion that there was "no credible evidence that Chrissy [had] been sexually abused." In August 1987, he awarded custody to Timothy Foxworth. Dorrie fled into the Mothers' Underground, a network of safe houses around the country. Mothers like Dorrie hid in basements, homes, and makeshift secret annexes, fearing the FBI's knock on the door and the pictures on milk cartons and the backs of advertising cards. Dorrie Singley hid in an outdoor pool house of a child advocate in Louisiana while Chrissy was sheltered by confederates in California.

Dorrie Singley died of a brain aneurism while she was in hiding and unable to get medical attention. The family with whom Chrissy had been living delivered her to child welfare authorities in San Francisco, who determined that she was an "abused child" and placed her in the home of guardian *ad litem* Donna Medley. Less than a month later, a written arrangement was made for Chrissy to be turned over to the Mississippi authorities by her California advocates and attorneys. The conditions included a neutral foster care setting in Mississippi, not with relatives; psychological and physical examinations; a qualified attorney as guardian *ad litem* in Mississippi; an abuse petition filed on her behalf in the Mississippi Youth Court before her return to that state; and no contact with her father until an order was issued by the Mississippi Youth Court. Judge Sebe Dale and the Commissioner of Youth Welfare Services, Thomas H. Brittain, agreed to those conditions in order to obtain Chrissy's return. District Attorney Douglass went to California and brought the child back to Mississippi. She spent one night in his home, where she was visited by her father and his family. The next day, Judge Dale ordered examinations by two doctors who had previously found Chrissy not to have been abused, and then he placed her in her paternal grandmother's home without the appointment of guardian *ad litem* and without any court hearings or orders. Shortly thereafter, the County Attorney and Youth Court prosecutor held a hearing at which no evidence of abuse was offered. Legal custody was promptly given to Timothy Foxworth, with his mother to care for Chrissy "on a daily basis."

Shortly thereafter, Chrissy appeared on television with her father and said that her mother had forced her to lie about abuse, and that meant that her mother could not go to Heaven. Garnette Harrison, the courageous *pro bono* children's rights lawyer from Mississippi who had fought for Chrissy and Dorrie in Judge Dale's court, and who was later disciplined by the Bar for her advocacy, remarked through her tears that Chrissy was instantly believed when she recanted but never believed when she disclosed.

Donna Medley, with the assistance of Sheila Brogna, of the Children's Law Offices, San Francisco, and Daniel S. Mason of Furth, Fahrner and Mason of that city, sued Judge Dale, the court, the prosecutor, and the Mississippi Department of Social Services. Their 81-page complaint brought in the name of the child began a groundbreaking battle in the federal courts, based on Chrissy's constitutional right not to be subjected to risk of sexual assault, or, to express it legally, not to be deprived of her liberty interest in her bodily integrity, health, and welfare, without due process of laws.

At first, the trial court dismissed the action, saying that Medley had no standing to sue on behalf of the child since she was not a parent or legal guardian in Mississippi. According to the court, only Timothy Foxworth could sue on Chrissy's behalf, because he was her custodial parent. Medley successfully appealed that decision, arguing that the father, who claimed the sole exclusive right to represent Chrissy's legal position, had a "conflict of interests" with respect to her rights since he was the named perpetrator of the sexual abuse previously alleged by her. The Fifth Circuit Court of Appeals then ordered the district court to appoint a guardian *ad litem,* or next-friend, for Chrissy, commenting that it might not be Medley, since they did not know her motivations, and Chrissy had lived with her in California for only two weeks. (The motivations of court-appointed guardians *ad litem* who have never even met the children are not ordinarily questioned.)

The federal court did in fact appoint Donna Medley as Chrissy's next-friend, and the legal team from San Francisco pressed on, insisting that the federal Civil Rights Act protected Chrissy's constitutional right not to be molested, even by her legal custodial parent. Chrissy lost again in the trial court in Mississippi, on the theory that federal jurisdiction would not attach to the case because custody law was the sole province of state courts. But the Fifth Circuit Court of Appeals reversed that decision in 1991, declaring that children did have federally protected rights not to be subjected to sexual abuse. The U.S. Court of Appeals ultimately found against Judge Dale and the other officials who had violated Chrissy's legal rights pursuant to the interstate agreement relating to her placement and treatment in Mississippi and the failure of the Mississippi authorities to evaluate the evidence of past sexual abuse.

That opinion, however, did nothing for the real child Chrissy, who was in her father's sole custody as a result of all the wrongs the courts later identified. The court merely observed that Chrissy was—as far as it knew—doing fine in her father's custody and that she would remain there, because there was no current evidence of continued sexual abuse!

Rachel was found by a court to be a free person because of certain peculiar circumstances that occurred while she was a slave, and because her lawyer prevailed. A few years later, this route was blocked for Dred Scott, who was declared not to have standing to sue for his own freedom *because* he was a slave. Mary Ellen Wilson was saved from abuse at a time when no laws were available to free her, but even after such laws were passed they did not avail Lisa Steinberg because the social services system did not use them in her behalf. In the same era, another social services agency employed those laws in the case of Joshua DeShaney, but it did not take responsibility for protecting him. Finally, in the Foxworth case, the law recognized an abused child's right to sue for failure to protect her, but even that recognition was an empty gesture, for the system was not required to restore her to safety.

WHAT IS THE SOLUTION?

Are any proposals presently under consideration capable of truly protecting children from incest, dependent as they are on systems that sbstitute judicial discretion for true emancipation of children? We think not, but in deference to the belief expressed by our colleagues that improvements will lead to solutions, we present the following examples.

The Bricolage Solution: "We need a new law that says . . ."

No new law that provides for a certain kind of evidentiary standard, a certain procedural safeguard, a certain factual requirement for judges, or a certain adjustment in the criminal or civil responses made to child sexual abuse can result in the protection of children's rights. The laws already on the books have failed to do so. We already have a law in every state of the Union that makes it a crime to sexually molest a child. Children are not "competent" to sign contracts in their own names, so they are not considered able to consent to sex with adults, and there are criminal and civil penalties everywhere to deal with that situation. American judges have ignored this law even to the extent of calling three-year-old children "seductive" and excusing adults for molesting them.

Tipping the balances of one law or another in an attempt to affect the whole problem of child sexual abuse and the law's failure to prevent it will never result in wholesale, unequivocal, effective protection. In fact, the reason that we now have a patchwork of laws that confound rather than protect is that each law was put into place by well-meaning legislators, informed of terrible individual injustices by well-meaning citizens and professionals, trying to solve problems resulting from those individual cases. The word "bricolage," adapted from the French word describing a home repairman's response to localized problems ("fixing leaks and patching cracks"), also describes our hundred years of trying to fix things for abused children. We have never inspected the soundness of the foundation. In fact, in the case of children's rights, we have never admitted that no foundation has been laid.

The Juridealist Solution: "We need to train these judges"

Lawyers most often adopt this position, led by the country's foremost jurist/advocate for molested children, Judge Charles B. Schudson of the Wisconsin Court of Appeals, co-author of *On Trial: Sexually Abused Children in American Courts.* Judge Schudson gives seminars to judges around the country on child sexual abuse and how to interpret what they hear from children and experts in courtrooms. Joan Pennington, Esq., founder of the National Center for Protective Parents, has meanwhile enthusiastically begun a campaign to educate lawyers to take pro bono cases for protective parents of molested children. Attorney Alan Rosenfeld of Vermont has traversed the country representing protective parents himself and has urged other lawyers to follow his lead. None of these attorneys believes that a proper response to the problem of children's rights or child sexual abuse can be made outside the courts. We, however, believe that the courtroom is the wrong forum for dealing with these matters, and, therefore, no amount of expertise on the part of witnesses or professionals can make it right. Judges who *wish* to understand the problems involved in "determining" whether or not a child has been molested will benefit from Judge Schudson's rousing and informative presentations; lawyers who *wish* to protect children's rights in the courts will certainly benefit from Joan Pennington's expertise and passion; and some children will be lucky enough to achieve protection as a result of efforts like these, just as the slave Rachel was lucky enough to be freed. But luck is not enough, and better judges will just give more children somewhat better odds.

The Federal Messianic Solution:
"We need federal jurisdiction"

Washington, D.C., legislative attorney Sherry Quirk has joined New York Congressman Gerald Nadler in calling for the federal courts to accept jurisdiction over civil rights cases brought on behalf of children who can prove they have been molested and deprived of their right to protection "under color of state law," modeled on the Foxworth case in Mississippi. In fact, the history of the Civil Rights Act, 42 U.S. Code Section 1983, is instructive in analyzing this proposed solution. Section 1983 was passed in 1871 to enforce emancipation because some states maintained slavery by manipulation of state laws and by out-and-out terrorism (the Ku Klux Klan) even after it was prohibited by the Thirteenth Amendment to the Constitution. Section 1983 provides that anyone who deprives a person of his constitutional rights "under color of state law" is liable for damages. The Eleventh Amendment, meanwhile, protects judges and other governmental agencies and officials from monetary damages, but allows injunctions against them. But the most significant fact about the successful use of Section 1983 is that it was passed and used *after* the emancipation of the slaves, to enforce the intent of Congress to set them free. In other words, federal jurisdiction for children like Chrissy Foxworth will become useful only after children have definable and undeniable rights, in their own persons and on their own initiative, for which to sue, denial of which can lead to damages. Since Chrissy did not have the constitutional right to refuse to live with her father, she could not gain it by Donna Medley's lawsuit on her behalf for her right not to be molested by him.

The Exposé Solution: "We need to open up the courts"

While it is true that publicity helped Elizabeth Morgan get out of jail and join her child in New Zealand, it does not follow that opening the courts will solve the problems faced by molested children. Right now, criminal courts hearing cases against child molesters are open, and cases like the McMartin Pre-school trials in California had no lack of public exposure. At times, all that is generated is news for the sake of news or even news that gives rise to regrettable reactions, backlash activities, and prurient interests. It has been suggested that child abuse proceedings be videotaped so that the conduct of judges and witnesses is open to public scrutiny, but the well-known videotape of the police beating of Rodney King did not change the fact that there are problems the law cannot solve. It would certainly be better to have a record of what is being done in the courtrooms than to leave history without such a testament. However, many judges have no particular desire to hide what they have done. Judge Gordon Mitchell of Miami voluntarily appeared on national television, saying that he had not seen "conclusive" evidence that an alleged molester had "put his penis in somebody's tush," so he ruled that the child in question should have unsupervised visitation with the alleged abuser. If each individual case has to be fought in the battle for children's rights, then each individual record will not necessarily avail the next endangered child. The result, at best, will be prolonged slavery with a more active underground railroad, sensitized by more exposure of decent people to horror stories from behind the lines.

The Judge Gill Solution:
"We need a constitutional amendment"

Slaves were freed by the Thirteenth Amendment to the Constitution in 1864. The Bill of Rights already said that all persons had the rights they later acquired, but slaves had been prevented from accessing those rights before they were emancipated. Women were given the right to vote by the Nineteenth Amendment in 1920, although the Constitution had never specifically excluded females from its coverage, and the English language had long used the word "men" to mean "mankind." Now, although the Constitution does not exclude children from its coverage *per se,* it has been suggested that the problems children face in the court system can be solved by putting them into the Constitution. Judge Charles Gill has been the primary proponent of this solution. A moving speaker, he has also written extensively on the terrible condition of children in America, pointing out that it is adult "ownership" of children that most seriously hampers efforts to protect them from mistreatment and abuse by adults. Critical of lawyers, Gill writes:

> Howard Davidson and Mark Hardin [of the American Bar Association Center on Children and the Law] wrote 179 pages of well-intentioned proposals in which the only parents not allowed to keep their children in zones of danger are dead ones! [1991:564]

> The innocent reader is led to believe that the problem is exaggerated, that children fabricate these stories [of sexual abuse], that we cannot really quantify abuse. Slick courtroom psychologists, with packaged presentations, make the circuit of family law and criminal defense seminars to peddle their contributions to the confusion of English-Majors-turned-judges in the family courts, and the reasonable doubt arguments to the jurors in criminal court. . . . How can a society which is thought to be so child-oriented have such a terrible record with regard to children, even in comparison with many third-world countries? [Ibid.:554–555]

According to the Gill Amendment, children's rights would include: 1. The right to a good, safe home; the right to adequate health care, adequate education, and a loving family or a reasonable approximation of it; 2. the right to testify in any legal proceeding about any person accused of abusing said child; 3. the right to have a judge receive evidence as to such child's developmental level as it pertains to that child's credibility, in any legal proceeding; and 4. the right to counsel in any legal proceeding that affects the child's interests.

These rights have a good ring to them. So does the standard "the best interests of the child," the words used by every judge who hands children over to alleged molesters. Even if the Gill Amendment passes, decisions about children's status and placement will remain with the judiciary, which would retain its broad discretion and its lack of accountability. The amendment would not change the fact that judges like Sebe Dale, in the Foxworth case, would be ruling on children's rights to live in "good and safe homes," and would be deciding which homes were "good" and "safe." Judge Gill admits that his constitutional amendment will probably not pass in his lifetime, and may never pass, but he believes that advocating for it is a worthwhile effort with positive implications for children. But the Gill Amendment does not grant children their fundamental human rights. It does not give a child the legal right to avoid living with, and being kept, against his will, under the control of someone he hates and fears; all he would gain would be the right to testify about his attitudes. Educational psychologist John Holt's (1974) vision of a free child living with people he loves would not result from passage of Judge Gill's amendment. It would still be true that a woman could divorce her husband for her own reasons, but a child could not divorce his parents.

The Oversight/Accountability Solutions:
John E.B. Myers, J.D.

In his recent book *The Backlash: Child Protection under Fire,* law professor John Myers describes a flood of media attacks on CPS and some of the results he attributes to this phenomenon. He makes recommendations based on his assumption that the CPS system can be improved by being strengthened—a reasonable enough proposal if weakness is the problem faced by the agencies. He emphasizes, also, that there must be accountability and oversight, and joins the American Bar Association in proposing evaluation of a nationally supported system of ombudsmen for children. The ombudsman idea is predicated upon the same underlying theory as the guardian *ad litem,* the court-appointed special advocate, or next-friend, mechanisms, whereby adults act in children's best interests and take up the struggle on their behalf. Myer also suggests an inspector general for CPS agencies, to operate like the inspectors general who "police" the military and other government offices.

In our view, strengthening our child protection system would not decrease, and might even increase, its unreliability and irresponsibility toward children. Myers mentions that parents must feel as though they are treated fairly within the system, but we are far more concerned with fairness to children. We feel naturally suspicious about the inspector-general proposal, since inspector-general investigations are not essentially different from investigations within the agencies inspected; thus, they may become part of the problem rather than alleviate it.

The ombudsman proposal is based on a concept that originated in Sweden. If an ombudsman were to represent a child's rights to choose whom to live with, whom to visit, and whom to depend on, we might find this idea workable. If, however, the ombudsman were to become yet another political force addressing the "conditions" under which one adult or another could make those choices for a child, we do not think it would change the ability of at-risk children to access protection.

The use of inspectors-general, ombudsmen, oversight committees, or complaint departments seems helpful, but this kind of provision works only if the system really wants to change. No amount of oversight can change an overt facade hiding a covert system with quite a different purpose; it will just provide a new level of cover for the covert system's real operations.

PART THREE
A PROPOSED
SOLUTION

11
Introducing CARCO:
CHILD AT RISK
CLASSIFICATION OFFICE

In this chapter we present the foundation of a federal system we believe could really begin to control the problem of incest in our society. The system would not depend on the enforcement of laws against undesirable adult behavior but would concentrate on the provision of benefits to children.

The fundamental problem with the present system is that it relies on absolute proof that a child has been abused—an unworkable premise because that possibility cannot be properly and safely measured.

Incest is a public health issue, not a legal one. It became a legal issue because society passed laws to prevent it. But they have not been successful; in fact, reported cases of incest are on the rise. Even when the crime is proven, the penalties imposed rarely prevent recidivism. Therefore, a more effective means of prevention must be devised.

When we rely on the law to handle incest the emphasis turns from the child and protection of the child to the accused and his constitutional rights. Placing incest and child protection into the judicial realm puts it on adult turf—the law—and especially into alleged molester turf, that is, criminal defense law. Our proposal would completely remove criminal prosecutions, and keep the problem of incest in the public health forum, away from the judicial forum altogether.

To help understand the ideas behind our proposal, consider the child who, in the opinion of the child protection authorities, needs emergency medical treatment but whose parents oppose it for religious reasons. According to case law in virtually every state, the parents' consent is not required, and the child's need for medical attention is considered paramount. The system first recognizes the parents' rights and then overrules them in favor of the child's need for medical help. Once the child's risk is removed, the parents' First Amendment rights to practice their religion and to teach their child that faith are restored and left undisturbed.

No less consideration should be given to the child at risk of incest, which produces negative consequences more serious than almost any other kind of injury, although its effects are often not as easy to see and appreciate. Current research holds that the psychological sequelae of incest are lifelong and can be completely debilitating. A child may recover more effectively from most major injuries than from rape. A patient with a physical illness is given sympathy and assistance, whereas a rape victim may be rejected, invalidated, reviled, and re-abused. A child who suffers incest is entitled to a solution that holds his rights and needs paramount, without competition from the rights and needs of others. No adult rights to visitation, custody, contact, or parental control should have any place in decisions about treatment once the child discloses or is found to be at risk of incest.

Our proposal is simple but radical: Remove criminal penalties and deal with incest in the context of the health needs of the child. Remove the issue from the courts, where competing legal interests of adults can easily overwhelm the needs of the child; place it under the purview of the public health system, implemented by a federally run network of offices designed to measure and diminish the risk of abuse of children.

We propose, therefore, a child-oriented risk-assessment agency completely administered perhaps by an office within the U.S. Public Health Service. It would replace the governmental social service agencies presently designated to make administrative "findings" about child abuse. The initial enabling legislation would set up CARCO (Child at Risk Classification Office) and divert funds to it from the present unwieldy and expensive child protective services. Periodic regulatory and review legislation would monitor the system and revise, as needed, the procedures to be followed uniformly in the individual CARCO facilities within the 50 states. As we write this, we are only too aware of the current political climate for downsizing the federal government. Our proposal is a search for a uniformly administered and enforced risk-assessment system for child abuse, which suggests action at the federal level.

CARCO is a national plan for the direct prevention (not rhetoric, not amelioration, not statistical analysis, not education) of child abuse. Its purpose is to identify and decrease risk. The word "abuse" has no place in either its name or its function. The CARCO plan seeks only to prevent intrafamilial child abuse; it does not aim to punish offenders, compensate victims, or make custody decisions. It starts with the premise that prevention of incest depends on two necessary conditions: 1. protection of children from persons who, by a showing of significant probability, may molest them; and 2. treatment of children who have been shown to be at significant risk—such treatment being designed to strengthen the children's own ability to decrease such risk. Thus, the CARCO system is very much like dealing with allergies: first, you determine if the patient is sensitive; then you remove significant allergens in his environment and start treatment to improve his physiological resistance and healing power.

The CARCO system might be part of and administered by the U.S. Public Health Service, which operates under the Department of Health and Human

Services. CARCO's job would be to classify and treat children who appear to be at risk of physical and/or sexual abuse. Included in the federal CARCO legislation would be the requirement that every public and private school, every child care facility, every clinic and hospital regularly tell children in age-appropriate terms that a local CARCO exists and teach them how to reach it. Every federal program involved in the welfare or health of children would take part in a massive campaign to inform children and their parents about the local CARCO.

The CARCO system would operate just as the specialized education system now functions to classify children with special needs because of learning disabilities, Down's Syndrome, or mental retardation. Once the criteria are met, the child is entitled to special services, even if the parents do not agree with—or even vigorously deny—the diagnoses made by the classification office.

Under the auspices of a government agency, local CARCOs would be administered in the same way as our present community health clinics and clinics for migrant workers and the homeless. A manual approved, reviewed, and periodically revised would provide uniform standards for the classification and protection of children at risk of abuse, known as CARKIDS. The real job of CARCO is to work with such children to decrease the risk and remove the risk factors until they can be declassified.

Since only the child is the CARCO client, the local office will not be a "family center" or a mediator of parental rights or concerns. Parents, significant others, and family members will be involved with and assisted by CARCO personnel to the extent that their participation is helpful to the child who is the CARCO client, and referrals for other services could be made for the family. But family members would be free to choose whether or not to take part in the work of declassification. Our response to the question "What about the family, and what about the parents' rights?" is: the function of CARCO is only to prevent and remedy child abuse. Providing for the rights of parents and saving families are outside its area of concern. If state governments want to perform those functions, they can do so, using other agencies and systems. If the federal government wants to help in that regard, it may of course do so, but our proposal is not that ambitious.

This sounds simple. But it will be hard for most Americans to grasp because it is not what we are accustomed to. The CARCO program is so revolutionary and so devoid of courtroom drama that it has been difficult to understand even by professionals in the field, who keep returning to the question of the constitutional rights of the alleged molester. CARCO represents a fresh way of thinking about children and their needs, one that corresponds more to the vision of child psychologists and educational professionals than to Supreme Court decisions about competing civil and constitutional rights. CARCO would be a public health agency designed and operated to decrease and prevent risk of child abuse, not a law enforcement or litigation support entity.

THE PROPOSED LEGISLATION

Federal funds presently support nearly every state Child Protection Service (CPS) agency in the country through grants from the Department of Health and Human Services for the prevention of child abuse and neglect and for treatment programs. By 1991, 47 of the 50 state CPS departments were dependent on federal funds. To qualify for these grants, the state CPS agencies must: 1. have in effect a state law relating to child abuse and neglect, including reporting provisions; 2. provide that reports of abuse will be investigated and, "upon a finding of abuse or neglect," take steps to protect the health and welfare of the child; 3. demonstrate that there are administrative procedures, personnel training procedures, and facilities available; 4. keep records confidential; 5. provide for cooperation with law enforcement officials and courts; 6. provide guardians *ad litem* for abused or neglected children in court proceedings; 7. fund their own agencies to a certain extent; 8. provide for dissemination of information to the public; 9. provide "preferential treatment" to "parental organizations combating child abuse and neglect"; and 10. include medical neglect as an aspect of child abuse or neglect that they address.

However, state agencies are using millions of federal dollars without being directly accountable for the results. Every state has laws relating to child abuse but no requirements for their enforcement. In fact, it was admitted during a 1994 New Hampshire case that a state's laws do not have to be "effectively" enforced; federal law only requires that they be enacted (*Eric L. By and Through Schierberl* versus *Bird,* 848 F.Supp. 303). Every state investigates reports of child abuse, but there are no national standards or quality control applied to such investigations; there is often a break-down in making "findings," so steps to protect children depend heavily on the discretion of agency personnel, who are themselves not accountable to any federal authority. The cooperation that CPS agencies give to law enforcement officials and courts is more often a block to effective protection of children than help. Confidentiality of records is not a problem since every state CPS agency is eager to keep its functions and work a secret. The provision of guardians *ad litem* for children who are the subject of CPS "findings" of abuse or neglect does not improve the accuracy of those findings or the follow-up. Worst of all, none of these provisions will keep a molested child out of custody court or out of the custody of the alleged molester, as we saw in Chrissy's case in Mississippi (see Chapter 10). The requirement that states disseminate information to the public is often viewed as an invitation to state agencies to do public relations for their own benefit. The requirement that state CPS agencies provide preferential treatment for parental organizations is more likely to impede than enhance the ability of incest victims to access protection, since these children usually need protection from their own parents.

Under the provisions of the U.S. Code (42 USC Section 5106), the states are receiving federal funds but are getting only vague guidelines for performing assessments and delivering services to children and families. As long as a state CPS agency follows its own procedures, complies with its own policies, and cooperates with its own state's judicial system, it may continue to receive these funds with no control over the results it achieves. Some states routinely place children in foster care for months while they evaluate sexual abuse allegations, spend large sums of money trying to determine whether the children were abused, and usually conclude that nobody knows. This money would be better used to set up and begin the operation of CARCO.

The U.S. Public Health Service seems the logical home for the CARCO program. As special needs have arisen, the Public Health Service has added new sections and provided grants to states or other organizations to address those needs. Sections have been added recently for PHS involvement in combating Sudden Infant Death Syndrome, Trauma Care, and AIDS, as well as to provide support groups for families of Alzheimer's patients. A special section authorizes assistance to children of substance abusers, while another provides for primary medical care to homeless children. Our proposal would add "assistance to children at risk of child abuse" to this list. What is required is the will to recognize child abuse as a national public health issue and to take action to prevent it.

The closest analog to the establishment of CARCO is 42 USC Section 254c, which set up community health centers under PHS during the 1960s. The first step toward this legislation was recognition of the need for such centers in medically underserved areas and to help special populations. PHS was the obvious governmental entity to handle this matter, although before enactment of this section of the law, it had never established or operated such centers. The community health centers now in place are administered by ten regional offices, which could easily house regional CARCO management offices as well.

With proper training, social workers and other professionals in the present CPS system could very easily work within the regulatory scheme for CARCO. The Uniformed Services University of the Health Sciences in Bethesda, Maryland, one of the most underused of all medical schools in the nation, could educate critical medical management personnel for the regional CARCO centers. Then CPS agencies could be invited to bid for contracts to operate local CARCO facilities, using members of their own personnel who were able to retrain and test into the CARCO jobs. No state CPS agency would be required to join the CARCO program, but there would be no more federal funding to child abuse prevention and treatment programs outside the CARCO program.

The cost of operating CARCO, after the initial start-up, would be less than that of the present system, since it would involve much less work, no lengthy court proceedings, and fewer expensive professionals. Child abuse cases involving 30 to 50 appearances in court (such as In re Marissa, in Chapter 2) would no longer be a drain on the system, with their use of public funds to pay private forensic psychiatrists, clinical psychologists, and lawyers arguing about fine points of evidence.

We recognize that there may be valid objections to this general idea. Louise Armstrong, the pioneer of the movement to identify and address incest, believes that the mental health community has failed so irrevocably and irremediably to deal with incest in a rational and moral way that the problem must be confined to the legal system. We have obviously come to a nearly opposite conclusion from our esteemed colleague. We agree that many members of the mental health community have betrayed victims and survivors of incest horribly. They are described in Chapter 9 as those professionals who play ritual roles in the covert system. We feel that they have failed so miserably because they focus not on the mental health needs of their patients and clients but on the opinions of judges, the actions of the courts, and the rights of parents. Forensic psychologists and CPS social workers who care about "evidence" rather than facts, and "evaluations" rather than treatment, have dominated the field of sexual abuse. If the mental health system were not influenced and driven by the legal adversary system, if public health needs were elevated over public appearance needs, our professionals would soon learn to behave differently. Armstrong's criticisms of the mental health system are valid, but we feel that the legal system has performed even more dangerously. Therefore, we choose the mental health model over the legal model with the knowledge that we are choosing the lesser of two obvious evils.

Another valid objection is that a federal system for child abuse prevention and treatment is the epitome of "Big Government" and, as such, undesirable. We would only agree that this was a serious consideration if CARCO were a legal system, in the judicial branch of the government, rather than a public health system, to be administered by the executive branch. Since CARCO would only be involved in the provision of benefits, not in the enforcement of law or in the administration of justice, the benefits of uniformity and the savings represented by a centralized system outweigh concerns about the removal of state power or the delegation of federal authority. There were no objections to the federal government's providing benefits to the children of alcoholics in many states, and the children of pedophiles are no less needing or deserving of assistance. In addition, individual states are limited in their ability to protect abused children by territorial jurisdictions. For example, a Public Health Service physician in New Jersey made a mandated report to the local CPS agency when she treated a migrant family's child who had been sodomized. The New Jersey authorities refused to investigate the case because the parents had moved to Pennsylvania. There was no follow-up, medical, legal, or social. At approximately the same time, two little girls in Pennsylvania reported sexual abuse by their father. The CPS agency in that state made a "founded case," indicating that the evidence was convincing. The father moved to New Jersey to avoid further investigation, so the Pennsylvania CPS agency closed its case. When the mother and children moved out of Pennsylvania, the father sued for custody of the girls and won. The State of New Jersey refused to investigate allegations of abuse because it had not taken place within its jurisdiction.

These technical problems arise from the patchwork jurisdictional nature of the two kinds of laws involved, those applying to custody and those applying to child abuse. The only reasonable solution to such a complicated system is a uniform system implemented by the various states in a standardized way.

HOW WOULD CARCO WORK?

A CARCO "walk-in" office would be set up in each school district. It might be most efficient to use school buildings for many CARCO functions from 4:00 P.M. until 8:00 A.M., on weekends and holidays, and during summer vacations. Local churches, synagogues, YMCA buildings, and other public agencies might also be able to house CARCO under the PHS section providing for shared facilities. Buildings now being used for other Health and Human Services Department purposes could also provide space for CARCO.

Children would be allowed and encouraged to visit the local CARCO at any time, in order to become acquainted and comfortable with it. A CARCO facility would ideally contain areas for private conversations, play, outdoor activities, a library, and age-oriented recreation areas. Community activities for different age groups (story hours and demonstrations of pets for young children, free movies for elementary school children, "rap sessions" about issues of concern to teen-agers) could take place at CARCO so that children are aware of their location and operations. Universities might offer course credit for practicum work in presenting recreational and educational activities at the local CARCO.

CARCO's official business would be conducted according to a manual drawn up by professionals (possibly members of the American Professional Society for Abused Children) and employed uniformly everywhere. The manual—which should be reviewed and revised periodically—would provide intake workers with a simple scale of risk—not of abuse. Every contact with a child would result in a measurement based on that risk-assessment scale. For instance, if a child discloses sexual abuse, an employee specially trained in the use of the scale and without discretion to decide whether or not the disclosure is "credible," must check the risk factor labeled "Child has disclosed sexual abuse." When the risk factors are added up, the child is categorized as "At Risk" or "Not at Risk."

A child at risk is immediately eligible for certain "entitlements": specific social services and health treatment, which continue until the child is declassified, a process that is carefully documented. Declassification would occur when the child had received all her entitlements and was no longer considered at risk. That would be the ultimate goal of CARCO in every case. No child could be declassified without a carefully conducted professional risk assessment, and no child could be declassified against her will if she still felt herself to be at risk—that would be her absolute right.

Step One: Invitation to CARCO

If a child discloses sexual abuse to an adult (parent or not), appears with marks and/or bruises that seem to indicate physical abuse, or gives any adult reason to suspect that she may be at risk of physical or sexual abuse, that adult is responsible for taking the child to the local CARCO or reporting that suspicion to CARCO. If the child is brought to CARCO, an initial risk assessment is done immediately. If a child is the subject of a report to CARCO, an intake worker asks responsible adults to bring the child to the office, where an initial risk assessment is done immediately. If there is a lack of cooperation from the responsible adults, the child is immediately classified as "Provisionally at Risk."

Step Two: Intake

On the first official visit to CARCO, the child and any protective adult accompanying her are introduced to an intake representative, who explains the office and the way it works. The child's first interview is meant to determine whether her situation is one of "E.R." (emergency risk). For instance, a disclosure of sexual abuse by someone in the child's household is automatically an E.R. situation, because the alleged abuser is living under the same roof. If the situation does not involve emergency risk, an intake is begun without pressure, and the initial risk assessment does not have to be completed on the first visit. That is, the child may want to learn about the local CARCO one day and return the next for an intake interview. She may decide to play in the game room for a while and not speak. She may start an interview and then discontinue it for some reason.

In an emergency risk situation, however, the intake worker is required to complete the risk assessment and fill out the entire form at the first visit, as expeditiously as possible without frightening the child. The manual will provide the exact questions to be answered by the intake worker, which will lead to a numerical risk assessment. For instance, on a scale of one to ten, a child who verbally discloses sexual abuse would immediately be assigned a score of seven. (This procedure would be determined in a uniform way and applied without variation in every CARCO facility, so there would be something tangible to refer to when describing risk.)

Why shouldn't the intake worker have the discretion to believe or disbelieve a child's disclosure? That is too much discretion for any one person to exercise when another human being feels afraid or at risk. If someone is afraid of heights, it is not reasonable to allow another person to decide that he should become a pilot. Each individual has feelings and experiences that he cannot, especially at an early age, communicate to another. The danger that an intake worker would disbelieve a disclosure that is true is far more serious than believing a disclosure that is not true. In other words, comparing the negative consequences of "false negative" and "false positive," a disclosure of abuse that was in fact invalid (that is, not factually accurate) might temporarily separate a child from a person who had not in fact abused her, whereas disbelief of a disclosure of abuse that was in fact valid (that is, factually accurate) would expose the child to risk of repeated sexual abuse by the same perpetrator. Inestimable harm is done to a child who discloses abuse, is disbelieved, is returned to the control of the molester, and is molested again and even punished for telling. The harm that ensues from the first scenario is the lesser of two evils, from the child's point of view, and, it is important to remember, CARCO is built exclusively on the child's point of view.

Step Three: Classification

A child who is classified is immediately informed of her entitlements. Appropriate terminology will be used, avoiding clinical and legalistic vocabulary. All CARCO personnel will receive specialized training and testing so they communicate effectively with the age group they serve. The child's entitlements always include, but are not limited to:

1. The right to continuing contact with CARCO.
2. Immediate and unequivocal protection from contact with the named abuser.
3. The right to stay with and/or live with a protective parent or guardian who is willing to keep or stay with the child, preferably in the same situation in which she already lives, unless it is impossible to make that into a safe environment (as when a named abuser is living in a house with the child and refuses to leave, in which case housing will be found for the child and the protective parent on an emergency basis).
4. Medical attention, at no cost if necessary, as needed by the CAR KID appropriate to the child's needs.
5. Therapeutic mental health services, at no cost if necessary, as needed by the CAR KID appropriate to the child's needs.
6. Social services, at no cost if necessary, as needed by the CAR KID appropriate to the child's needs.
7. Protection from negative legal or economic consequences of the classification.
8. Educational assistance if needed.
9. Adjunct social services to other members of the family if such services are feasible and if they will enhance the child's chances of declassification.

10. The right to be informed about the CARCO process at any time, and the right to question and participate.

Step Four: Declassification

Now the real work begins. A child who is classified At Risk needs to have that risk diminished, to the point of disappearance if possible, and needs to have her defenses to risk shored up so that she will not be a vulnerable child in the future or grow up to be a vulnerable adult.

The first step in declassification is an attempt to get cooperation from the adults in the child's life. For instance, if the child has been classified as At Risk of incest by an older stepsister, the adults in charge of her family must cooperate in an arrangement whereby the child does not live in the same home (or visit in the same home, unsupervised) with the stepsister. If she has been classified At Risk of incest by her father, the most helpful cooperation will be from him.

Could CARCO hope to gain such cooperation? We believe it could, for two important reasons. The first is that there are no criminal penalties for incest under CARCO. If a child accuses a gym teacher of molestation, that may be handled by law enforcement authorities. But if a child reports sexual abuse by her father, that is not the same, technically or realistically, as an "accusation." It is more logical to think of it as a "disclosure" or even a "confession," in psychological terms. It is a plea for help and a revelation of terrible pain experienced by the child. There need be no criminal elements in the solution to the problem of incest, since criminal penalties have never been effective in preventing or treating its sequelae. Under the present legal and social circumstances, an accused incest perpetrator has every reason to deny molestation and has very little reason to admit it. This feeds into the general psychological denial that is an unfortunate psychological attribute of most pedophiles, who cannot seem to tolerate their own obsessional behavior and who live double lives in order to hide it. So the first reason that CARCO could expect cooperation even from a sexually abusive father is that he faces no risk himself, if he admits he has molested his child.

The second incentive for an allegedly sexually abusive father to cooperate with CARCO is that cooperation would lead to declassification of his child, whereas a refusal to cooperate, in the face of knowledge that CARCO believes his child and is prepared absolutely to protect her, means she will not be declassified until her eighteenth birthday, and may have no contact with her father until she is an adult!

Since most parents, even those accused of incest, will want to cooperate with the CARCO office, we can now turn to what developments CARCO can accomplish with that cooperation. It is presumed for these purposes that one of the parents (usually the protective mother) is non-offending, supports the child's disclosure, and works with CARCO without resistance.

After a child is classified and housing and exposure problems have been handled (with foster care in the case of two abusive parents or no available protective adult guardian), the child begins to form her alliances with CARCO. She has "reps" at CARCO who handle her needs on a regular basis so she is not shuttled from person to person. It is of primary concern that one person is in charge of seeing that all services are being rendered as needed. The child's CAR REP would help her find and keep a therapist she could communicate with, and would provide liaison to other medical and mental health personnel. Her CAR REP would also try to make her named abuser understand the process by which his influence on her life could be changed from the category of Risk to the category of No Risk. This could take years. If possible, the position of CAR REP should not change during the classification, even if other personnel have to change. CAR REP applicants should be screened very carefully before being assigned to that very important position, so that as far as possible, persons with longevity and accountability are employed. CAR REP positions might have to be filled by individuals who enlist in the Public Health Service for a specified period of time, so that there would be less likelihood of turnover.

In the event of a false allegation, with the cooperation of the falsely accused parent and a comparatively brief period of therapy and supportive assistance to the family members involved, a quick and relatively painless declassification should follow. Since no criminal penalties are involved, the temporary separation from the accused parent would not require the child to defend a "false allegation" because of the harm she had done by "lying." The CARCO process does not involve blame but offers treatment; thus the innocent family member would be involved voluntarily in conjoint therapy with the child, and problems between them could be worked out amicably. Since there would be no incentive to continue a situation that was not beneficial to either parent or child, and since all recriminations that generally accrue in these cases concentrate on injured parental rights and indignant parental reactions, we feel that the number of genuinely wrong classifications will be minimal. Most studies of sex abuse allegations show that deliberately false allegations occur in less than 15 percent of all cases, with larger more reliable samples showing smaller percentages (see Chapter 6).

Although declassification for a child whose molester admitted the abuse would be painstaking, it would be eminently possible. The child would need psychotherapy, but the length of that therapy is an individual matter. She would probably need social services to support her protective parent and to help her recover from economic or educational hardships that resulted from the abuse itself or from the family separation. She might need medical attention and special care. Her molester would definitely need therapeutic assistance and a strenuous behavior modification campaign so that he could relate to his child in a non-threatening way and would not make her feel guilty. He would need to learn new ways of coping with his obsession:

education, sympathy, support, and an unwavering insistence upon his dealing with, rather than denying, the problem.

According to social workers now in the public social service agencies, parents who have admitted abusing their children can be assisted in avoiding such behavior in the future. The declassification of a CAR KID can begin when the molester has availed himself of all resources conducive to stopping his offensive behavior and has benefited from therapy and other support. When the child-victim is strong enough and the perpetrator is frank enough and helpful enough, the relationship can be reestablished and supported so that it can continue on noncoercive but declassified terms.

For the declassification documentation process to continue, the child must, first and foremost, feel free of risk and capable of managing her own situation. Her therapist must believe that she has come to the point of safety as well. If she and her therapist agree, she takes a brief, age-appropriate course in how to reinstate her CARCO classification in case she feels at risk again in the future. She must not feel shame in returning for more CARCO assistance, should that occur. If her therapist believes that she will not shy away from reclassification if it becomes necessary, the child and her therapist can ask the CAR REP to draw up a declassification contract. The past offender will join in that contract, which will set forth the terms under which the risk is managed by all participating parties, children and adults. Every six months, the declassified child will be called in for a follow-up report on the progress of the declassification. If risk rises again and reaches an unacceptable number, the child is reclassified and the cooperative parent or parents are again asked to assist.

The insoluble problems that plague the CPS system will not appear in CARCO, but there will be new challenges. The fact that Congress reviews CARCO periodically assures that they will be addressed. Meanwhile, most of the obvious errors have been eliminated.

What can derail or interrupt the CARCO process? Nothing. If an alleged perpetrator should want to get custody of the CAR KID, that is his prerogative, but he will have to wait until the child is declassified. During the child's classification, no legal proceedings are permitted to interfere with either her placement or her progress through the declassification process. Should a father who is considered a risk factor for a classified child sue for custody, CARCO, like a federal bankruptcy court, would place an automatic stay of proceedings on all litigation until it could be proven that such litigation would not interfere with her access to her entitlements or endanger her classification. If the alleged perpetrator was the financial support of the family and he refused to support her because of the allegations, that could be handled by other social service agencies, such as support enforcement divisions of the Department of Justice. Not only would litigation not be effective in preventing classifications, it could not short-circuit the provision of children's needs and entitlements once classifications were made. On the other hand, the classified child would not be encouraged to engage in aggressive litigation for damages. The rights of the classified child to redress later in life are outside the purview of CARCO.

HOW WOULD CARCO HAVE AFFECTED OUR CASE HISTORIES?

To show how CARCO, as opposed to the CPS system, would solve or prevent the known problems, let us subject the five cases described in Part One of this book to CARCO procedures.

In the Mary H case, the CARCO system would have eliminated the need for a state appeals court to restrain two judges from enforcing bizarre and erroneous orders. Another state's CPS system would not have had to intervene to protect a refugee from "justice," and a protective mother would not have had to give up her own right to medical attention while hiding from the law. Dan H would not have been a convicted child-molester under CARCO. Debbie would have gone to CARCO when she was molested, before Shari was born. Her disclosure would have classified Shari as At Risk upon birth. Dan H admitted to molesting Debbie, and experts agree that child-molesters present a definite risk to all children. Unsupervised visitation would never have been forced upon Shari, and any failure on Dan's part to cooperate in the continuing efforts to declassify his child and stepchild would have been met with immediate and absolute protection of the family from contact with him. That goal was met once the press reported the story and the Commonwealth of Kentucky stepped in, but it could have happened in such a way that would have saved Mary's life as well as thousands of tax dollars for the people of Kentucky and Maryland.

The Linda Jamison case provides one of the most eloquent arguments for CARCO legislation that can be imagined. Marissa disclosed sexual abuse over and over again to a validator who had a national reputation. Her refusal to validate what she was being told repeatedly is proof that uniform standards are a must in this area of danger and discretion. If there is no absolute test of the validity of a child's disclosure, it must be taken as valid, at least initially; if one must err, it must be on the side of caution. Descriptions of outrageous conduct will naturally sound outrageous, but implausible acts are the stuff of which incest is made. Any professional who invalidates a child's disclosure for describing outrageous and implausible acts, when incest is the subject of the interview, is acting recklessly, without adherence to acceptable standards. Under the CARCO system, no one, not even a well-respected person, can suddenly "go wrong" on a case and invalidate a disclosure because he or she finds it (for unspecified reasons) unbelievable. A CARCO intake form will not ask if the interviewer believes a disclosure. No form in use for any other government system asks officials to make such discretionary decisions about information filed with them. CARCO will have ironclad protections against individual employees suddenly taking the law (and the facts) into their own hands; their job is to follow the procedures in the manual, procedures that are legislated and uniform, not dreamed up by individuals and subject to whim.

What would have occurred if Karen Carter's daughter, Jesse, had CARCO's help when she was nearly two years old and first revealed sexual abuse? Her CAR REP would have arranged for a physical examination. Jesse had mentioned vaginal penetration; but since she was not as verbal as an older child, extra confirmation would have been helpful in finding out what, if anything, had happened to her. Immediately upon getting evidence of vaginal penetrating injury, Jesse would have been classified, even though a perpetrator could not be identified. Karen would naturally be expected to function as the protective parent because Jesse did not like to be separated from her, and she was already living with her 50 percent of the time anyway. Obviously, Karen would have agreed. Since Jesse was expressing fear of going to Bob's house, CARCO would have offered Bob a chance to cooperate in Jesse's declassification. If he agreed to do so, even though he denied molesting her, he would be involved in trying to find out who had actually molested her and why she thought it was her daddy who did it. If another person had molested Jesse, the therapist who had gained her confidence would probably have been able to help her reveal that. No lawyers could have inserted themselves into the classification process. Bob would have been free to consult lawyers, such as guardian *ad litem* Donald Harper. They might have helped Bob choose a course of action for himself, but that would not have affected CARCO's course of action. Bob could also have decided not to work with CARCO. Karen and Jesse would have eventually identified the abuser. If the abuser was not Bob, he would benefit from the declassification by being reunited with his family immediately. The CARCO office, with Bob's and Karen's help, would probably have located the perpetrator quickly and that person would have been brought to justice while Jesse healed. If the abuser was Bob, Jesse would have been protected from him until and unless he chose to work toward declassification within CARCO guidelines. If, on the other hand, he cooperated with CARCO, he might have discovered or admitted that he had molested his daughter, taken advantage of the course of treatment for parents who had abused their children, and patched up his relationship with Jesse in time. Karen Carter would not have had to go public, and the people of Iowa would never have heard the name Bob Fulton in the same sentence with the word "rapist." Jesse might have been declassified fairly quickly and would probably be visiting with her father already.

Under CARCO the Backman case would have saved more than one state money, and would have eased the burden on Catholic Charities in Canada. Since both Tina and her little sister disclosed sexual abuse by the same father/stepfather, Renee's role would have been minor in terms of proving a case of incest. Tina could have approached CARCO with her little sister instead of running away. There would have been no war of attrition, no litigation, and no convening of grand juries. Once Tina disclosed her own abuse, the CARCO process would have protected all the children in the family, as well as assisted Stew Johnson in reevaluating his parenting goals. Had he chosen to cooperate with CARCO in Mississippi, he could have facilitated Tina's declassification and re-established a relationship with his younger daughter fairly soon. Perhaps, under those circumstances, Tina could have been the visitation supervisor for Renee with Stew Johnson, so her initial goals of protecting her little sister would have been part of a therapeutic process supported by CARCO. Tina would have been able to continue her college career. She could have felt proud about protecting her younger sister, but she would not have had to sacrifice her own welfare to do so.

The Sandy Moore case provides an even more persuasive argument for CARCO. Since the jury that sent Sandy to jail for life actually believed that her son had been molested by his father, the death of one man, the crippling of another, and the destruction of an entire family could have been avoided if there had been a local CARCO, operating according to federal guidelines, instead of a local CPS office that had "discretion" to mishandle the case. Instead of the CPS paper chase and a dozen confused memos, the CARCO intake would have necessitated only one session, at which Willie A would have been made comfortable with a male interviewer. His disclosure would not have been challenged; there would have been no CPS attempt to make him recant; and there would have been no custody battle based on the defensive paternal family's need to protect its reputation. Willie A would not have been hospitalized or institutionalized, since his mother would have cooperated with CARCO to help protect him from further risk and to declassify him. Texas would have saved a lot of money on that case and on the lifelong incarceration of a woman who was only trying to protect her son from sodomy.

WHAT-IFS?

What if innocent parents are prevented from being with their children because CARCO believes children's disclosures and not all of them are true?

The American Bar Association has discovered that very few allegations of child sexual abuse, even in the context of bitter custody disputes, are deliberately false. Among those, there would be a high degree of remedy as the CAR KID was involved in supportive therapy. As long as there are no criminal penalties for alleged perpetrators, a child who has made a false allegation can grow to reverse such a position without guilt and shame under CARCO. Dad has not been arrested; Mom has not been called a liar; no custody battle has been started; a flock of lawyers have not descended on the family; nothing irreversible or irremediable has happened. In therapy, a child who has made a misleading comment or even a false allegation can declassify herself without having to recant or be pressured. Does a child really have incentive to separate herself from a father who has always loved her and never hurt her? If she does so to please an angry mother, will that work for long?

What if bad staffing causes a CARCO office to misfunction?

There will be real controls over the conduct of CARCO employees, and, ideally, there will be accountable U.S. Public Health Service personnel running every local office. Now, CPS workers are almost immune to criticism for their actions in individual cases because of the secrecy of such proceedings. CARCO workers will be under full supervision, so that abuses will not be allowed to continue past the point of being reported and investigated. If a local CARCO fails to comply with the manual, the regional Public Health Service office will investigate. A shoot-out on a ranch and a national scandal will not be required to keep the local CARCO clean.

What if a named perpetrator decides not to abide by the CARCO rules? If there are no criminal penalties, what will prevent criminal conduct while the classification takes place?

The CARCO proposal removes criminal penalties for incest, but not for any other criminal activities. If a named Identified Risk Person (the labels "alleged abuser" or "accused perpetrator" are not helpful to an understanding of the process) chooses to cooperate with the CARCO declassification effort, he will sign contracts limiting his actions and his contact with the Child at Risk. If he chooses not to cooperate with CARCO declassification efforts, the Child at Risk and the rest of the family will be shielded immediately by the issuance of firm protective orders, which the local CARCO would be authorized to issue if it could not gain the cooperation of an Identified Risk Person during a classification. Any violation of a CARCO contract or protective order will be a felony; even a first violation of such an order would carry a mandatory jail sentence. A second violation would carry a severe penalty. A recidivist who repeatedly violated CARCO protective orders might be barred from further CARCO involvement and face termination of parental rights. Prosecutions for violating CARCO protective orders would not be like the lengthy and unpredictable jury trials of sexual abuse allegations with frightened children as complaining witnesses. They would be cut-and-dried cases, often with police as witnesses, and with clear evidence: either this person was on the porch at that house on a certain evening at 8:00 P.M. or not; either this person came to a child's school and accosted her or not; either the crime of violating the order happened or it did not. No validator, no second opinion, no mixed evidentiary standard, no scuttle fish, no equivocation.

What if a child is at risk of sexual abuse by a member of the family who does not live in the household—will that be a CARCO case or a crime?

The answer lies in the delineation and identification of risk, just as the classification of the child lies in the assessment of risk. If a mother's boyfriend has been accused, the risk to the child, as well as the classification of the child, will depend on whether the boyfriend is still present and is still presenting a risk. If the mother supports the child's disclosure, takes all necessary steps to remove the boyfriend, and assists her child in the recovery process, there is no need for a classification because the boyfriend cannot sue for custody and the risk is no longer a factor. If the police investigate and the prosecutor chooses to press charges, the prosecution would be no different from a stranger-molester trial. If the Identified Risk Person is a maternal uncle, and the mother, who is otherwise protective of her child, chooses not to isolate the child from him, CARCO would classify the child and try to involve the Identified Risk Person in the declassification process, just like any other relative. If he refused cooperation and the mother still included him in family activities, two protective orders would be issued: one forbidding the uncle from contacting the child and another directing the mother to prevent all contact. The mother would be as vulnerable to criminal penalties for endangering her child as the uncooperative uncle.

Won't CARCO classifications endanger many children who are unrelated to the Identified Risk Persons, since many perpetrators will escape criminal penalties and go on to molest other children?

We do not think there will be an appreciable difference in risk to unrelated children. In our present system, because of the enforced secrecy of child sexual abuse proceedings, nobody knows who among their neighbors has been under investigation for incest. In New York, a man who has twice been named in the State Child Abuse Registry for child sexual abuse of his own daughters, is a social worker who directs a large agency with programs for parents and children. The local family court judge protected him vigorously, as did the local agency; he got sole custody even after one daughter was seen in the emergency room with multiple vaginal lacerations. He sued people who tried to inform his neighbors and clients that their children were also in danger. In Kentucky, a prominent law professor was retained by CPS to represent the agency in handling a high-profile, sensitive incest case. He had been cited by CPS for psychological and physical abuse of his own daughter; sexual abuse had originally been among the findings, but the agency chose to play that down so as not to damage his reputation. A commercial airline pilot defending himself against charges of incest in court filed an affidavit saying that he was an excellent father and a friend of children, and that whenever he learned that there were unescorted children on his domestic flights, he brought them up to ride in the cockpit with him. Although the airline that employed him was notified of the founded incest case against him, it did nothing to restrict his access to children. In case after case, under our present system, alleged perpetrators escape notice by outsiders, even by the parents of their stepchildren, as was illustrated in the Karen Carter case. Ironically, Mary H was forbidden by the Maryland judge to tell her youngest child about her own father's criminal record for abusing her older sister. Even within the family, word was not getting out. Under

CARCO, proceedings will be open and above board, denial will be discouraged, treatment will be made available, and classifications will not be considered stigmatizing to the CAR KIDS. These remedies will engender a greater sense of safety than can be achieved by the present system of gag orders and refusals to prosecute.

What if the CARCO system degenerates into another version of CPS?

CPS has not degenerated so much as it has failed to get its land legs. The reasons have been debated by many. Some say workers are overworked and underpaid, under-trained, poorly trained, overwhelmed, burned out, incompetent, biased, inept. But it is undeniable that CPS has been unable to act independently of the courts. The cry of the hard-working, well-trained, competent, caring caseworker often is "I can't do my job; the judge won't let me." Caseworkers who last at CPS are those who can adjust to the idea that it is adversarial litigation, not child protection, that requires their primary attention. The people at the CPS offices now are those who can tolerate being political rather than useful; the people at the local CARCO will be those who welcome accountability and can do their jobs in accordance with clear mandates. The way that CARCO will avoid the problems that have besieged our social services system is by giving the office its own job to do (the protection of children at risk) and its own way to do it (classification and declassification), independent of judicial or political interference.

Isn't it unfair to undermine the entire legal system because of a few or even a lot of bad judges?

Although the conduct of judges has come under harsh criticism in this book, we are neither condemning the system because of their mistakes nor blaming them for the system that empowers them to commit those mistakes. We are just being pragmatic. It is not possible to educate judges to act in a way that is inconsistent with the system they represent. South African jurist Johann Krigler recently said, "Ultimately a court cannot be much better than the society it serves. . . . The future of that society will be determined less by the quality of its Bench and more by the sense of justice in its civil society." A judge who rules that there is "no evidence of sexual abuse" in spite of solid forensic evidence is responding to a society that does not wish to see solid evidence that it has been tolerating the rape of its children. People who care about the welfare of children more than they care about the pride of the Bench may regard a change in forum—away from the courts and into a more child-friendly environment—as a positive step for our child protection system in this generation and, in the next, for our civilization.

REFERENCES

Adler, J.; Beachy, L.; Seligam, J.; Rogers, P.; Azar, V.; McGinn, D.; and Gordon, J. Unhappily ever after. *Newsweek*, August 31, 1992, p. 57.

Anderson, K. *Chain Her by One Foot: The Subjugation of Native Women in Seventeenth Century New France*. New York: Routledge, 1993.

Armstrong, L. *Kiss Daddy Goodnight*. New York: Hawthorn Books, 1978.

Armstrong, L. Daddy dearest. *Connecticut*, January 1984, pp. 53–55, 127.

Arnold, R. A star cries incest. *People* 36/13 (1991):84–88.

Barron, James. Striking back, Woody Allen denies child sex-abuse allegations. *New York Times*, August 19, 1992, pp. B1, B4.

Bass, Ellen, and Davis, Laura. *The Courage to Heal: A Guide for Women Survivors of Child Abuse*. New York: Harper and Row, 1988.

Benedek, E.P., and Schetky, D.H. Clinical experience: Problems in validating allegations of sexual abuse. Part 2: Clinical evaluation. *Journal of the American Academy of Child and Adolescent Psychiatry* 26 (1987):916–921.

Besharov, D.J. "Do something" about child abuse. *Harvard Journal of Law and Public Policy* 8 (1985):539–589.

Besharov, D.J. Gaining control over child abuse reports. Public agencies must address both underreporting and overreporting. *Public Welfare*, Spring 1990, pp. 34–47.

Bloom, Sandra L. Psychodynamics of preventing child abuse. *Journal of Psychohistory* 21/1 (1993):54–67.

Blush, G., and Ross, K. Sexual abuse in divorce: The SAID syndrome. *The Conciliation Courts Review* 25 (1987):1–11.

Bowers, Carol L. Judge delays custody transfer: Girl, 5 was to be handed over to her father, a convicted sex abuser. *Hartford County Sun*, May 24, 1992, p. 2.

Bresee, Patricia; Stearns, Geoffrey B.; Bess, Bruce H.; and Packer, Leslie P. Allegations of child sexual abuse in child custody disputes: A therapeutic assessment model. *American Journal of Orthopsychiatry* 56/4 (1986):560–569.

Briere, John, and Runtz, Marsha. Symptomatology associated with childhood sexual victimization in a nonclinical adult sample. *Child Abuse and Neglect* 12 (1988): 51–59.

Brigham, John C. Commentary: Issues in the empirical study of the sexual abuse of children. In Doris, 1991:110–114.

Browne, A., and Finkelhor, D. Impact of child sexual abuse: A review of the research. *Psychological Bulletin* 99 (1986):66–77.

Burgess, Ann W., and Grant, Christine A. *Children Traumatized in Sex Rings*. National Center for Missing and Exploited Children, U.S. Department of Justice and School of Nursing, University of Pennsylvania, March 1988.

Burton, K., and Myers, W.C. Child sexual abuse and forensic psychiatry: Evolving and controversial issues. *Bulletin of the American Academy* 20/4 (1992):439–453.

Butler, S. *Conspiracy of Silence*. San Francisco: New Glide Publications, 1978.

Carrier, J.M. Mexican male bisexuality. In F. Klein and T. Wolf, eds., *Bisexualities: Themes and Research*. New York: Hayworth Press, 1985. Pp. 75–85.

Ceci, Stephen J. Some overarching issues in the suggestibility debate. In Doris, 1991:1–9.

Ceci, Stephen J., and Bruck, Maggie. Suggestibility of the child witness: a historical review and synthesis. *Psychological Bulletin* 113/3 (1993):403–439.

Ceci, Stephen J.; Leichtman, M.; Putnick, M.; and Nightingale, N. Age differences in suggestibility. In D. Cicchetti and S. Toth, eds., *Child Abuse, Child Development, and Social Policy*. Norwood, N.J.: Ablex, 1993. Pp. 117–137.

Chesler, P. *Mothers on Trial: The Battle for Children and Custody*. New York: McGraw-Hill, 1986.

Clarke-Stewart, A.; Thompson, W.C.; and Lepore, S. Manipulating children's interpretations through interrogation. In G.S. Goodman, Chair, Can Children Provide Accurate Eyewitness Reports? Symposium at the biennial meeting of the Society for Research on Child Development, Kansas City, MO, April 1989.

Coleman, Daniel. Doubts rise on children as witnesses. *New York Times*, November 4, 1990, pp. C1, C3.

Coleman, L. False allegations of child sexual abuse: Have the experts been caught with their pants down? *Forum* (published by the California Attorneys for Criminal Justice), January-February 1986, pp. 12–22,

Collins, Judy. *Trust Your Heart: An Autobiography*. Boston: Houghton-Mifflin, 1987.

The Committee for Justice for Women and Orange County North Carolina Women's Coalition. *Contested Custody Cases in Orange County, N.C. Trial Courts 1983–1987: Gender Bias, the Family, and Law*. 2d revision, November 1991.

Conte, J.; Sorenson, E.; Fogarty, L.; and Della Rosa, J. Evaluating children's reports of sexual abuse: Results from a survey of professionals. *American Journal of Orthopsychiatry* 61 (1991):428–437.

Cook, A.I. Gender bias: Push grows for study, action. *The National Law Journal*, May 19, 1986, pp. 30–31.

Corwin, David L.; Berliner, Lucy; Goodman, Gail; Goodwin, Jean; and White, Sue. Child sexual abuse and custody disputes: No easy answers. *Journal of Interpersonal Violence* 2/1 (1987):91–105.

Cramer, Jerome. Why children lie in court. *Time*, March 4, 1991, p. 76.

Crewdson, John. *By Silence Betrayed: Sexual Abuse of Children in America*. Boston: Little, Brown and Company, 1988.

De Beauvoir, Simone. *The Second Sex*. New York: Alfred Knopf, 1953.

DeBellis, Michael D.; Chrousos, George P.; Dorn, Lorah D.; Burke, Lilian; Helmers, Karin; Kling, Mitchell A.; Trickett, Penelope K.; and Putnam, Frank W. Hypothalamic-pituitary-adrenal axis dysregulation in sexually abused girls. *Journal of Clinical Endocrinology and Metabolism* 78/2 (1994):249–255.

deMause, Lloyd. *The History of Childhood*. New York: The Psychohistory Press, 1974.

deMause, Lloyd. The universality of incest. *The Journal of Psychohistory* 19/2 (1991):123–164.

De Panfilis, Diane, and Salus, Marsha K. *A coordinated response to child abuse and neglect: A basic manual*. U.S. Department of Health and Human Services Administration for Children, Youth, and Families, National Center on Child Abuse and Neglect. DHHS publication No. (AFC) 92-30362, 1992.

Doris, J.M., ed. *The Suggestibility of Children's Recollections*. Washington, D.C.: American Psychological Association, 1991.

Drakich, Janice. In search of the better parent: The social construction of ideologies of fatherhood. *Canadian Journal of Women and the Law* 3/1 (1989): 69–87.

Dziech, B.W., and Schudson, J.C.B. *On Trial: America's Courts and Their Treatment of Sexually Abused Children*. 2d ed. Boston: Beacon Press, 1991.

El Sadaawi, Nawal. *The Hidden Faces of Eve: Women in the Arab World*. Boston: Beacon Press, 1980.

Engels, Frederick. *The Origin of the Family, Private Property and the State*, edited by Eleanor B. Leacock. New York: International Publishers, 1972.

Everson, Mark D., and Boat, Barbara W. False allegations of sexual abuse by children and adolescents. *American Academy of Child and Adolescent Psychiatry* 28/2 (1989):230–235.

Fahn, M. Allegations of child sexual abuse in custody disputes: Getting to the truth of the matter. *Family Law Quarterly* XXV/2 (1991):193–216.

Faller, Kathleen C. *Understanding Child Sexual Maltreatment*. London: Sage Publications, 1990.

Faller, Kathleen C. Possible explanations for child sexual abuse in divorce. *American Journal of Orthopsychiatry* 6/1 (1991):86–91.

Faludi, Susan. *Backlash: The Undeclared War against American Women*. New York: Anchor Books, 1991.

Fernandez-Marina, Romon. Brief communications. *Psychiatry* 24 (1961):79–82.

Finkelhor, David. *Child Sexual Abuse: New Theory and Research*. New York: Free Press, 1984.

Finkelhor, David. Commentary on "The Universality of Incest." *The Journal of Psychohistory* 19/2 (1991):1219.

Finkelhor, David; Hotaling, Gerald; Lewis, I.A.; and Smith, Christine. Sexual abuse in a national survey of adult men and women: Prevalence, characteristics, and risk factors. *Child Abuse and Neglect* 14 (1990):19–28.

Firestone, Shulamith. *The Dialectic of Sex: The Case for the Feminist Revolution*. New York: Bantam, 1970.

Flicker, Bernard. Psychohistorical roots of the war against children. *The Journal of Psychohistory* 21/1 (1991):69–78.

Foulks, Edward F. The Bimin-Kuskusmin: A discussion of Fitz John Porter Poole's ethnographic observations of gender identity formation in a New Guinea people. In L. Bryce Boyer and S.A. Grolnick, eds., *The Psychoanalytic Study of Society*, Vol. 12. Hillsdale, NJ: The Analytic Press, 1988. Pp. 157–169.

Fox, Robin. *Kinship and Marriage*. Harmondsworth: Penguin Books, 1962.

Fox, Robin. *The Red Lamp of Incest*. New York: E.P. Dutton, 1980.

Fraad, Harriet. Children as an exploited class. *The Journal of Psychohistory* 21/1 (1991):37–51.

Gardner, R. *Sex Abuse Hysteria: Salem Witch Trials Revisited*. Longwood, NJ: Creative Therapeutics Press, 1989.

Gardner, R. Differentiating between bona fide and fabricated allegations of sexual abuse of children. *Journal of the American Academy of Matrimonial Lawyers* 5 (1989):1–27.

Gill, Charles D. Essay on the status of the American child, 2000 AD: Chattel or constitutionally protected child-citizen? *Ohio Northern University Law Review* XVII/3 (1991):543–579.

Glueck, Bernard C. Early sexual experience in schizophrenia. In Hugo G. Beigel, ed., *Advances in Sex Research*. New York: Harper and Row, 1963. P. 253.

Goodman, G.S., and Aman, C. Children's use of anatomically detailed dolls to recount an event. In M. Stewart, Chair, Anatomically Detailed Dolls: Developmental, Legal and Clinical Implications. Symposium at the meeting of the Society for Research in Child Development, April 1987.

Goodman, G.S., and Aman, C., Children's use of anatomically detailed dolls to recount an event. *Child Development* 61 (1990):1859–1871.

Goodman, G.S.; Rudy, L.; Bottoms, B.; and Aman, C. Children's memory and children's concerns: Issues of ecological validity in the study of children's eyewitness testimony. In R. Furvish and J. Hudson, eds., *What Young Children Remember and Know*. New York: Cambridge University Press, 1990. Pp. 249–284.

Goodman, G.S.; Wilson, M.E.; Hazan, C.; and Reed, R.S. Children's testimony nearly four years after "an event." Paper presented at the meeting of the Eastern Psychological Association, Boston, March 1989.

Goodwin, J. Credibility problems in multiple personality disorder patients and abused children. In R.P. Kluft, ed., *Childhood Antecedents of Multiple Personality*. Washington, D.C.: American Psychiatric Press, 1985. Pp. 2–19.

Gordon, D. Female circumcision and genital operations in Egypt and the Sudan: A dilemma for medical anthropology. *Medical Anthropology Quarterly* 5/1 (1991):3–14.

Gordon, Linda. *Heroes of Their Own Lives*. New York: Penguin, 1988.

Gray, Ellen. *Unequal Justice*. New York: Free Press, 1993.

Green, A. True and false allegations of sexual abuse in child custody disputes. *Journal of the American Academy of Child Psychiatry* 25 (1986):449–456.

Hechler, David. *The Battle and the Backlash: The Child Sexual Abuse War*. Lexington, MA: Lexington Books, 1988.

Hechler, David. Danger ahead: Sex abuse cases. *Washington Journalism Review* 13/7 (1991):37–40.

Herdt, Gilbert H. *Guardians of the Flutes: Idioms of Masculinity*. New York: McGraw-Hill, 1981.

Herdt, Gilbert H. Fetish and fantasy in Sambia. In G.H. Herdt, ed., *Rituals of Manhood*. Berkeley: University of California Press, 1982. Pp. 46–98.

Herman, Judith L., and Hirschman L. *Father-Daughter Incest*. Cambridge: Harvard University Press, 1981.

Herman, Judith L.; Perry, J. Christopher; and Van der Kolk, Bessel A. Childhood trauma in borderline personality disorder. *American Journal of Psychiatry* 146/4 (1989):490–494.

Hewlett, Sylvia Ann. *A Lesser Life: The Myth of Women's Liberation in America*. New York: William Morrow, 1986.

Hlady, L.J., and Gunter, E.J. Alleged child abuse in custody access disputes. *Child Abuse and Neglect* 14/4 (1990):591–593.

Holt, John C. *Escape from Childhood*. New York: E.P. Dutton, 1974. Pp. 13–30, 109–114.

Honeycutt, Valerie. Court upholds shielding girl from molester father. *Lexington Herald-Leader*, November 13, 1992, pp. Al, A7.

Hosken, Frank P. *The Hosken Report: Genital and Sexual Mutilation of Females*. Lexington, MA: Women's International Network News, 1979.

Jacobi, Marianne, and Wright, Rosalind. Mothers who go to jail for their children. *Good Housekeeping*, October 1988, pp. 158, 234, 236–238.

Jones, D.P., and McGraw, J.M. Reliable and fictitious accounts of sexual abuse of children. *Journal of Interpersonal Violence* 2/1 (1987):27–45.

Jones, D.P., and Seig, A. Child sexual abuse in custody and visitation cases: A report of 20 cases. In E.B. Nicholson and J. Buckley, eds., *Sexual Abuse Allegations in Custody and Visitation Cases*. Washington, D.C.: American Bar Association, 1988.

Jumper, Shan A. A meta-analysis of the relationship of child sexual abuse to adult psychological adjustment. *Child Abuse and Neglegt* 19/6 (1995): 715–728.

Kahr, Brett. The sexual molestation of children: Historical perspectives. *The Journal of Psychohistory* 19/2 (1991):191–214.

Kerrison, Ray. Pleas for a dying child go unheeded. *New York Post*, November 9, 1992, pp. 7, 14.

Kinsey, A.C.; Pomeroy, W.B.; Martin, C.E.; and Gebhard, P.H. *Sexual Behavior in the Human Female*. Philadelphia: W.B. Saunders Co., 1953.

Kluft, R.P. First rank symptoms as a diagnostic clue to multiple personality disorder. *American Journal of Psychiatry* 144 (1987):293–298.

La Fontaine, Jean. *Child Sexual Abuse*. London: Polity Press, 1990.

Leacock, Eleanor. Women's status in egalitarian society: Implications for social evolution. *Current Anthropology* 19 (1978):241–255.

Leventhal, John M. Have there been changes in the epidemiology of sexual abuse of children during the 20th century? *Pediatrics* 82 (1988):766–773.

Lewis, Oscar. *La Vida: A Puerto Rican Family in the Culture of Poverty—San Juan and New York*. New York: Vintage books, 1965.

Lightfoot-Klein, Hanny. *Prisoners of Ritual: An Odyssey into Female Genital Circumcision in Africa*. New York: Harrington Park Press, 1989.

Little, Marilyn. *Family Breakup*. San Francisco: Jossey-Bass, 1982.

Loftus, E.F. The maleability of human memory. *American Scientist* 67 (1979): 312–320.

McClendon, David. Mother of tot "not credible" judge says in court documents. *Rockland* [New York] *Journal-News*, June 20, 1993, pp. Al, A6.

McGough, Lucy S. Commentary: Sexual abuse and suggestibility. In Doris, 1991: 115–117.

McGraw, J. Melbourne, and Smith, Holly A. Child sexual abuse allegations amidst divorce and custody proceedings: Refining the validation process. *Journal of Child Sexual Abuse* 1/1 (1993):49–62.

MacIntyre, Ben. Allen case reflects growth of abuse claims in custody battles. *Times* (London), August 20, 1992, p. 8.

Mann, Judy. Stepping over the line. *Washington Post*, August 28, 1992, p. E3.

Manshel, L. *Nap Time*. New York: Kensington Publishing, 1990.

Masson, J.M. *The Assault on Truth: Freud's Suppression of the Seduction Theory*. New York: Farrar, Straus & Giroux, 1984.

Mead, Margaret. *Male and Female: A Study of Sexes in a Changing World*. New York: Morrow, 1950.

Meiselman, K.C. *Incest: A Psychological Study of Causes and Effects with Treatment Recommendations*. San Francisco: Jossey-Bass, 1986.

Miller, B.D. Wife beating in India: Variations on a theme. In D.A. Counts, J.K. Brown, and J.C. Campbell, eds., *Sanctions and Sanctuary: Cultural Perspectives on the Beating of Wives*. Boulder: Westview Press, 1992. Pp. 173–183.

Moore, Henrietta L. *Feminism and Anthropology*. Minneapolis: University of Minnesota Press, 1988.

Myers, John E.B. Allegations of child sexual abuse in custody and visitation litigation: Recommendations for improved fact finding and child protection. *Journal of Family Law* 28/1 (1989–90):1–41.

Myers, John E.B., ed. *The Backlash: Child Protection under Fire*. Beverly Hills: Sage, 1994.

National Center on Child Abuse and Neglect, Study Findings: National Study of the Incidence and Severity of Child Abuse and Neglect. DHHS Publication # (OHDS) 81-30325, Washington, D.C., 1981.

Olafson, Erna; Corwin, David L.; and Summit, Roland C. Modern history of child sexual abuse awareness: Cycles of discovery and suppression. *Child Abuse and Neglect* 7 (1993):7–24.

Orthner, Dennis K., and Lewis, K. Evidence of single-father competence in child-rearing. *Family Law Quarterly* 13 (1979):27–47.

Padilla, E.N. An agrarian reform sugar community in Puerto Rico. Ph.D. diss., Columbia University, 1951.

Paquette, Catherine. Handling sexual abuse allegations in child custody cases. *New England Law Review* 25 (1991):1415–1446.

Paradise, Jan E.; Rostain, Anthony L.; and Nathanson, Madelaine. Substantiation of sexual abuse charges when parents dispute custody or visitation. *Pediatrics* 81/6 (1988):835–839.

Polikoff, Nancy. Gender and child custody determinations: Exploding the myth. In I. Diamond and M.L. Shanley, eds., *A Feminist Dialogue on Women and the State*. New York: Longman, 1983. Pp. 183–202.

Pollock, Linda A. *Forgotten Children: Parent-Child Relations from 1500 to 1900*. New York: Cambridge Univerity Press, 1983.

Pribor, Elizabeth F., and Dinwiddie, Stephen H. Psychiatric correlates of incest in childhood. *American Journal of Psychiatry* 149/1 (1992):52–56.

Quindlen, Anna. The good mother. *New York Times*, December 10, 1994, p. 23.

Raskin, David C., and Esplin, Phillip W. Assessment of children's statements of sexual abuse. In Doris, 1991:153–164.

Rosen, Leora N. Male adolescent initiation rituals: Whiting's hypothesis revisited. *Psychoanalytic Study of Society* 12 (1988):131–155.

Rush, Florence. *The Best Kept Secret*. New York: Prentice-Hall, 1980.

Russell, Diana E.H. The incidence and prevalence of intrafamilial and extrafamilial sexual abuse of female children. *Child Abuse and Neglect* 7 (1983):133–146.

Russell, Diana E.H. *The Secret Trauma: Incest in the Lives of Women and Girls*. New York: Basic Books, 1986.

Sack, David A. *No More Secrets: Understanding Sexual Abuse and Emotional Disorders*. Washington, D.C.: The PIA Press, 1990.

Saywitz, K.; Goodman, G.S.; Nicholas, E.; and Moan, Susan F. Children's memory for a physical examination: Implications for reports of sexual abuse involving genital touch. *Journal of Consulting and Clinical Psychology* 59/5 (1991): 682–691.

Schafran, L.H. Documenting gender bias in the courts: The task force approach. *Judicature* 70/5 (1987):280–290.

Schetky, D.H. Editorial: Emerging issues on child sexual abuse. *Journal of the American Academy of Child Psychiatry* 25 (1986):490.

Schouler, J., and Blakemore, A. *Marriage, Divorce, Separation and Domestic Relations*. Vol. 1. 6th ed. Albany, NY: Matthew Bender, 1921.

Schudson, Charles B. Antagonistic parents in family courts: False allegations or false assumptions about true allegations of child sexual abuse? *Child Abuse and Neglect* 1/2 (1992):111–114.

Sisco, Rebecca. Courting disaster: When divorced mothers charge incest. *The Minnesota Women's Press*, September 9–22, 1992, pp. 1, 6, 8–9.

Sitomer, Curtis J. Abusing the law: Falsely charging molestation. *Los Angeles Daily Journal*, August 31, 1986, p. 6.

Smith, Lynn. Houses divided. *Los Angeles Times*, September 3, 1992, pp. E1, E7.

Sommerville, C. John. *The Rise and Fall of Childhood*. New York: Vintage Books, 1990.

Sowers, Leslie. Child abuse and the courts. *Houston Chronicle*, November 11, 1990, pp. G1-4.

Stager, L.E., and Wolff, S.R. Child sacrifice at Carthage: Religious rite or population control? *Biblical Archeology Review*, January-February 1984, pp. 31–51.

Summit, Roland, C. The child sexual abuse accommodation syndrome. *Child Abuse and Neglect* 7 (1983):177–193.

Szegedy-Maszak, Marianne. Who's to judge? *New York Times Sunday Magazine*, May 21, 1989, p. 30.

Teischer, Martin H.; Ito, Yutaka N.; Glod, Carol A.; Schiffer, Fred; and Ackerman, Erika. Possible effects of early abuse on human brain development, as assessed by EEG coherence. Paper presented at the 33rd Annual Meeting of the American College of Neuropsychopharmacology. San Juan, PR, December 15, 1994.

Thoennes, Nancy, and Tjaden, Patricia G. Child sexual abuse: Whom should a judge believe? What should a judge believe? *Judges Journal* 27/3 (Summer 1988):1–4.

Thoennes, Nancy, and Tjaden, Patricia G. The extent, nature, and validity of sexual abuse allegations in custody and visitation disputes. *Child Abuse and Neglect* 14 (1990):151–163.

Tuzin, Donald F. Ritual violence among the Ilahita Arapesh. In G.H. Herdt, ed., *Rituals of Manhood*. Berkeley: University of California Press, 1982. Pp. 332–355.

Van Derbur Atler, M. The darkest secret. *People* 35/22 (1991):88–94.

Wakefield, H., and Underwager, R. *Accusations of Child Sexual Abuse*. Springfield, IL: Charles C. Thomas, 1988.

Warshak, R.A. *The Custody Revolution: The Father Factor and the Motherhood Mystique*. New York: Poseidon Press, 1992.

Webster, Paula. Matriarchy: A vision of power. In R.R. Reiter, ed., *Towards an Anthropology of Women*. New York: Monthly Review Press, 1975. Pp. 141–156.

Weitzman, Leonore J., and Dixon, Ruth B. Child custody awards: Legal standards and empirical patterns for child custody, support and visitation after divorce. *University of California Davis Law Review* 12 (1979):471.

Weller, Sheila. Abused by the courts. *Village Voice*, December 1, 1992, pp. 31–32, 37–38.

Wells, Gary L., and Loftus, Elizabeth F. Commentary: Is this child fabricating? Reactions to a new assessment technique. In Doris, 1991:168–171.

Wibler, N.J., and Schafran, L.H. Learning from the New Jersey Supreme Court Task Force on Women in the Courts: Evaluation, recommendations and implications for other states. *Women's Rights Law Reporter* 12/4 (1991):313–318.

Wyatt, Gail Elizabeth. The sexual abuse of Afro-American and White women in childhood. *Child Abuse and Neglect* 9 (1985):507–519.

INDEX

LEORA N. ROSEN

earned a doctorate in Social Anthropology from Witwatersrand University, in her native South Africa, and a Masters of Public Health from Columbia University. Her research has been in the fields of psychiatric epidemiology, anthropology, and social psychology. She took part in the campaign to free Elizabeth Morgan, was one of the founders of Alliance for the Rights of Children, and helped start Operation Z, a child advocacy organization.

MICHELLE ETLIN

is a volunteer activist and advocate for mothers and children. She comes from a family tradition of public activism and has been involved most recently with children's rights. She is a philosophical founding mother of Operation Z and has appeared on national television programs on custody and child abuse, including *Geraldo,* CNN *Cross-Fire,* and *Headlines on Trial.*